How to Start Your Own Forex Signal Service

THE NEXT STEP EVERY FOREX TRADER
SHOULD TAKE TO BUILD AN AUTOMATED
PASSIVE INCOME STREAM

Rimantas Petrauskas

A Currency Trader & Programmer

Book Layout ©2014 BookDesignTemplates.com

How to Start Your Own Forex Signal Service / Rimantas Petrauskas —1st ed.
ISBN: 978-609-408-562-8

Contents

Disclaimer

Any and all opinions, commentary, news, research, analyses, prices, or other information contained on this book are provided as general market commentary, and do not constitute investment advice nor a solicitation and there are no guarantees associated with them. We are not liable for any loss or damage, including without limitation, any loss of profit, which may arise directly or indirectly from use of or reliance on such information. We have taken reasonable measures to ensure the accuracy of the information on the book.

Foreign Exchange market (FX, Forex) is very speculative in nature, involves considerable risk and is not appropriate for all investors. Therefore, before deciding to participate in off-exchange Foreign Exchange trading/Forex, you should carefully consider your investment objectives, level of experience and risk appetite. Investors should only use risk or surplus capital when trading Forex because there is always the risk of substantial loss. Most importantly, do not invest money you cannot afford to lose. Any mention of past performance is not indicative of future results. Account access, trade executions and system response may be adversely affected by market conditions, quote delays, system performance and other factors.

Commodity Futures Trading Commission: Futures, Options and foreign currency trading have large potential rewards, but also large potential risk. You must be aware of the risks and be willing to accept them in order to invest in the Forex/futures and options markets. Don't trade with money you can't afford to lose. This is neither a solicitation nor an offer to Buy/Sell Forex/futures or options. No representation is being made that any account will or is likely to achieve profits or losses similar to those discussed on this web site. The past performance of any trading system or methodology is not necessarily indicative of future results.

CFTC RULE 4.41: HYPOTHETICAL OR SIMULATED PERFORMANCE RESULTS HAVE CERTAIN LIMITATIONS. UNLIKE AN ACTUAL PERFORMANCE RECORD, SIMULATED

Introduction

Congratulations! If you are here it means you want to be more than just a Forex trader. It means that you have the mind of an entrepreneur and you are just a few steps away from creating your own trading signals service. This book, "How to Start Your Own Forex Signal Service," is the story of how a currency trader was able to make money with just a demo trading account, and also includes a road map for building a fully-automated trading signals business. I will share the exact same steps I have been using, and even those things I've seen other websites using, to build and run a signal services business. I will also happily share this Forex trading signals service with you in a separate chapter.

Obviously, starting such a business is not a 1-click process and it requires a lot of work and effort, but even if you are a hard worker and you do put in a lot of effort, you still need a map. This book is all about the map—the guide that will show you what things you really need to make this business successful and how you can accomplish them. Before you begin, I want you to be completely serious about this. If you are not serious about becoming a signal provider then obviously I won't be able to help you become one.

I am going to share my story of struggle when I was creating my trading signals business, and in this you will learn what I did and what things worked well for me. All the techniques that I share with you in this book will not work without implementing them. This is not some get rich quick business model. It often takes weeks or even months to start, but once you have it running, the customers will start coming in and your success will grow month by month. So be prepared to work, and let's begin.

Forex is the art of trading currencies for a profit. With a daily turnover of over 4 Trillion US Dollars, the Foreign Exchange market is the largest trading venues on Earth and can provide an incredible opportunity for building a lasting and profitable business. Now I am sure you already know what the Forex market is, and I definitely won't waste your time explaining it. If it happens that you have no idea what Forex is, then I encourage you to find and study a Forex beginners guide. You can find many on Google pretty easily, and I would say the most convenient place to start would be Pips School created by babypips.com.

There are three ways to leverage the Forex market. Option number one, you can become a currency trader and invest your own money. Second, you could manage money on behalf of others. Option three, you can start your own Forex Signal Service. Of course, there are a few other ways also, like becoming a Forex broker, but today I am going to talk about the fact that starting your own Forex signal service can be a lucrative endeavor and a path to financial security. Nowadays, software has made it easy for entrepreneurs to build a solid Forex signals delivery service. The other option where you can manage other people's money is a great opportunity as well, but I would say that comes only after you have lucrative and successful trading signals business.

In the section below, I'll go over the tools that are needed in order to start your very own signal service.

MetaTrader 4 Expert Advisor (EA) software or Forex Robot

This software will be the foundation of your trading business. The Expert Advisor, or EA for short, is a trading software that is designed specifically for the MetaTrader Platform. The EA can provide advice to traders on which trades to take or not take.

This software can also be programmed to carry out the execution of trades automatically, without any input from the user. If you don't want to use an EA, or you don't want to trust your account to a trading robot, you can always find signal providers willing to share trading signals for a subscription fee or even for free.

It is not a surprise that not everyone likes the MT4 platform. This is just common life practice, so I encourage you to be more open minded and give this platform one more chance. My book is mostly about this platform as my business is built around this platform. This trading platform has allowed me to create so many tools that serve traders that it might be a big mistake if you reject it just because of a few inconvenient things it has to offer. Nothing is perfect and as is the MetaTrader 4 platform, but with the help of 3rd party tools, you can overcome most of the limitations.

Signal Delivery Software

The signal delivery process involves using trade copier software. The copier will follow the trading actions made on your account and duplicate them in the accounts of your clients. There are many of these apps available, and of course, we will get to know most of them here in this material. Every software has its own pros and cons, so it is always wise to learn about each solution so you can choose the one you like the most and will serve your business the best.

What trading signals you can send to customers?

To send trading signals you will first need to generate them. Now if you are a trader yourself then that is easy for you, especially if your trading method is profitable. Now in this book I will show you many ways to find profitable sources of trading signals that you can sell to your customers, so don't worry if you are not yet a profitable trader. To start and run this business you don't have to be a professional Forex trader with 20 years of experience. Of course, that would be truly the best platform for this business, but you have many possibilities without as well.

Domain

Having your own domain name is a must. There is not much to explain on this one, but I will still explain where and how you can get your own domain name.

Build a Customer Base

Before proceeding any further, take a moment to consider what your targeted customer base is. How can you attract them? Would you consider giving away free signals as an incentive to buy your Forex products? What are the other methods you can use to create clients out of your target demographic?

I will share several methods with you on how to attract new customers. I use some of them in my trading signals service too.

Website

The website represents the virtual store of your Forex signal service. It should include all the important information, such as a trading track record, an easy sign up process and most importantly, lots of information for the customer to explain what services you offer exactly.

I will show you the main things you should add to your website. I will also share my knowledge with you about what things work and what things do not.

Payment Gateway

Payment processors like PayPal and ClickBank take the hassle out of managing your customers' payments and free up time you can use to work on other parts of your business. You should integrate a reliable payment processor to your website and secure your payment transactions with a security certificate.

This is, of course, not required in many cases when running a signals service, but if you are going to start with monthly based subscription payments, I can tell you that the easiest way to implement this is with a PayPal account.

Marketing

Online marketing can provide that needed boost to your forex signals business. Forum posting, affiliate marketing, social media and PPC are the hottest marketing tools right now.

It is important to understand that it's best to use as many of them as possible. You never want to "put all your eggs in one basket". If you just use your Facebook page to market your service, and that page gets blocked, you will end up in trouble for sure. Now if you'll have 3 or more other sources where people are coming to your site from, then your business won't get affected too much if one of those sources gets shutdown.

SEO

Lastly, don't forget to make your web pages search engine friendly. A little SEO helps search engines like Google, Yahoo, and Bing to find your website and send user traffic your way. You can get a lot of potential customers and more sales this way. Don't get too crazy about this right from the start though. At first, I recommend using only a few simple strategies, most of them are even available online for free. I will definitely explain to you what I mean by that and share with you from my experience so that you can avoid wasting thousands of dollars on SEO like I did.

Also in this book I will share with you my interview with the founder of the aforex.com signal providers. This site belongs to the company which was the first to offer trading signals offline, now many years ago. The available technology was not very good back then, but they still were still a very successful company, and are to this day also.

So what are we waiting for? Let's begin.

My Story

Life is a well. Everyone gets as much water as they draw out with their own strength. Do not believe that it is impossible to draw more than everyone else, and do not forget to share with others.

- Rimantas Petrauskas

How I Started My Forex Signals Business

When I tell people that they can earn money in Forex, even with a practice trading account, they usually just smile at me. After a few moments, when they saw my face is still serious, they say, "Are you serious?" Yes indeed, I am serious, and I have been doing this very thing for the last few years now.

"So how do you do that?" they ask. The short answer is, I deliver trading signals from my practice (a.k.a. demo) trading account to my customers. While my practice account balance and equity grows, my customers' accounts grow too. I get paid monthly and my customers earn income in their trading accounts by following my signals.

Now the long answer is in this book, and if you read it from top to bottom, you will learn how to start your own trading signals service. You will see what tools you will need to deliver trading signals automatically, in order to make this business run without human intervention. You will see how easy it is to setup a sales/company website, as well as understand the whole process from beginning to end of such a service.

This is exactly what I did. I started a successful trading signals business with a MetaTrader 4 practice account. I couldn't afford to open a real money account when I first was getting started so I did this on a demo. I had a trading system that worked and a dream to earn enough money to fund my real account. Now I have paying customers and I earn additional income from monthly payments. The cash flow from this business helped me earn enough money to open my first real account.

Most people think that you need a real money account to start a signals business, but my story is proof that this is not the case. I still use my practice account to send the trading signals and I've been in this business for a few years now. This is while I use the same trading system on my own personal real money account.

Other people think that it's hard to create a website. But these days with the advancement in technology this is as easy to do as sending an email. WordPress can help you create your own website and you can pick up a professionally looking website design from www.themeforest.net for a small fee.

Designs like these were priced at $2000 back in the day. Now you can get them for as little as $50. You can create a website with zero programming knowledge.

What people say about this book?

"It's been 16 years since we first started offering Forex education, which later included Forex signals, to Forex traders all over the world. All I can say is "If only this book was available then, it would have saved me thousands of dollars and you can't even count the savings in time". This book is absolutely superb and covers perfectly from A – Z everything needed to know about starting an online Forex service. It covers every aspect involved in setting up a Forex business and sending Forex signals, and the information is especially valuable these days with the explosion of popularity in automated Forex trading. This book is an

absolute must have for anyone looking to enter this field and specifically getting involved in online Forex signals."

- Ben Lewis, USA, ForexSignal.com

"I was quite surprised myself about how straightforward this business could be to build. I had had this idea in mind a couple of years before, but never knew the very first steps to take. In my mind, this was a very complicated business and one that was 'off in the distant future' but now I am grateful for this book helping me to see the tangible steps along the way."

John R, Virginia, Unites States

"I'm a professional full-time forex trader with a successful performance record and I'm thinking of starting a forex signal service. I want to do it seriously so there are still a lot of important decisions I have to make (domain, sales strategy, etc.), but I am pretty sure about 2 things:

1) reading this book helped me to clarify a lot of issues and

2) that my signal delivery software will definitely be the Remote Trade Copier from ea-coder.com."

Juan Manuel Velilla, Spain

"I've been working in the Forex industry for a long time, and I only wish when we were first starting out that we had this book to guide us through the steps of operating a Forex signal service. I highly recommend this book for anyone wanting to sell Forex signal services or improve their current Forex signal business. And to make your life even easier and your Forex signal business more successful.

I highly recommend ea-coder.com to execute your Forex signal service. Don't waste your time with anything else out there, this book and ea-coder.com are essential tools to running your own Forex Signal website and service."

Teri Patterson, California, United States, aforex.com

"How to Start Your Own Forex Signal Service" is a great book for anyone seriously interested in starting their own Forex business. Whether you are a veteran Forex trader or a newbie it give fantastic insight into "trading robots" and step by step guide on how to set up a signal service. I myself as a trader have been interested in this service for quite a while and have never known exactly how to get into the market. This book has provide me with enough knowledge and tools to start.

Darren Gray, Australia

Story about my struggle creating trading signals service

I do not want you to think that there is zero work involved when starting this business. Be prepared to work hard, unless you want to start just another mediocre service that struggles to get customers.

The internet is already full of such websites where people sell trading signals that charge a few hundred dollars a month without even giving any proof of their trading results. I have tried many of such services myself, and in the end (usually in the first few days) it starts to be clear that the results on the website do not match the trading that I am seeing in my account. Or there are some other tricks involved, so that the vendor stays out of hot water when they deliver trader that do not match what was promised.

When I was starting my signals business, my main goal was not to look like or be like those dishonest services that just trick newbie Forex traders. To be honest, it wasn't easy. When I first started I was creating websites by using PHP, HTML, MySQL and other programming languages. Since I'm a programmer, this is something I'm very familiar with. But the process wasn't easy, even for someone with my programming skills. It took me 2 months to finish my first website and creating it was hard work.

I didn't know about WordPress, I knew nothing about design templates and I didn't know about all the useful plugins that make a website owner's life much easier. With a couple of mouse clicks, these plugins will finish a task in mere seconds. Some of these tasks took me hours to complete back in the day. With no clue about the existence of these tools, I thought that I needed to create everything from scratch.

The hard work didn't end here however. A website alone is not enough to sell signals. You need software to deliver those signals to your customers. After you figure out all of this stuff, you need to implement a payment solution that has the option to charge customers on a monthly basis.

All I had was a trading system that made virtual money on my practice account and a dream to help other people make money in the forex market. I was working hard and doing my best to make this happen. I couldn't get the idea that I can make a living from this out of my head.

Imagine all the lives that I can change. Imagine all the people who can earn additional income by following my trading signals. Imagine their families living the lives they've always longed-for, not bound by money problems.

Finally I found a solution

I wanted to make everything as automated as possible. The idea was that my subscribers could enjoy life and not bother themselves with copying my trading signals. What if a signal was delivered at night while they were sleeping or while they're spending quality time with their families?

There are so many trading services that still send signals by just email or sms. People often contact me asking if I could create a software that can transfer those text messages to their MetaTrader 4 accounts automatically. This shows how inconvenient such signal services are for many currency traders. They want a solution that can be automated and work with as little human intervention as possible.

In other words, people are tired of signals delivered as text messages. Unfortunately, such software is something that requires a lot of work to build well and also costs a lot of money.

This led me to create a special software, which among Forex traders, is known as a trade copier. I like to describe it as a trading signal delivery software. It not only copies trades to customer accounts, but can also take care of the payments, the registration, email notifications and much more.

There are a lot of methods that you can use to start selling trading signals. In this book I will be focusing on the task of running a trading signals business with the help of the Remote Trade Copier, created by yours truly. Although, after reading this book, you will learn the main things you need to create to run a trading signals business, using any signal delivery method. So please do not feel like I am selling anything to you, I use my RTC software as an example because this works for me and dozens of other trading signal providers. It's the solution that I know best and that is why I will use it as an example.

Even today, I still use this piece of software and it continues to perform really well. My whole signals business is completely automated and everything runs without any human intervention. All I have to do is answer my customers' emails when they have questions or they need help with the software.

Myths about Forex Trading Signals Business

A lot of people think that you need a huge staff to run this kind of business. This isn't true at all. I'm doing this alone. Well, I do hire one person that helps me answer emails and provides support to my customers, but that's it. Everything else is taken care of by the signal delivery software.

A lot of people say that before you start a signals service you first need to find a successful trading system. In my opinion, this is not necessary; I think you can find this part later. It takes time and effort to setup everything, to learn how to operate and work with all of these new tools. The preparation process is very time intensive and you should be ready to start selling signals as soon as you find that profitable trading system or robot. Later in this book, I will offer a lot of ideas on how you can find profitable systems for trading the Forex market.

Traders who are just beginning to explore this opportunity may think that they need a large amount of money to start a forex signals business. But what they fail to realize is that when they get customers they will have their money back in no time.

If you have a great trading system that turns a profit every month, do you think that you could sell those signals for a monthly subscription of 50 dollars? This is a very low fee for trading signals, but even charging this small amount could potentially earn you thousands of dollars with just 100 customers.

Taking into account the fact that there are hundreds of thousands, probably even millions of forex traders out there, most of who are not profitable, don't you think that you could entice just a hundred of them to subscribe to your trading signals?

And don't forget the fact that you can start selling signals from your practice account, just like I did. Sure, for some customers it may look suspicious, but my consistent trading and profits proved that it is a reliable system. My first investment into the signals service business was just a couple hundred dollars.

You can start small. There are many options that can help you do this. There are trade copiers with a monthly subscription based on the number of clients. Other copiers offer a lifelong license for a one-time fee. You could get a trade copier for a one-time fee of $50 that will deliver signals to your first customer. This can be your only investment made at this point.

I believe that there are even free trade copiers available. As you grow bigger and get more clients, you can upgrade your business to the next level with a proper signal delivery software and be prepared to deliver signals to thousands of subscribers.

Tips for success

Let me share some tips and ideas with you on how you can make your website stand out from the crowd and get attention from potential customers. Also, you will want to make your website leaves a good impression and not look like just any other signals website. There are so many websites out there that charge huge amounts of money and don't even offer a refund guarantee in case things are not as promised.

Here are few tips to make your website look more professional and to-the-point. You will find them discussed in detail in the coming chapters.

- Avoid anything on your site that will make it look spammy.
- Post your trading history on MyFXBook.com or some other 3rd party verification site.
- Make things personal. People are more likely to buy from other people.
- Don't confuse people—educate them. Inform them of important rules that relate to your system like scalping/spreads, hedging, etc.
- Set and manage their expectations. Explain briefly how your system works and what they can expect.
- Do not put advertisements on your site, especially ads of a 3rd party competing products or services.
- Look professional from the start. Make your website look nice using a modern design template.
- Show confidence in your services by giving at least a 30-day free trial and/or money-back guarantee.
- Be realistic and do not shout to the world that you are the number 1 signals service. I am sure there are other traders out there managing billions of dollars. Do you think that you are better than they are?
- Use fancy design elements to introduce important things. In other words, have a strong call-to-action on your home page so people can start testing your service quickly.

Begin Today

Now take a pen and a piece of paper and write down some numbers. How profitable is your trading system? If you don't have a system yet, read this book to learn more about how to find one. Next, think about how much would you charge in a month? Or perhaps you want to charge on a weekly basis?

My book will help you realize the possibilities of this business, so please continue reading. In the pages below I will go over the process of setting up a trading signals business in great detail. I will also give my personal experience with setting up my own business.

I won't hold anything back and I will freely share what worked and didn't work for me. If you're interested in setting up your own trading signals business, or if you're just curious to learn more about this topic, read on.

Chapter 1 Takeaways

Tools needed in order to start your very own signal service business:

- MT4 EA or Forex Robot
- Signal delivery Software
- Trading signals to send to customers
- Domain
- Customer base
- Website
- Payment Gateway
- Marketing
- SEO

Chapter 1: My Story

- How I Started My Forex Signals Business
- Hard work is involved when starting this business
- I started a successful trading signals business with a MetaTrader 4 practice account
- When my practice account balance and equity grows, my customers' accounts grow too
- I get paid monthly and my customers earn income in their trading accounts by following my signals
- Myths about Forex Trading Signals Business
  - You need a huge staff to run the business
    - You can do it alone
    - Everything else is taken care of by the signal delivery software
  - You need to find a successful trading system
    - You can partner up with a professional trader or buy a profitable EA
- Tips for success with your online presence
  - Avoid anything on your site that will make it look spammy
  - Post your trading history on MyFXBook.com or some other 3rd party verification site.
  - Make things personal.

- Don't confuse people—educate them. Inform them of important rules that relate to your system like scalping/spreads, hedging, etc.
- Set and manage their expectations. Explain briefly how your system works and what they can expect.
- Do not put advertisements on your site, especially ads of a 3rd party competing products or services.
- Look professional from the start. Make your website look nice using a modern design template.
- Show confidence in your services by giving at least a 30-day free trial and/or money-back guarantee.
- Be realistic and do not shout to the world that you are the number 1 signals service. I am sure there are other traders out there managing billions of dollars. Do you think that you are better than they are?
- Use fancy design elements to introduce important things. In other words, have a strong call-to-action on your home page so people can start testing your service quickly.

CHAPTER 2

How the Trading Signals Business Works

"Things are difficult before they become easy. Most things worth doing require effort. As you do the task, you learn, gain experience and begin to understand. Then we call it easy."

- Rimantas Petrauskas

I assume you already know what Forex is, but still, let me write a few words about it.

Forex is a term derived from "Foreign Exchange" and is the process of trading different countries' currencies.   In other words, this is the trade between one nation's currency and another. Currency traders are continuously looking to buy or sell a currency pair and profit from the change in price. If we can guess correctly the direction that a currency value will go then we stand to make a profit from the exchange. And as traders, we are looking to take some money that we have (capital in our trading account) and use it to buy and sell these currencies in the hopes of increasing our account equity (the amount of money that is in our trading account).

Nowadays it is incredibly easy to begin trading foreign currencies. In the past it was very difficult and required working with telephones and newspapers in some cases, fax machines and snail mail in others. Trading currencies might have even involved telegrams, if you go far enough back in history. The GBPUSD (Great Britain Pound / United States Dollar) pair gained its nickname the "CABLE" because there was a time when a giant cable—a data and communications line—stretched between the UK and United States (in the Atlantic Ocean) that would relay the prices of the currencies and other information between the two countries.

Most of us who are reading this book will have never known the days of phone and newspaper information and ordering or especially the days of the telegram to notify our brokers of a buy or sell order. We are currency traders of the modern computer age.

Most of have a lot of experience with computers and have not known any other way of trading currencies. Nowadays, it is even possible for a teenager, with their parents' permission, to open up a currency trading account online and begin trading within hours—using real, live money. It is certainly possible to open a demo account and begin trading within 5 or 10 minutes. This comes as a direct result of the revolution of the Internet and now we, as currency traders, are able to make or lose fortunes within a few hours or a few days' time.

It takes years to become profitable forex trader. This is chief reason why the majority of people would rather buy signals and generate a profit on their account that way than go through a 10 year learning process on how to trade currencies. This is one of the most important reasons why this business is so lucrative.

Forex signals are an easy way for regular people and novice traders to make money in currency trading. By subscribing to automated trading signals they can allow a professional forex trader to take control and initiate trades on their account.

People are interested in following trading signals that have potential. Investing in a signals service may turn out to be the best financial decision of their life, but it can also end in tears just as often. Just as is the case with traders, the majority of signal providers will not make money in the long run. In fact, very few signal providers make it past a couple of years.

And I don't know why, but the majority of signal services that you can find by running a simple search on Google usually get you to those websites that promise a lot, but deliver nothing more than another broken dream. Maybe it's because they do not care about the profitability of their signals and just focus on marketing. Maybe this just proves that the majority of new Forex traders get sold by those websites only to find disappointment later and lose faith and trust in Forex overall.

Due to the high failure rate, trust is very important in the signal service business. People need to have faith in the service before they join and offering a 30 day trial is an essential step to establishing that trust. I will talk more about this in an upcoming chapter.

How does Forex signal business work?

The process is simple. You initiate trades on your own account, I call this account the master account or the signal provider account. With the help of a trade copier software, your customers will receive those same trades automatically copied to their accounts. I call these accounts the slave accounts or simply the followers. When you make profit your clients make a profit as well.

You can trade currencies manually or by using a trading robot. Now I know many of you do not like trading robots, but allow me to share a few thoughts with you. Don't let go of the trust for trading robots just because there are hundreds of them that do not work. As I write this chapter. I am sitting in front of a Christmas tree and when my family and I were looking for it, we choose it from 100 trees. Others were too small, or had broken branches, or was of some funny shape, etc. My point here with this is that there are millions of Christmas trees out there that look ugly or are not quite right, but we still were able to find the one that looks just gorgeous in our living room and is perfect in shape and size.

I prefer to use a trading robot because in this way you can setup everything on autopilot. This is exactly what I'm doing. And yes, I created one myself using my own trading strategy. Even if you do not know how to create trading robots, you still can build one by hiring a programmer.

Alternatively, you could ask a professional trader to come and work with you. You could establish a kind of a partnership where he would be responsible for providing profitable forex trading signals and you would handle the process of trade copying, marketing the service and getting clients to subscribe. The usual fee for a monthly subscription to a signal service ranges from $49 - $99 per customer. Having just 100 subscribers could generate close to a 10,000 dollars income on a monthly basis.

When you have very little money to invest and can only afford to take trades on a demo account (or a small $500 real money account, for example), isn't this a much better option than trading? As you keep earning money in subscription fees you can transfer those funds to your trading account. Now you've potentially created two income streams for yourself.

A signals business can generate a significant amount of extra income. Making 10,000 USD per month with trading would be close to impossible to do on a 500 USD account. Even if you happen to stumble upon a great trading system that makes 10% profit per month, you would still need a 100,000 USD account to earn a 10,000 USD profit.

You can start a forex signals business with a couple hundred bucks. In all my years of involvement in the forex arena, I have yet to find a system that could allow you to make enough money to live on by trading from a 500 dollars account. Don't have enough money to open a real account? No problem, I already told you that you can even start a signals business by sending trades from your practice (demo) account. I keep repeating this so you will finally believe it's possible.

Will people buy my trading signals and what I need to begin?

There are thousands if not millions of currency traders who do not earn and even lose money in the Forex market each day. Majority of them maybe do not even know that there is a possibility to follow someone's trading signals and make an income in Forex in such a way. Your job to demonstrate that and teach them how to invest their money in your trading signals so they could earn money together with you.

The benefits of following trading signals for customers are huge. When you trade with signals it is like having a calm and experienced mentor watching over you and guiding all that you do. In the heat of the trading day and all the pressure it can bring, having this support will keep you on track and your profits growing. After a while you may even feel confident enough to allow the signals to automatically place all the trades for you, allowing you to focus your time on other markets or other life pursuits.

There is nothing confusing in this type of service actually. Just do what I do and you will get the results similar to mine. Do not tell them that they will get exact the same results as you do, because that is not possible, but obviously if they follow your trading signals they will get similar results too. Now make all this process automated and you have the service which will be of interest to many traders.

It does not matter how you are doing this, what software you use and what payment structure or system you are applying. It also does not matter if you are just a beginner or a professional trader. As long as you make profit in Forex trading and sell your signals people will follow you. Money makes more money, everybody knows that and serious or even amateur investors will find you if you can make money for them.

However, you should pick your audience. Do not advertise or try to sell your service to everyone. Even selling this to any investor would seem a bad idea. Hardly the person who is investing in a real estate will be interested in your trading service. Although that is possible, you will still get more people sign up if you just try to reach Forex traders.

It is a wise idea to try reaching people interested only in the same trading style as you use. Say if your trading system is a long term it will not be of interest to Forex scalpers who are looking for systems that make a lot of trades and aim for a couple of pips profit only. The same can be with day traders or swing traders. People who are more comfortable with the long term systems will not be that much interested in a day trading systems. Keep this in mind when you will be reaching for the customers.

Another important thing to consider is to discover the needs of your prospects. Being a trader of some certain style will have its own needs and requirements for the strategy. Like for example day traders will be looking just for a trading system that opens and closes orders the same day. That what your potential future customers would need and look for. Personally I do not like scalping systems and you can sell me that all day with no luck.

Before offering your signals tell them your story how you created your strategy. Every one of us have a story about how we stumble upon that magical trading technique that finally make us money. Every single Forex trader starts with no knowledge and do not know what system to use. You may even heard the fact that if you give a profitable trading system that works to someone who is just a beginner or simply is not enough disciplined trader, the system won't work. This only proves that every single one of us are struggling for years or even decades before we learn to trade and find something that works.

You do not need to reveal your secret, just tell them your story. My story is that I was creating trading robots based on my crazy ideas and I had a lot of them created in many years. Finally, one of them, the Daily-F trading robot proven to be making money on a demo account for a few months in a row and I focused on that one. Months later I started my trading signals using that demo account as a master account to deliver signals.

So I have tested enormous amount of ideas before I found something that works for me and now this earns money not only for me, but for my customers as well. So have your story and be honest telling it.

Now to illustrate their problem to make money as a problem you need to tell a story how you struggled to make money in Forex before. Once people see that you have come from the place they are in right now, they will listen to what you can offer to them. And of course you will offer a solution to their problem.

So look at your profitable trading as the solution for investors. It is important to understand, that your service, the product you are going to sell is your solution to make money. You will need to show that your strategy makes money for you so they would see that as a solution to their problem, which is they do not know how to make money in Forex.

Now there is a lot of information that you should share with the traders to demonstrate your knowledge and expertise in Forex trading. And you may already know that the best way to present this information is on a website. This way everyone will be able to find you and your service online at any time from any place on earth.

That's a no brainer, right? But believe me I know so many websites that look just horrible or they do not have a website at all. I know people who were managing funds of tens of thousands of dollars and do not have a website. In my opinion it is a complete disservice to people who are looking to make money in Forex.

With so many scam websites in Forex there is no doubt that we need more genuine traders offering their services. We need more honest people running businesses and offering services and solutions to Forex traders. Hundreds of thousands of currency traders need guidance and help and you are saying that you better manage accounts for 5 people, even if that sums up to a million dollar fund, than offer your trading solutions to masses? I encourage you to start your own trading signals service so you could reach masses.

In this book I will show you what you need to start your own website and what software you need to deliver trading signals. I will show you different methods to run this business and I hope you will finally take action and go out to the world and help others to reach financial freedom just the way you did. Even if you are struggling right now with no money to invest in your real live trading account for your successful trading strategy, you will be able to start earning income with just your demo account.

The main piece missing to start this business for Forex traders is usually the lack of self-confidence as it may seem that it is very difficult to sell trading signals. Do not let this fear of not knowing how to do this stop you from creating your business.

Let me share with you one of my favorite quotes that I keep in mind a lot.

> *"The best time to plant a tree was 20 years ago. The second best time is now."*
>
> *– Chinese Proverb*

This quote helps me to not stop and keep moving in many areas of my life including business. There will be times when you learn something new and you set yourself a new goal in life, so the best thing you could do is to follow that quote and start reaching for that goal right now. Now is the best time to create a signals service because there is so much technology that allows us to do things with just a few clicks and just a couple hundred of dollars. There were many things before that were so complicated, but now they are so easy to do—like creating a website or sending trading signals automatically and directly to your customer's trading platform.

I know you will have a lot of questions on how to build this business and you will also likely have many doubts, but I did my best to address as many of these concerns as possible in this book so you would have as much knowledge as possible.

One of the questions people ask me often is which is better—to charge your clients monthly or to charge them a percentage from the profits (a.k.a performance fee). People will wonder which one to choose and this keeps delaying them getting into business.

In my opinion it is not worth to charge monthly based on performance if you plan to sell trading signals. It is a good decision and a good way to get paid for your service, but if you want to go this path you should go with a PAMM/MAM type account where the broker does everything for you. They charge a percentage and pay you through your account. I will discuss this in detail in the upcoming chapters.

Imagine if someone has to pay you $5000 by credit card, because you made profit for him last month. Do you think a lot of people have credit cards that can handle such payments? People will have to deal with credit card limits and will need to go to the banks to raise them, etc. That will result in a delay or simple failure to pay and need to look for alternatives fast.

Right now on Vavatrade I charge 100 EUR/month. This happens regardless to what account size customer has and regardless to how much of my service he uses. There are customers who use only email notifications and I do not even see their accounts. There are customers with $500 accounts, which are way too small to make a profit to even cover the expenses of the monthly payment. I would not get any profit from such customers if I were charging a performance fee.

However, there are customers who have big accounts and I wish I could charge them a percentage-based performance fee, but at the end of the day I just keep it the way it is for now. I mean, this is trading signal business, not a money manager business. I am in a process starting a MAM account with one of the Forex brokers, and charging a percentage on performance, but I think that will run as a 2nd business for clients with bigger accounts. I will offer both options for my customers.

So, in conclusion, both ways are good to earn money and each has its own advantages and disadvantages. I think it is not possible, or at least truly very hard, to get noticed by big traders so they would invest in your trading and your MAM account. Now if you start small with $500-$2000 accounts or so, and grow by charging fixed monthly fee, then after some time—usually a few years or several months—you naturally get proposals from brokers to have your MAM account and they will drive you customers with big money. This is how you grow—at least this is the way that I have found it to be.

So my advice would be to start your own trading signals service, grow to 100 or even 1000 customers paying you 50-100$ a month and then grow into a MAM money manager with some huge broker to manage millions of dollars.

I know many of you wonder how much you should charge monthly for your trading signals service. Don't make such a big about this. Know that you can always change the price as you go along.

You should charge as much as you feel your clients are willing to pay. If you operate your business and are surrounded by rich Forex traders, then charging a couple hundred of dollars a month sounds pretty fair. If you just starting, with no investors on your radar, you should be looking at the price point below $100.

In my case, many customers say my Vavatrade is expensive, but those that come with at least $5k or $10k accounts do not feel this way. I have customers with accounts above $50k and they made enough profit in their first month to cover their whole year's expenses for my service. They do not even think about the monthly price. Often such investors ask to pay annually at a discounted rate to save some fees.

So charging a larger amount of money will eventually attract more serious investors. If you charge smaller amounts you will be seeing a lot of Forex novice traders. A lot of investors will be not as serious so you just focus on those who are serious enough to invest.

The majority of Forex traders who keep looking for that perfect "holy grail" of trading signals (or trading strategy) will have accounts that are not more than $1k or so. So the lower monthly price will definitely get their attention as they will be able to afford it for testing.

Speaking of getting people's attention on your service... it is very important to show your trading record clearly on the front of the home page of your website. People often ask me if it is vital to add a verified trading record to the website to show the trading system performance, and most certainly it is.

Performance is something that will get visitors attention. It's a must and should be visible as soon as they visit your site. MyFXBook is the most trusted for this. Some don't trust even MyFXBook and ask for a MT4 investor password.

I was sharing this investor password some time ago with my customers and potential investors, but later I've found this to be very inconvenient. After some time you will want to change the investor password, and this will bring you a lot of trouble, as you will need to update that password every place you are publishing it. If you publish your trading record on FPA and MyFXBook, you will need to update them with your new investor password as well, every time you change it.

Now one of the biggest questions I receive is people asking me what the potential of this business is. They ask me how many clients I think they could have per month.

This is truly hard to answer, but I can assure you that your client number can be unlimited. Really. Yes, I mean it. When I started Vavatrade, I had only a few customers, but once I started to invest time marketing it, giving 30-day trials and updating my website with the answers to the most frequently asked questions, my numbers started to grow. Recently, I read a press release from iFexx signal service and they claim to have about 600 customers. This truly can get to be a very serious business with lots of monthly paying customers.

When you attract more and more people, your business will go viral for sure and the big investors and Forex brokers will notice you. So this business is not only about signals. If you are making money with your system, you will get noticed by brokers and other institutions as well.

There is no limit for sure and if you make money all depends on how you market your services. You cannot afford to keep your trading system just to yourself, there are thousands of Forex traders that are waiting to invest their money into a system that makes consistent profits. Isn't this something you've been looking for yourself the whole time? If you give that to the world it will pay you back a fortune.

After releasing the new version of the popular MetaTrader 4 trading platform, MetaQuotes said there are over 7 million MT4 and MT5 users. This means there are that many Forex traders in the world. Do you think you could attract 0.001% of them? That would be 7000 customers which would be enormously huge business and income for you.

Now let me tell you what the best part about this business is. The thing that I like the most is that there is no competition. In every other business you will have competitors, but not with a Forex trading signals business. I don't think signal providers are really competing with each other. If someone were to find 2 profitable signal providers, the initial thought of the user is, "I should find a way to run both and diversify".

And of course this book would not be complete without helping you to answer the most frequently asked question by Forex traders, prospects and your website visitors. This one is usually asked by those who have experienced serious losses before or someone who is wary of everything and even skeptic about all signal providers.

That question is "Why don't you trade and make money yourself with your system instead of selling signals?"

Be sure that you will get a lot of people asking you this. Now the most important part here is that you would answer this question in your own words and from your own position and make sure your answer is honest and pure truth.

But let me answer this one for you with what I say to my customers when they ask me this question.

I am just a simple guy from a small town in a small country where no one around even knows what Forex is and for many years I have been living on a salary and did not have any money to invest into Forex trading. Risk disclaimers tell you not to invest money you cannot afford to lose, but to tell the truth, I even did not have any money at all. Having my own real money account seemed to be an unreachable goal at that moment. But I had good knowledge on how to make websites and create software. So this allowed me to create a trading signals service from the ground up where I had to invest only a couple of hundred dollars or so.

Even now, when I have this business running on autopilot, and have it as my passive income stream, I cannot afford to invest $100,000 or so to get the monthly returns that could provide for my family. My goal is to get to that level and beyond, but right now I am still moving towards this. Even when I reach that level I may still manage money for my customers—earning for them and getting paid for that as well. There is no limit to how big this can get, but we all know that it all starts with the first step and for me that was a demo account and a trading signals business.

A journey of a thousand miles begins with a single step.

- Lao-tzu, The Way of Lao-tzu, Chinese philosopher (604 BC - 531 BC)

For someone who can afford to invest thousands of dollars just to trade Forex, and make a living out of it, may sound as a great opportunity, but I believe that the majority of Forex traders, especially the new ones, start with small capital.

Chapter 2 Takeaways

Chapter 2: How Trading Signals Business Works
Forex Trading
- Foreign Exchange Trading is the simultaneous buying and selling of a currency against another currency. Traders profit from the change in prices.

Forex Signals Business
- With a profitable trading strategy, you can use your live trading account or a demo account as the master account to initiate trades. The trades will then be copied to your customer's accounts or the slave accounts. Customers must subscribe to your service to avail of the trading signals and pay a regular subscription fee.

Why People Need My Service
- Ninety percent of Forex traders lose money in the markets every day. Most of these losing traders prefer to invest their money to trading signals. If you can generate profit from your strategy, they too can earn profit by copying your trades.

Source of trading signals and to whom to market the signals
Trading Strategy
It doesn't matter if you're a beginner or a professional trader as long as you make profits in trading.
Customers
- Pick your specific customers that trade the same style that you use. If you're a day trader, target to market your service to day traders.
- Illustrate the solution to your prospect's trading problem
- Present all the information about your service in a website
- Grow your trading performance record

CHAPTER 3

Forex Trading Signals Delivery

"Living a life without a purpose is like walking down the pier on a beach. Eventually it will dead-end and you will need to come back and look for another path."

- Rimantas Petrauskas

How would you feel if you built a large, highly-successful trading signal business and were able to help thousands of other traders succeed because of your efforts? Maybe this has been your exact goal... You have a vision in mind of building a large business by providing trade signals to clients. You envision a large, monthly recurring income from the signals and the account growth that you can offer to your customers. The ability to share trades with other traders is now very possible, thanks to advances in technology, and the creation of several different types of trade copying services that I'd like to share with you here.

Your trading account is capable of sending out signals to your clients. These signals can "tell" them which currency pairs to buy or sell. They can inform your clients about the current currency ranges or alert them of an imminent breakout. Brokers and trade signal providers often send out these types of alerts or signals through SMS, email or instant messaging.

However, there are obvious drawbacks to these now rather antiquated methods.

Constant monitoring by the client. These types of alerts require traders to be logged on to the PC or cell phone to monitor texts and email messages.

Time zone issues. Currencies can move tens, sometimes even hundreds of pips within a few seconds or minutes. Traders who live in different time zones are more likely to miss these alert updates. They could be sleeping, working, shopping or walking the dog while there is an alert occurring.

Add to this the speed delay from different email providers as well as the delay from needing to manually enter the orders and you have a pretty unreliable and slow system of communication!

Automatic signal delivery software (also called a trade copier or account copier) can help eliminate these problems. A trade copier will greatly reduce the time you need to spend fiddling with your Forex account. For you this might mean no more long hours staring at the computer screen. If you are a signal provider, the copier will send out the signals to your clients' accounts as soon as changes are made on your own account.

Advantages of automatic signal delivery software

Here are some of the benefits of using trade copier software in your business to send out automatic signals to your clients/fellow traders/followers:

Automated trade copying software helps you stay connected with your clients at all times.

Automated trade copying software copies the trading actions from your account to the account of a client in real time. As soon as you make changes to a trading position, that same action will get replicated to your client's account.

Most of the trade copier programs are easy to install.

Automated trade copying software can allow you to run a trading signals business on autopilot.

Customers just need to setup the software on their account and leave it to do the rest of the work.

By now you can probably see how these automatic copiers can make Forex trading simpler, better managed and more efficient. It can take incredible weight off your shoulders and make this business more fun.

What is a trading signals delivery software?

A trading signals delivery software is a special computer application that takes trading signals from a master account and copies them to customer accounts (also called slave accounts). This is also known as trade copying or copy trading. There are many different applications for trade copying and they can operate online or offline, and on both a large and small scale alike.

You usually have to purchase this type of software, but once you start receiving a monthly income from trading signals, the software will easily pay for itself. I have customers who earned back all the expenses they paid for setting up their business in just the first week of operating their trade signal business. This included not only the cost for the software, but also the server and domain registration fees. There are free trade copying solutions out there and most of them are not very good, so usually you just end up "feeding the brokers" by paying spreads and earning just breadcrumbs.

I recommend to have a trade delivery software already setup on your server BEFORE you find a profitable signal source. Trust me, when you do find those profitable signals, you will want to launch your business and start selling the signals as soon as possible.

An added benefit to setting up the software beforehand is that when you launch your business you will already know how to operate the trade copier because you have already been using it for a while. You will have gone through the instruction manual and now you are able to help your clients if they encounter any issues with the software.

Or maybe you will take care of all the technical details yourself and make your service available to a bigger audience, especially to those who don't know how to use computers or software applications all that well. The ideas are numerous on how to setup and run a forex trade signal provider service and we are going to look at a number of them right here in this material.

Find a Signal Delivery Software

You could also do it the other way… Once you find a source of profitable signals (or you can also create your own profitable trading system) proceed to the next step and start looking for a signal delivery software. While you're searching for the right piece of software, your trading record will continue to grow. By the time you have everything setup and ready to go, you'll have a nice past performance record that you can present to potential customers.

Note: The performance record of your trading signals is one of the most important parts of your success in running a trade signals business. The longer the performance record you have the better. Customers will compare your performance record to that of other signal providers and trading services. Use a service like MyFXBook.com to show off your trade signals' performance and provide authenticity and credibility.

Important Warning: Please make sure that you do a lot of research before buying your signal delivery software. Look at online reviews, and ask on public forums for other people's opinions. This is something of a big decision, and one that you will potentially be using for years to come, so make your decision carefully. After purchasing and setting up the trade copier, spend some time with the software and understand thoroughly how it operates. I am going to show you many different trade copying options in this book so that you can see what is out there and have enough information to make a wise decision.

There are many ways that you can use to sell your trading signals. You can use old-fashioned delivery methods and simply send signals by email or through sms. Or you can use modern technology and deliver the signals automatically by using special software designed especially for trade duplication/replication. This latter option is what we are going to be researching here in this material.

The most popular methods to deliver trading signals

Let's take a closer look at the most popular methods for delivering and selling trading signals. Each of these options could serve as the basis for a strong and profitable trading signal business, but some are much better than others. Some will provide you with a more hands-off approach and limited control while others will allow you to take hold of the reins and control every aspect of your signals business. Here is an example of one method that I have used to build a trade signals business. You will find the method that works best for you, but these are the most services out there these days for trade copying...

Using Zulutrade.com to deliver signals

Are you a profitable Forex Trader achieving consistent trading results? Do you have proven strategies and excellent trading skills? Or perhaps you're a professional trader with years of experience in the Forex market. Did you know that you can share information about your trades and get paid for it?

With a service called ZuluTrade, you can potentially earn $100 up to $1,000,000,000 per month by just using the web based point-and-click platform and executing trades (which are then shared with others). This depends, however, on your performance and popularity. If you are confident that your strategy and trading advice are interesting enough for other ZuluTraders, then be one of the company's professional and talented signal providers and you can earn extra money by helping others profit in Forex.

However, you can earn such a huge income only if you have hundreds or thousands of followers, so don't expect to make a fortune just by sending your first signals to ZuluTraders.

As a signal provider, you would develop and provide live Forex trading signals and systems to ZuluTraders ("followers").

You either trade a demo or live account at your chosen brokerage firm while ZuluTrade publishes your trading results and statistics publicly through the website.

With the advantage of the web based point-and-click platform, your trade is automatically copied from your broker and broadcasted and executed at your followers' demo or live trading account at their respective brokerage firm. This allows ZuluTraders the possibility of following all your trading activity.

ZuluTrade trader ranking boards help promote you to trade followers

With the ZuluTrade leader board, as long as you are consistently profitable, you don't have to spend time in recruiting your followers. Once you sign up and are accepted to this program, your account appears on ZuluTrade's list of signal providers. Traders who are interested in your service will just choose you from the list and can start to follow your trades. Your positions are automatically executed in your followers' accounts without their personal intervention. When new traders sign up for Zulu, one of the first screens they will see is a 'fast start' invitation to follow a few traders. If you are one of the top providers on Zulu, you will appear on this list and will likely have many new traders flocking to your service and following your trades.

If you are able to provide profitable trades, then more and more followers will be enticed to join you and your compensation will increase. To help ZuluTraders find the best signal provider, your performance is constantly ranked through ZuluRank and the ZuluTrade social community. The best signal provider for any given time period appears on top of the list. Zulu also tracks, compiles and shares trading statistics, number of followers and live money capital following each trader to help their traders make informed decisions.

Note: The ZuluTrade system provides a pretty good service for their followers and signal providers. It recognizes the fact that due to the different configuration and trading interfaces of various brokers, a follower's trading account may have the possibility of an orphan trade. Wherein a signal provider may have closed a position but it wasn't executed at a follower's account. This trade may have been left open at one or more followers' live accounts due to various causes. The signal provider may have gained but the followers end up losing their money. Zulu-Trade provides the authority and tool to signal providers to both monitor and close their followers' orphaned positions. This extra tool can give confidence to your followers to trade with you as their signal provider.

Another variance of ZuluTrade from others is providing the possibility of you opening a demo account and then becoming a signal provider. You can trade with virtual money, while your followers' may trade demo or live funds, provided that you follow the demo trading compliance rules. You are limited only to 30 markets and 30 pending orders within 24 hours. Signals in excess of these will no longer be broadcasted to followers. In comparison to a live trading account, you can open unlimited number of orders at all currency pairs within 24 hours. (Note: Most trading systems will never need these types of trade numbers though.)

Earning Extra Income through ZuluTrade

The greatest advantage of becoming a ZuluTrade signal provider is the extra income you can potentially generate by letting other traders follow your trades. That's what you get of course. While trading your own account or money, you let others take advantage of your success and get paid for it—from $100 up to several million per month without having to manage their portfolios. You will earn 0.5 pips per lot, per transaction, from a live follower account.

A Signal Provider's compensation is calculated on a monthly calendar basis. So, if a trader follows 100 of your trades during the month using 1 standard lot per trade, you will earn $500 from this. (Note: This is just an estimated amount of dollars earned since pip value varies according to Forex pairs traded.) ZuluTrade will pay you the rate as posted on the company's website. Payment requests can be withdrawn through PayPal, bank wire transfer, and the ZuluTrade MasterCard. In cases that you may have incurred losses in your trading account in a month, you will not receive any compensation. Also, you are not accountable for any followers' accounts in cases that your followers incur losses in copying your trades.

Downside to followers when signal provider traders use demo accounts

Even though becoming a signal provider of ZuluTrade has also its own disadvantages, its apparent benefits far outweigh the drawbacks. Its biggest disadvantage lies on the possibility of becoming a signal provider through a demo account. It's an advantage compared to others but there is a huge difference between trading a demo and a live account. A demo account doesn't have the strong emotions of real money. As traders, emotions must be separated from money. To address this need, money management and risk management must be mastered to really profit in Forex trading. Even if you tried to treat your demo account as a real one, the truth is that there is no real monetary risk on a demo account. You may have the best equity curve, outstanding performance and rank with the best traders, but in real world of Forex trading, past performance is not a measure of future gain. That's why elite Forex traders always keep their emotions in check to avoid harming their live trading account. You can suffer a few losses here and there but, at the back of your mind, you have nothing to lose if you will blow your demo account. How about your followers? Well, they lose real money on their live trades. Of course, followers were warned about this and it's their decision to follow a demo account.

There is also a large potential downside for your following traders in the way trades are copied between different brokers. It is advised that you start a demo account yourself and follow some top system providers yourself to see if you can make money with this system. Sometimes the difference in broker spreads and execution time alone is enough to put a 'trade copying system' in jeopardy. Always test with a demo account first and notice how your profitability differs from that of the signal provider, and then only after strong testing, proceed with a small live account.

Interesting fact: On the top 100 list of ZuluTraders there are only 4 signal providers that are using live, real money accounts to send trading signals to followers. Now this proves that you can make money or even a fortune by selling trading signals from a demo account. Although, that is not the best for the followers. Also this kind of proves that signal providers are not very serious about their signals. If your strategy would get published there with a real money account and make profit, I am sure you will get lots of followers.

ZuluTrade bird's eye view

Traders who have consistent results trading live accounts can earn additional money from their followers. ZuluTrader is one of the best platforms that gives competitive payments to its signal providers. To meet the requirements set by the company, you must have a profitable trading strategy. It is best that you have already developed a profitable strategy to build a winning account in a short period of time. Your trading equity curve will reflect on your account statistics. If you have excellent performance, more and more followers will believe in you and follow you. You must strive to be ranked among the globally competitive professional and talented traders and generate more money for your followers. Your followers' success is also your success, here with Zulu, but also in general with all signal providing. So keep developing your trading skills, demonstrate it in your own live account and then you will have more and more ZuluTraders following you.

It's good news that you can sell your signals on Zulu-trade.com. A lot of traders and signal providers use Zulu-Trade—it is one of the largest social trading networks. There are no fees for using the service. The site makes money by acting as an IB (introducing broker). Basically brokers pay a commission to ZuluTrade for every trade customers take. The website, in turn, pays some of that money back to the signal providers.

Everything is done automatically. After a customer opens an account with one of ZuluTrade's recommended brokers, his/her account can begin to follow trading signals from the hundreds of signal providers operating on the website.

The good news also is that anyone can become a signal provider. The problem with this kind of openness is that there are a lot of signal providers who try out random systems or EAs in a bid to create a trading record and thus gain more followers. If the trading system fails they just open a new account and start from scratch with another strategy. For the signal provider it is just another trading system that doesn't work, but their followers lose real money in the process.

Note: Lately, though, I saw that ZuluTrade changed the rules and now they accept only high quality traders. I think this happened after the MyFXBook.com launched their Autotrade service where only traders with a profitable and proven trading history are welcome.

Two more Zulu advantages

There are two other major advantages to using Zulu-trade.com. The first one is that there is no need to install any software on your computer in order to start sending or receiving trading signals. The second major advantage is the large pool of forex signal providers present on the site. As a follower, you will have a lot more options to pick a good signal provider.

Before choosing a provider, make sure to thoroughly check their trading record. Is he/she profitable in the last 12 to 24 months? What was his biggest drawdown during that time period? Note: The leading traders on ZuluTrade seem to shift a lot. This is the nature of trading, yes, but can make it difficult to determine the best traders to follow.

On a risk adjusted basis, the performance of a signal provider that makes 5 percent per month with a 1 percent drawdown is equal to the performance of a provider with a 50 percent monthly gain and a 10 percent drawdown. Make it a habit to always check a trader's drawdown along with their profitability, and not just over the past month, but look at as much history as possible.

Look for providers that have been trading consistently profitable for a long time

Longevity is also incredibly important when selecting a trader to follow. A provider who has been in the forex business for 3 years is lot less likely to blow up an account when trends/markets change, compared to a trader who's been profitable for the last 3 months only. Markets always change and shift—it is just a fact of this business. An experienced trader/signal provider will know how to handle this situation and adjust to the new market conditions.

For a new signal provider, it can be really hard to get subscribers on ZuluTrade. Even if your system makes a decent amount of profit, you still need to compete with the signal providers at the top that have hundreds or thousands of followers. It can be difficult to move to the top and get noticed, but consistent profitability (with low drawdown) is the key. Your long term results will be better than your short term results.

The model of ZuluTrade, as previously mentioned, is that you get paid a small commission fee for each trade that your subscribers choose to follow in their accounts. If you only have a couple of followers and their accounts are small, your income will be small as well. But as you build your followers and your track record then you will be in a position for great profits in the years to come.

Sell trading signals and software
on the MT5 marketplace

MetaTrader Trading Signals is a social trading service that allows amateur traders to follow and copy trades of professional traders. Traders can subscribe to the signal feeds of other traders directly in the MetaTrader platform regardless of their broker. Each trade executed by the Signal Provider will be copied on the Subscriber's trading account. What this potentially means is that you can sit back and receive the trades of highly successful traders while you watch your account equity grow.

How to become a signals provider in MetaTrader

First, you will need to register and activate an account at MQL5.com. Next, connect your MT4 or MT5 account to your MLQ5 account through your platform. Launch your MetaTrader platform then click "Tools" menu then choose "Options". Under the "Community" tab, enter your MQL5 username and password then click "OK". Then, register as a Signal Provider by opening your platform's navigator window, right click on your account, and click "Register as Signal". This will take you directly to MQL5.com website. Note that your MetaTrader account, broker's trading server name, and your MetaTrader terminal type (MT4 or MT5) were already set up for you. All you have to do is specify a unique name of your signal, enter your MetaTrader investor password, and subscription price. Signal Providers have the choice of how much they charge for their signals.

Note about pricing: Pricing can be a funny thing. If you price your signals too high then people may not be able to afford them or think that they are not worth the money. However, price them too low and you also run the risk of not having the credibility of a more expensive signal provider.

Making your signals public

Upon registration as a signal provider, your profile becomes available to the public. Throughout the subscription period, your MetaTrader password should not be changed and the transmission of your signals must remain failure free. Your trading signals will be transmitted through MetaQuote's signal service on a free-of-charge basis. All your instant execution trades will be broadcasted and executed to all subscribers' trading terminals. Pending orders are not transmitted until they are triggered in the signal provider's account.

Charging for signals

Free Signals become immediately available for subscription after a successful registration. You may change your Signal from free to a fee-based at any time. However, you need to register as a seller and you will be subjected to a one month testing period.

For the paid signals, you need to register as a seller. Traders can subscribe to your trading signals after one month—the test period, provided that you have executed at least 5 trades during the qualification period. If you're been approved, your signals become available for subscription and can bring you profit. Information about your signal will be available in all MetaTrader terminals around the world and each MetaTrader user can subscribe to your signal. If you do a good job trading then you will likely gain many followers over time.

You will automatically receive the subscriber's payment for your paid signals upon the expiration of each subscriber's subscription period. You can manage earnings from MQL5's internal Payment System and you can withdraw it through WebMoney and PayPal. MetaQuotes charges Signal Providers 20% of the fixed monthly subscription fee.

How to subscribe to MetaTrader trading signals?

MetaTrader traders can subscribe to any signal issued by providers. To subscribe to any signal provider, all you have to do is open an account at the MLQ5.com website. Next, launch your MT4 or MT5 terminal and specify your login and password from your MQL5.com account. To do this, click "Tools" at your terminal main menu and choose "Options". At the Options window, click "Community" tab. Enter your MQL5 community login and password then click "OK".

To select a suitable signal and subscribe to it, follow these simple steps. First, open your MetaTrader's terminal window by clicking "View" then "Terminal" at the main menu. At the Terminal window, click the "Signals" tab. You will see the list of all the available signals and their summarized details. Double click on the best signal you would like to subscribe to. Note: You will see a more comprehensive detail of the signal provider including the growth statistics, current open positions, trading history, author's name, and other information. By clicking the author's name, you will be able to check the author's MQL5 profile and you can directly communicate to him. By clicking the signal name, complete trade statistics will be shown such as the equity curve, risk profile and reviews.

To subscribe, click the "Subscribe" button near the top of the signal name. In the confirmation window, check the box marked "I Agree to the terms of use of the signals service", enter your MQL5 community password and click "OK". The "Options" window will appear. With the preselected "Signals" tab, it's important to specify the percentage of your trading account equity to be used for trade execution based on the trade volumes of the signal provider. Specify the allowable difference between the execution price and the price of the trade copied from the provider, and the minimum value of the trading account equity at which the execution of trading signals will stop and all open positions will be closed. Then click "OK". From this point, all trades made by your selected signal provider will automatically be copied on your trading account. Your trading terminal must always be up and running in order to receive trading signals in real time.

Paying for signals

To subscribe to a paid signal, you must have sufficient funds in your the MQL5 community account to pay the fee for the entire subscription period (a week or month). Upon subscribing, your account is automatically charged for the Subscription fee. Money can be deposited to MQL5.com's internal Payment System through PayPal, WebMoney, and Gate2Shop.

A subscriber is always in full control of his subscription and trading account. At any time, you can cancel, freeze, and renew your subscription directly from MetaTrader. You can unsubscribe to your current provider and subscribe also to your new provider. You are allowed to subscribe to only one signal provider. It is also important to note that an account that is currently subscribed to another Signal cannot be used to create a Signal or become a Signal Provider.

You can also control your subscription from MQL5.com. Using "My Subscription" option under "Signals" section, you will be able see your subscription information. You can suspend or unsubscribe by clicking the "Unsubscribe" toggle button on the rightmost side of the expiration date. This allows you to manage your subscription at anytime and anywhere.

With the MetaTrader for mobile devices (iPhone, iPad, Android), you can receive all kinds of notifications right at your mobile device. You will be updated with real time notifications anywhere and be fully aware of all trading activities happening in your trading account. MT4 and MT5 mobile terminal has a unique ID used for notification service. Notification service can be enabled at your MetaTrader terminal. Under the "Tools" main menu, click "Options". At the "Options" window, click "Notifications" tab. Tick the "Enable Push Notifications" checkbox. Specify the unique ID of your MetaTrader mobile terminal at the "MetaQuotes ID" textbox, then click "OK". Once done, you will receive any notifications in your mobile device every time a trade is executed.

Advantages of MetaTrader signals service

The MetaTrader Signals service is a simple and built-in solution for MT4 and MT5 platform. You can subscribe to any Signal Provider in just few clicks in your MetaTrader. A Signal Provider can easily start sharing their signals to all MetaTrader users around the world.

It offers complete transparency for both Subscribers and Signal Providers. Subscribers can access the Signal Providers' profile which contains the complete trading history and real-time statistical performance.

Subscribers and Signal Providers are completely independent. This means there are no required agreements between them. Signal Providers sell their trading skills while Subscribers choose the most suitable ones. No need to sign paper contracts or complex agreements between Signal Providers and brokers. All the processes are executed inside the MQL5.com system and no paperwork is required.

MetaTrader Signals service is completely free for all traders. No commission is charged by MetaQuotes to both subscribers and Signal Providers giving free Forex signals. Subscription charge to subscribers will only come from Signal Providers for their paid signals. Signal Providers are charged by MetaQuotes for 20% of the monthly subscription fee. This commission is used to maintain the technological infrastructure of the Signals service.

Using this platform for hosting your signals business

The MT5 marketplace is an online signals market created by MetaQuotes, the makers of the extremely popular Meta-Trader 4 and MetaTrader 5 trading platforms.

If you decide to run an independent trading signal service you can use the MetaTrader 5 marketplace as an advertising platform. You could entice people to notice you and your business by offering free trading signals.

For example, let's say you trade and deliver trading signals on five currency pairs in total on your main website. You can offer free trading signals from one of these pairs on the MT5 marketplace. As people subscribe to your free signals and make money with them, they will start gaining trust in your signals service. These traders will be more inclined to join your full service looking for more profitable signals.

Forex robots gain popularity among traders

Forex trading software or "Robots" are now becoming popular among Forex traders who want to automate their way of trading. It is one of the biggest opportunities this trillion dollar industry has opened to Forex traders and computer programmers. A simple Google search for "trading robot" will turn up well over a million search results. The dominance of these relatively new market analysis tools and trade-execution programs shows a shift in the Forex trading market overall.

Are you a trader but are tired and sick watching your charts and waiting for signals to place a trade? You might have a perfect strategy that suits your trading style but you are always late to place an order. Or perhaps you have other daily commitments and always miss the best trading opportunities. Maybe a trader friend has shared with you all the details of his proven money-generating strategy, but it just does not work for you because you have a hard time following the rules. Or maybe your trading emotions and attitude hinders you towards trading success. It could just be that you want to automate your trading and sell it to other traders. Trading automation answers all of these concerns.

The MT5 marketplace is a gathering point for traders and robot developers

The MT5 market is a great Forex community wherein you can develop, sell and download proprietary MetaTrader 4 and MetaTrader 5 trading software. As might know, the most common trading platform among Forex traders are the MetaTrader 4 and MetaTrader 5 platforms (MT4 and MT5). They are used by numerous brokers and traders worldwide. MT5, which is an updated version of MT4, offers the possibility of using MQL5 programming language to codify and automate your Forex trading strategy.

Although this programming language can be learned, it is more suitable if you have a background in computer programming or software development. Learning a new programming language for programmers is pretty easy, but quite difficult if you do not have a very technical mind. In this article I assume that you are a trader who knows how to manipulate the MetaTrader Platform. You may visit the official website of MT5 Market to learn about mql5 programming language and to develop trading strategies.

In order to access the advanced features of the MT5 market, you need to register for a free account. Members can access the market directly from their MT4 and MT5 terminal window. Numerous articles were written by MQL5 community members to help you develop and program your own robot. Of course, coding your trading strategy requires arithmetic skills and you must be able to understand the MQL5 programming language. You are not limited only to Forex robots and Expert Advisors (EA), you can also develop your own proprietary indicators, scripts, and utilities. After you have developed a working and error free trading software, you may publish it at the MQL5 marketplace.

MQL5 market tends to attract high quality traders and programmers

The internet is full of garbage Forex trading software developers selling scam trading robots. But with MQL5 marketplace, it is a secure environment to buy or sell different trading tools which are compatible with MT4 and MT5 platforms. Before your system can be accepted for publishing, it will be verified for one month before being approved on the market and a demo version will be made available to be used by traders for testing before official purchasing.

You can share it for free or otherwise traders will pay you the amount you specify. Your trading software will be included in the list according to its category (indicator, expert advisor, analytic tool, script, or MT5 utility). Most other systems available on the internet do not offer a demo version to traders. Only descriptions of the product and screenshots of the past trades are available in many cases. Others make claims of no losses or very little losses, while others even use fraudulent screenshots that have been manipulated by graphic design software.

As a legitimate trading software marketer in the MT5 community, you are concerned with the welfare of others and not just to make money through the community. This is the reason why your trading software must pass through several rounds of testing before it will be allowed for release into the MT5 community. This is a good 'safety feature' of the community.

Given the above difference of MT5 marketplace from a lot of other trading system marketers, another great advantage is the ability of the purchaser to rate, write a review or post comments about a system's performance. In this way, the MT5 marketplace will attract more traders to download or buy your trading software. MT5 marketplace offers the transparency of the system from third party references which are traders themselves. Your software will market itself in a certain way. Also, this MT5 marketplace allows each purchase of the product an activation on at least five personal computers, and this is more generous than most other trading software sources. You, as the developer can also set the available activation numbers. Since the MQL5 market is directly connected to the members, any update messages about your product will be delivered automatically to members' MT5 terminals that is activated with your software. In this way, MT5 marketplace helps ensure your continued support to your buyers.

Challenges with software piracy and MT5 marketplace protection

Probably the greatest disadvantage of marketing your trading software thru MT5 marketplace or any other Forex marketplace is widespread software piracy. Once you release your software to the world, pirates can reproduce and distribute it under a different name. With the advancement of technological tools, software can always be unlocked and recopied, repacked and distributed on a massive amount of personal computers and/or to traders as 'legal' trading software. This software reselling piracy can be very difficult to identify due to the very sophisticated manner in which the software is duplicated and presented. Even incorporating the most advanced anti-redistribution software algorithm in your software, it can be very hard to safeguard your trading software. This trading software piracy is beyond the scope of MT5 marketplace. There are external laws that govern software piracy and this differs in each country. This law, however, is very challenging to enforce with such a global marketplace.

However, MQL5 marketplace offers a high protection level to MQL5 applications and with the new MetaTrader 4 Build 574 release in the beginning of 2014 the MQL4 protection has raised to the MQL5 protection level. So actually, selling apps on MQL5 marketplace gives you the ability to protect your intellectual property and licence your apps properly to customers.

Despite this seemingly undetected piracy, the MT5 marketplace offers a great place for traders who desire to learn how to program and automate their trading. It has a wide variety of Forex mql5 programming articles categorized according to your needs. Although mql5 programming requires mathematical and programming skills, you could probably even ask someone from the MT5 community to help you with the programming. For skilled MT5 Forex software developers, this marketplace is the best for you to publish your EAs and indicators if you are looking for feedback and testers.

This marketplace has gained the trust of traders since it provides a good avenue for promoting software. Traders can scrutinize your product's performance before and after purchasing it. The best software will top the list and will attract more traders to buy. If you believe in your trading strategy and it can be automated, you can share it with other traders here. And if you want to sell it to other traders too, then program it or ask help from MT5 forum and community and put it up for review/demo/sale.

Note: The MT5 marketplace is a great spot to promote software, yes, but also to find great trading software too. If you are in need of a fantastic trading system, browse the marketplace and read the reviews of the top-performing trading systems. One or more of these systems might make for a great addition to your forex signal providing business (if you gain usage permission from the owner of course).

Autotrading on MyFxBook.com

MyFxBook.com recently started offering an autotrading feature to the visitors of the site. This service is very similar to ZuluTrade, but they state that it has some distinctive qualities that make it better than any other Autotrade service online. What I can tell you is that you won't earn a lot of money by using their autotrading service unless you have thousands of followers. The brokers and MyFxBook.com will take a big cut just like they do on ZuluTrade. Basically, you will get paid a small portion of the spread. If you have thousands of followers with live trading accounts, and you generate hundred trades or more per month, then you will earn good income. Otherwise you will just be earning breadcrumbs and the greater profit is to be found elsewhere.

Wouldn't it be better to have each of your followers paying you $50 a month? When you reach thousands of customers you basically become a mass product offering company, and can offer very competitive low prices... perhaps even as low as

$25 a month or so. And if you chose to work with a single broker, just imagine what a good relationship you would have by bringing them so much business. And you act as an Introducing Broker (IB) and also get paid for each transaction (trade) placed by those referred customers, you will be earning a very nice income. In this case, you don't need to share profit with any 3rd party like Zulu or MyFXBook. Yes, you have more responsibility this way, but it is worth it. We'll talk about this more at a later point in this report.

Back to MyFXBook.com's autotrading community

MyFXBook.com is a professional social community for traders. You have likely heard me reference this site many times before. It offers unparalleled metrics and account performance tracking. Its Autotrade system offers free services for Forex traders, enabling them to analyze their own Forex trading account, share trades, publish their market opinions, find a money manager, audit results and review Forex brokers. It provides a way for experienced or newbie traders to tap into successful trading systems. It supports several brokers with MetaTrader platforms and with a growing number of registered traders. Their autotrading system is much smaller than most other platforms, due to their relatively young age, but I believe they will grow quickly since so many people are familiar with MyFXBook.com.

How does the Autotrade system work?

Like many other social trading networks, experienced traders with proven track records of Forex trading success can become an Autotrade provider and can earn money per winning trade. Although registered traders are not charged when copying trades, their respective brokers, who are connected to MyFXBook, add additional commissions on the spreads, which the trader automatically pays from his profit for every trade taken.

Note: Spread is the price that traders pay to the broker which basically the difference between ask and bid price. This will automatically be deducted from the profit of every trade executed. But it is reported that with FXCM, one of the partnering brokers, that they don't add any additional amount on the spread. Most brokers will charge an additional fee (as spreads) to each and every trade, whether a win or a loss.

Skilled traders can offer their service to MyFXBook.com Autotrade and can earn as much as 0.5 pips per lot traded. This is an impressive opportunity for successful traders to share their trading system with others in order to profit from significant commissions. MyFXBook provides registered traders with tools to help them determine whether a system is worth copying or not. The active discussion and community features also help traders and Autotrade providers to learn, compare and improve their own trading skills and strategies.

How is MyFXBook Autotrade different from other systems?

Unlike other similar systems, demo traders are not allowed to become signal providers. Trading with a demo account versus a live account has a very significant difference, especially when it comes to money management and trading psychology. Demo trading has no real trading emotions and has a high possibility to trade beyond a safe risk threshold. MyFXBook only allows Autotrade providers with proven track records of success who also trade a real money account. For Autotrade providers, MyFXBook have additional incentives for every profitable trade.

MyFXBook provides accurate statistics with their advanced statistical analysis tools. The best systems are ranked according to the result of in depth analysis. On the contrary, losing systems are filtered out of the list altogether.

What is the biggest advantage of MyFXBook?

The biggest advantage of MyFXBook is the trading transparency and security it provides to both Autotrade providers and copy traders. The Autotrade platform shows if the track record of the provider is verified. In setting up the MyFXBook tracking platform, the Autotrade provider can mark their account as a demo or real account. In the trade copier's platform, demo or real account can be seen in the provider's profile. Because of slippage and requotes, some trading systems work only with demo accounts and will not work on real accounts. More often, a demo account has a faster execution compared to a real account because no actual trade is placed (it is all just numbers on a computer with demo accounts). However, real money orders can lag, especially during times of high volatility like during big news events and also during times of very low volatility. These differences between demo and live accounts can be very disastrous to a copier's real trading account.

Also, the individual trade tracker informs the trader about the AutoTrade provider's trading performance or statistics, whether the trader has a strategy or whether the trader is just hitting and hoping. Tools such as the monthly analytics allow traders to sort trades taken in a specific month by profit, pips, and percentage. An AutoTrade provider who has had a long enough success history of trades can easily be spotted. The longer the track record the better of course.

Another extra feature of MyFXBook is the ability to check your trade results by day. This tool shows which trading days are the best and the profitability of each. It shows best trades, holding times, and best hours to trade as well.

What is the disadvantage of MyFXBook?

One major drawback of MyFXBook is that it supports a limited number of Forex brokerages.

In MyFXBook, Autotrade providers can hide their losing trade history, which is not a good thing for those are trying to investigate a system. Although this sounds to be an advantage of providers in hiding their current trades or recent trade history, the overall trading history should be accessible to trade copiers. Autotrades can hide overleveraging accounts, holding onto losing trades for over a thousand pips or other high risk strategies. Other schemes that can be hidden include funding an account when it has closed due to a drawdown. With these in mind, a trader who is copying trades must be cautious on selecting an Autotrade provider to follow. Diversifying providers can also be a great way to profit from the combination of top trading strategies. Of course, traders are allowed to undertake measures to limit their risk from each provider.

Who can be an Autotrade provider?

Only experienced traders are allowed to be an Autotrade provider. There are several criteria that a potential Autotrade provider must achieve before they are approved to be on the list. He/she must have a connected, real and verified Meta-Trader 4 account with MyFXBook and at least three months of trading history. Trading history should include no drawdown of more than 50% and a return of at least 10% (and higher than the largest drawdown). Every trade must have an average of at least 10 winning pips. Also, the trade balance should be at least $1000 and also have taken at least 100 trades in the past 3 months. This means a constant trading activity must be kept to achieve this minimum number of trades.

The requirements are very strict and aim to protect traders from unreliable providers. Since Autotrade providers are growing in number, it is worth noting that there are only few highly skilled traders meeting these criteria and at the top of the list. Those who are curious about the Autotrade program can try out a risk free demo before putting and real money on the line.

Tradeo Social Trading Network

Social Trading is becoming widely accepted as an interesting new way for Forex traders to make money. This platform is another of these social trading networks designed for retail traders and investors to access the financial markets and ride the coattails of successful traders and fund managers. Tradeo is one of the growing social trading networks which allow registered traders to follow the trades of these top traders and literally have the same trades as these 'big boys' copied into their own accounts. It connects traders from all over the world, regardless of their brokerage firm and trading platform, into a network to share their views, strategies, and trades in real-time. Although traders can copy a top trader's position for free, top traders receive payments from Tradeo which is basically a percentage from the trader's profit.

Any registered trader of Tradeo can become a leading trader using his/her live trading account or through a demo account. The condition you must prove is a good trading performance in a minimum of one month trading period. You must have at least 15 closed trades within 30 days and the max drawdown should be no larger than 25%. If you were able to meet these benchmarks and your performance statistics show greater than 10 percent gain, you will be included in the top traders list. Tradeo will continuously monitor your performance and rank you in the list accordingly. As a top trader, you can trade currency pairs (e.g. EUR/USD, USD/JPY, AUD/USD, etc.), commodities (e.g. gold, silver, oil), indices like the DAX and Dow Jones Industrial Average, interest rates, bonds, futures, CFDs, and company stocks too. The amount you get paid is totally dependent on the number of your followers and the lot sizes they trade. Tradeo pays you 1 to 5 USD per trade per lot traded in your followers' accounts.

Compared to other systems such as eToro's Social Trading platform, Tradeo operates on a broader scale. It runs across numerous trading platforms which include ActTrader, FXCM, MT4, and MT5. It integrates 60 of today's top Forex brokerages. With Tradeo's free 'Cloud Trader', a trader has a choice of whether to follow your trade automatically or copy the trades from other traders manually. This can be done on the web trader platform in just few clicks. Also, Tradeo's web trader platform is compatible also with mobile devices. This means you can trade and receive valuable information from other top traders, regardless of your location. Although your positions are copied by your respective followers, the Dynamic Leverage system allows the followers to change the trade parameters set by you. For example, if you have a live position with a lot size of 0.5, your follower or copier can have your trade executed in his platform with a custom lot size set by the follower.

Through its advanced social trading platform, a top trader can discuss with other top traders. Facebook, Twitter, and LinkedIn are also taken advantage by Tradeo as a tool for trade collaboration. This feature allows you, as one of the traders, to learn the strategies and market views of other high-ranking top traders. You can also share your ideas, not just to top traders but also to your followers and copiers. Tradeo does not just "spoon feed" followers, it allows top traders to educate them on their strategies and teach them how to trade independently. Even top traders need to advance their Forex education through the help of other top traders. Trading collaboration is one of the goals of Tradeo's social trading network.

Aside from the payment, social networking tools, and the number of brokerages to choose from that Tradeo offers to top traders, another advantage of becoming a Tradeo trader is the easy-to-navigate web trading page. It has an excellent user interface, full trading capabilities and also an intuitive functionality. As a top trader, you want to have more followers and Tradeo has made it easy for prospective trade followers to do so. It is packed with great tools such as trending indicators, Fibonacci retracement charts and many more. On your followers' web trader platform, lists of your live trades are seen as they are executed. Suggestions from professional traders are posted on all Tradeo traders' platforms. Tradeo excels at charting functionality as followers can see who, when and what trades are being opened, right on the exchange rate chart, which is very impressive and gives a clear overview of the activities.

On the other hand, Tradeo's disadvantage lies with the absence of trading activity. It has a very impressive web trader platform, competitive payment to top traders, and is partnered with numerous top Forex brokers but only a few traders choose to trade with Tradeo. Comparing to ZuluTrader and eToro OpenBook, Tradeo has fewer registered and active traders.

Also, prospective followers would be frustrated to continue signing up an account since Tradeo has a poor customer service support. The chat box has no use since no operator is continuously monitoring it. Answers to trader's concerns would take several hours to be answered. Communicating to Tradeo's customer service supports would be the easiest way to gather information on becoming a trader with the company because the website offers somewhat limited information. Although the signing up process is a step-by-step, rather easy to navigate process, many traders do not just sign up without knowing the pros and cons first. The same is true with a professional trader who wants to sell his trading via Tradeo—he needs to know how exactly Tradeo's system works. Sadly, at a first glance to the website, you cannot easily figure out where to find this information.

Tradeo is a very good start for anyone aspiring to be a top trader, given that he/she has a profitable strategy. Again, this is one of the platforms with not a huge number of traders and the trading platform itself is quite difficult to navigate (this could be a likely reason they do not have as many traders as sites like Zulu). Active traders claim that veteran top traders are just a few clicks away. Tradeo social trading network offers you a great opportunity to make some extra money with your trading skills, especially if you want to trade opportunities other than currencies alone. Top Traders, however, must have already a profitable strategy in order to be on the top list. The more consistent you are in your trading statistics, the more traders will follow you and the more earnings you can have. Results and consistency will obviously be the main factor traders use when they decide whether to copy your trades. However, because of the "social" aspect, you may also get some additional followers if you communicate actively and professionally with your followers.

FX Copy

FX Copy is a Forex social trading network headquartered in Sydney, Australia. It is a site where experienced and newbie traders can follow, learn and copy trades from top performing traders for free. It supports the MetaTrader4 (MT4) platform and has over 6000 traders in their community and growing. Although it is owned by Enfinium Pty Ltd who operate the Vantage

FX and Enfinium brands, FX Copy remains broker independent. Traders can choose from any of the supported brokerages. With FX Copy, a trader can choose to Auto-Copy all the trades of a FX Copy Leader. A trader can build his portfolio and becomes a pro trader, lead the way and be rewarded with cash rebates.

How does FX Copy work?

Just like other social trading networks, FX Copy allows you to connect, interact and share ideas with other registered traders. It provides valuable insight to traders and to watch and engage directly with top traders. Registered traders can successfully track, monitor and directly copy trades of profitable traders on the user-friendly platform. FX Copy is a nice social trading network for both trading beginners and advanced traders.

With the tools and the detailed trading histories, performance charts and statistics, you can analyze and monitor other trader's performance through this system. A trader's performance can be broken down into more detailed statistics over certain periods of time, and similar to myfxbook.com, how their performance varies between each currency pair. Copy traders can set to Auto-Copy or manually copy all the trades of top performers. All registered traders must download and install the FX Copy EA into their MetaTrader 4 platform in order to transmit/receive trades. All copied or auto-copied trades will reflect automatically into the copier's MT4 platform. All copied trades are tracked by the system and kept synchronized with the leader or the copied trader's account.

Leading traders are rewarded for sharing and interacting in the social community with rebates. You will earn a rebate from every FX Copy registered trader who copied your trade. Through the Lead and Earn Rebate Program, a copy trader has a chance to become a leader. Live account leader traders whose broker is a platinum partner of FX Copy can earn a rebate of $2 (Australian Dollars) per standard lot on an auto-copied trade. Since rebates are based on volumes, a leader can receive a rebate whether the trade is profitable or not. The more copy traders are following, the more the leader can earn.

How is it different from other systems?

With other social trading networks, a trader can be a signal provider as long as his account is supported by the network. But before becoming an FX Copy Leader, a trader must have opened a live account with any of the platinum partner brokers. At present, these are the only platinum partners: MXT, Vantage FX, and LandFX. All other supported brokers are not platinum, and therefore, a leader with a live account with these brokers will not earn any rebates from any of his copied trades. Also, live trades on Binary Options, Indices and Commodities are not included in the Lead and Earn Rebate Program.

To fully enjoy the capability of FX Copy, a trader's MT4 platform must be always online and the FX Copy Bridge must always be attached to the chart for the AutoCopy to work. A Virtual Private Server (VPS) is highly recommended for traders.

Compared to other systems that a signal provider can use a demo account for issuing trades, a demo account in FX Copy cannot be used for copying. Although FX Copy offers demo trading, it is only allowed for copy traders. Demo trading will remain as demo and therefore, will not lead to real earnings. The leader and trade copier must be trading on a live account for rebates to be earned.

FX Copy Advantage

Traders with live accounts with the platinum broker partners can take the advantage of becoming a leader with this network. This will limit the fierce competition between trade leaders as compared to other social trading networks with tight competition among signal providers. Therefore, leaders of FX Copy can earn more money with the increasing number of non-platinum broker traders. For a trader with a non-platinum brokerage to be a leader, he must shift to one of these preferred brokers, or otherwise fund a new account at any of the three platinum brokers. Viewing the easy to analyze statistics of traders using the

FX Copy platform, it is very impressive that several traders have made such remarkable returns. A number of highly skilled traders are using the platform although FX Copy has far fewer registered traders than most of the other big players. A trader's performance can be broken down in detail, highlighting the certain periods of profit and loss between currency pairings. However, it is still somewhat difficult to find out how risky a particular leader is.

FX Copy Disadvantage

The disadvantage for traders with non-FX Copy's platinum brokers is that they cannot be a leader, and therefore, cannot earn extra money. Hopefully FXCopy will change this in the future, as programs of this nature are almost always growing and improving with time. Although the great rebates program is very attractive because you can earn with your copied trades whether a profit or loss, it is not easy for an aspiring leader to shift from his original broker to a platinum broker, if a track record has already been established with a different broker. This has probably stunted the growth of the social network, as it will have certainly put some traders off. Of course, aspiring leaders wanting to "sell" their trading skills are looking for more active social networks with a large number of potential followers. The long term success of a social trading network largely depends on the number active registered traders. Also, on the side of copiers, the more active profitable leaders there are to be followed, the more copiers will flock to the network.

Compared to the leading social networks that have incorporated live customer support into their platforms, a potential FX Copy trader would have to rely on the limited information in the company's website. Email support is provided, but a live chat would be a far greater tool to attract new traders.

Who will enjoy using FX Copy?

FX Copy is for traders whose brokers are the platinum partners (MXT, Vantage FX, and LandFX) only. Non-platinum registered members with proven track records of trading success will never earn rebates even though they have thousands of copiers. Also, it is only for traders with MT4 platforms. FX Copy only supports MT4 as it is the most popular trading platform amongst traders. Other platforms are not supported although FX Copy is looking to add other trading platforms such as MT5. Again, as all platforms grow, so does their technology generally. Hopefully we will see growth here soon.

Currensee

Currensee is a social trading network which is very unique and completely different from the others. It is designed for serious investors. Like other social trading networks, Currensee gives registered traders an access to top performing traders' live trades. Its web-based social trading platform offers traders the ability to see top traders' trades and communicate with them through several means including instant messaging, Facebook, and email. The biggest difference here with this platform lies in the account equity minimums required....

How the Currensee trade copying system works

Any Forex trader wanting to take advantage of the benefits of social trading can sign up for the Currensee Trade Leaders Investment Program and can automatically follow and copy trades of other traders. Currensee offers only Forex traders with proven track records of trading success, called Trade Leaders. Each Trade Leader must pass the strict criteria, which includes live monitoring of performance and controlled risk management.

Traders must have a live account with one of the supported brokerages and must integrate the Currensee bridging software into their MetaTrader 4 platform. Each trader must select which Trade Leaders they want to add into their portfolio. The Leaderboard provides investors with statistics about the Trade Leader's strategy and risk management rules. Then, the investor must decide how much money he may allocate to copy the Trade Leader's trades. Every trade the Trade Leader executes will automatically be copied in the investor's platform in real time. The Dashboard gives traders access to information re-garding the number of traders (Currensee members) who are currently in long and short positions with each currency pair. This information is quite important for traders using technical strategies, or who want to follow along and try to learn from the copied trades.

For you to become a Trade Leader, a Trade Leader appli-cation (download form from Currensee website) is needed to be completed and submitted back to Currensee. A live account must be opened with one of the supported brokers. A demo account is not possible for both Trade Leaders and investors. You must have a live account from one of the brokers, funded with real money. You must have a minimum of one year trading history with a 10% ROI in a live Forex trading account, and also maintain a consistent track record of positive trading perfor-mance.

After Currensee links your trading account to your broker, your trading performance will be tracked for at least six months. Traders with positive net performance will be accepted as Trade Leaders. Once you're approved to be a Trade Leader, investors can start to follow and copy your trades. You don't need to recruit your followers since Currensee makes it easy for other traders to find and follow your trades. You will be fea-tured on the Currensee Leaderboard and investors can easily view your profile and performance history.

Signing up as Trade Leader and maintaining your member-ship has no cost. All you must do is consistently trade success-fully and manage your risk responsibly. And of course, you will receive compensation for every trade that was copied from you.

How the system is different from other systems

Currensee does not operate like the traditional social trading network. It reinvented the wheel to solve many of the problems that copy traders encounter on other social trading networks. Since the market is full of people claiming to be experts and trying to sell their strategies, Currensee Trade Leaders back up their claims with long term consistent performance and their own real money. The Trade Leader has full transparency to investors which enables the latter to gauge who the real experts/profitable traders are. Currensee is very diligent with their monitoring of their trade leaders.... After all, the Forex market is so unstable and a profitable trader today may not be a profitable trader in three months' time. Leaders are evaluated on a daily basis on both performance and risk strategies to ensure the success of Currensee investors.

Currensee targets serious traders who want to invest in a long term and high yielding investment. Trade Leaders must have an account funded with $10, 000 or more. Minimum investments of your followers depend on your specifics. As each Trade Leader has a unique strategy, the leader identifies the amount of capital needed to trade safely. Investors must have certain minimum account balances (according to the leader's specifications) to be able follow a certain strategy. This makes Currensee something of a 'reserve club' where only those with larger accounts can play. This helps to develop long term perspectives and traders who will not jump ship at the first sign of a drawdown.

Another crucial way in which Currensee differs from others is that the investor is charged with a 2% fee annually (as a maintenance fee) on his/her deposited funds. Also, 20% of profits are taken away and paid to the Trade Leader as a success fee. On other networks, commissions are taken from copiers based on the lot size traded. This makes Currensee more of a 'fund manager' than a social trading network.

Advantages of Currensee

The major advantage of Currensee for investors is that Trade Leaders are heavily monitored on a daily basis. Performance is based on cumulative and annual trade performance, length of history, risk management procedures, maximum drawdown, daily volatility and percent of days losing. This means that Currensee investors have a higher probability of success overall.

Currensee's advance controls, such as the volatility metric tools, are provided for Trade Leaders and investors to help assess the risk of each trade. Risk management in terms of percentage are gauged automatically from the Trade Leader.

Another benefit of Currensee for investors is that Trade Leaders are only paid for the profits made. Losing trades will not be paid on. Trade Leaders will receive a success fee, each month, of 20% of the profits they generated on the investors' accounts that copied their trades. For example, if you have successfully generated $100,000 in one month for the accounts that invested in you, then you would be looking at a paycheck of $20,000 that month, not to mention the gains you would have made on your own live account as well.

Disadvantage of Currensee

The major drawback of Currensee is the high initial investment required for Trade Leaders, which is a minimum of $10,000. Although minimum investments for investors depends largely on the Trade Leaders, it is more likely that they must have a minimum of $10,000 also to fully copy the trades, though there are some accounts that require less. If an investor wants to diversify his method through copying several leaders, then he must fund his account with more than $30,000, for example. Also, there is the two percent maintenance fee, as mentioned, plus the 20% success fee, which can be very expensive for investors. But in reality, this is not a lot of money charged for a fund manager.

Currensee also doesn't offer demo accounts. Although an investor can review all the available data on the Leaderboard about each leader, still the data is not complete. Each trader differs on risk tolerance, which means traders differ in the amount of money they can afford to lose. A trade leader may be comfortable with high leverage but his followers can only stomach lower leverage positions. Also, the Leaderboard has no way for investors to view the current open positions of the Trade Leaders, which is often a nice thing to see on other platforms. A trade leader may leave his open position for over a month and investors will not be able to see these types of trades.

Who will enjoy Currensee the most?

The Currensee Trade Leader opportunity is most appropriate for professional traders who have strong and successful Forex trading performance. As stated on the Leaders Investment Program, money managers and fund managers with a real and proven history of positive performance and strong risk management are allowed to become candidates. These traders must have a good understanding of investing concepts and financial markets. The program is only going to be of interest to those who have funded their account with over $10,000 and don't mind the 2% management fee which is included with the program. Retail traders will have no real possibility to become Trade Leaders.

SimpleTrader

The SimpleTrader Forex Trade Copier is a distinctive web based trade copier which allows traders to sell trade signals through their Commercial Trade Copier or to manage private accounts through their Private Trade Copier. It is built on a strong infrastructure to take full advantage of server uptime, allowing traders to completely leave copied trades unattended.

How does SimpleTrader work?

You may choose to become a commercial signal copier and sell Forex signals to the general public. The copier platform doesn't need to be installed on your client's MetaTrader 4 platforms. They don't have to worry about installing EA's onto their charts. They don't need to subscribe to a Virtual Private Server provider since SimpleTrader is directly connected to their brokers. This saves the client a monthly cost of maintaining a VPS and can increase your profitability as an independent signal provider at the same time. SimpleTrader promises a constant connection of clients' accounts.

Special Note: SimpleTrader will simply host MT4 platforms with a special trade copier Expert Advisor on their own VPS servers so you or your customers don't need to do that. Then they call it a 'direct broker connection' and on the customers' end it looks like it is. For customers and signal providers, this is a wonderful solution, there is no doubt about it. If I hadn't created my own trade signals delivery software then I think SimpleTrader would be my choice as well.

There is no upfront payment in subscribing to the commercial signal copier. Once you have started to attract customers, you will be charged for integrating the platform with your business. The price is a nominal $15 per month per platform connected, billed at the end of the month. This is not a bad price at all.

Like other signal providers, your track record of performance will be monitored and will be shown to clients. Signal providers are categorized into two types: those who have been approved and those who are under evaluation. Once you're approved and have clients, your trades from your trading account will be also copied to your clients' accounts. Your trades are directly executed with your clients' respective broker servers, bypassing the need for the clients to run a MetaTrader platform. All trade parameters are copied such the market entry price, stop price and the exit price.

For traders who want to manage a handful of client accounts, they must choose to sign up as Private Trade Copier. This is for those who want to copy a master account to multiple accounts. The trade copier platform maintains a constant connection with the master and the slave accounts—without the need for the MT4 platform of each account to be opened. As an account manager, it is your job to connect each account to the master account, utilizing the web based control panel of SimpleTrader. Trades executed at the master account will automatically be copied on each slave account.

How is SimpleTrader different from other systems?

There is great simplicity in this particular trade copying system. The commercial signal copier has a direct broker connection and so no additional bridging EA will be installed on each client's MetaTrader account. There is also no need to use a VPS hosting service for clients. If the signal provider is using an Expert Advisor or a Forex robot to trade, he would want a VPS to maximize his profits and protect against any power loss or internet connection instability. Unlike other companies offering similar trade copying services, the clients don't need to worry about the same. Clients don't need to have a VPS since the trades bypass even the need for clients to run MT4 platforms. Everything is executed directly to the broker's server and this makes it a very simple and efficient copying system.

Unlike other systems, SimpleTrader provides two different services to choose from. If you want to be a signal provider in which clients will evaluate your performance, then choose the commercial Trade copier. But if you'd rather manage their accounts directly, then use the Private Trade Copier option. If you are looking to simply build your own signals business where you manage both sides (recruiting successful traders and also signing up investors) then this is a great platform for you.

Other brands created from the SimpleTrader platform and technology

ConnectForex, SimpleTrader VPS, and MyLiveAccount are powered by the SimpleTrader platform which provides VPS hosting, as well as a vehicle to sell your trading skills. These companies are called White label companies. These companies work much the same as SimpleTrader but there are slight differences on some rules, monthly subscription fee, and signal provider's transparency.

Advantages of SimpleTrader

Although SimpleTrader is a web based platform, it copies and executes trades with a very fast execution time of 10 to 50 milliseconds. Its IT infrastructure ensures that all accounts are connected 100% of the time. This facilitates a high reliability of signal transfer.

Each client's account has individual money management settings. They have full control over their live accounts and trading signals. The lot size and stop-loss can be modified in each account depending on account size and risk threshold. Processing of trade signals can also be disabled.

Interested individuals can white-label SimpleTrader and run their own signal provider company under a different name giving themselves a great system under their own brand, even though everything remains hosted by SimpleTrader. You can then use your company name to attract new signal providers to sell their trading skills. Manage your own brand and attract new clients to register by reviewing and posting your signal providers' performance.

SimpleTrader provides 24/7 client support. Should any client have any concern about the platform, a live chat and ticket support is available 24 hours a day, 7 days a week. This ensures that your clients are satisfied with any service or assistance they may need.

Disadvantages of SimpleTrader

Perhaps the biggest drawdown with the SimpleTrader platform is the fact that it is not a large trading community where thousands of trade copier customers are waiting to join you and subscribe to your trading signals. This really is a system for those who want to build their own signals company from the ground up and maintain full control over their client base.

If you are a Private Trade copier, you are charged with $10 USD per slave account per month. However, one slave connection is totally free. Payment is not based on profits they were able to generate in a specific month nor is it based on spread charged to the client. For some new business startups monthly payment sounds scary.

For whom SimpleTrader is best

SimpleTrader is suitable for traders who want to build an independent trading signals business. With SimpleTrader, you can be a commercial trade copier and create your own brand, and then impress clients and sell to them your trading services. It is also great for account managers who want to automatically duplicate their trades on a master account to several slave accounts. Account managers will not bother themselves with opening trades on all the slave accounts; they will just focus on their trading activity and SimpleTrader will take care of the rest.

Local Trade Copier

The Local Trade Copier (LTC) is a software which is used to copy Forex trades. These trades that are copied can be between two or more MetaTrader 4 accounts. This software, which comes in the form of an Expert Advisor installed on a MT4 chart, is used by traders to automatically duplicate trades of a signal provider's account (master) to several clients'MT4 accounts (slave). This EA works regardless of how many master and slave accounts are connected. It has a boatload of features and can be used for several different purposes.

How does Local Trade Copier work?

The Local Trade Copier software must be installed on a computer or on a Virtual Private Server (VPS). A VPS is an externally hosted server used to manage trading connectivity, which ensures the trading platform is running 24 hours a day. The software is designed to work for any accounts with an MT4 platform, can be used with any Forex broker, and can copy trades on any currency pair. The LTC copies trades and pending orders from the master account into its slave accounts. Master and Slave accounts must be running on MT4 platforms and must be located on the same computer or VPS server.

LTC is capable of duplicating master and slave accounts in a one-to-one, one-to-many, many-to-one and many-to-many setup. There are many different options that can filter trades, which is very useful for traders using Forex robots and also for account managers managing several accounts. This filtering option can also help to 'cherry pick' trades from trade providers/robots who may trade well some times of the day but not others.

Slave accounts can filter trading signals by using external indicators and also Global Variables. For Example, LTC can be customized to copy long positions (buy trades) only when the market price is above a Moving Average indicator. You can set it up to skip and not copy any of the short positions if the market price is approaching a stochastic oscillator's overbought zone, for example. Several MT4 indicators can be used by LTC as a trade filter indicator. These trade filters can be applied to any number of currencies. Trade filter indicators can also be modified to only copy trades of certain currency pairs.

Master and slave accounts can also filter trades by "Time Range Filters". This filter works by drawing a rectangular object on the chart. LTC can be configured so that both master and slave accounts will not send and receive any trades during a specified time period. This is very useful for traders avoiding the abrupt market price surge during important economic new releases. For example, It can prevent the master account, which is using Forex robot, from sending new trades during a specified time of the day. This is nearly impossible to accomplish without the LTC if the robot has no such feature.

For example, you want your robot not to take trades 15 minutes before and 15 minutes after an economic news release at 12:00pm, you will simply need to create a rectangle object with a start time of 11:45 and an end time of 12:15. During this time period, the robot will not be able to execute trades which may lead to unexpected losses.

How LTC is different from other systems

The Local Trade Copier is different from other types of trade copiers and better in several ways, mostly due to the advanced options it offers. There are two different types of this copier: Local Trade Copier and Remote Trade Copier, which will be discussed in the next section. A remote trade copier utilizes the internet in order to communicate with other MT4 platforms that don't reside on the same computer. The client accounts may even be located in other countries! The signal provider may be in Tokyo whilst the client traders may be in London, and they may have different brokers also. Hundreds of client/slave traders, with different trading platforms, may be located all around the world and still they will be able to receive trades from the server/master account in real time.

Local Trade Copier, as its name implies, operates on a singular computer and can be used with any broker with a MT4 platform. It communicates between the two or more platforms or trading accounts on the same computer to relay trade signals. Let's say you're a manual trader and you have several different trading accounts, perhaps each with a different broker. With the LTC software, you could place one trade on your primary account, and then that trade will be automatically copied and transferred into your other accounts.

Advantages of the Local Trade Copier software

Account managers primarily benefit from LTC with its automatic copying of trades because it allows them to manage several trading accounts with little effort. Unlimited numbers of MT4 accounts, from any broker, and any account size, can be duplicated. Without LTC, an account manager would have to bear the burden of manually placing multiple trades of each client's account on different MetaTrader platforms. But with LTC, you only need to focus on your account and LTC will take care of relaying your trades to the accounts you're managing. All the accounts will receive the trades at the same entry price in a perfect market conditions, but important to understand that slippages will occur, which is normal in the Forex market and with any kind of trade copier application. Trade parameters of each account can be set up to a specific lot size or risk percentage settings.

The software can copy pending orders together with their expiration values, and the copier even can be set in a way that the pending orders will only be executed if they get triggered on the master account. All trades are copied at lightning speed—a fraction of a second. All the accounts will be at the same entry price, or within a fraction of a pip. Trade parameters of each account can be set up to a specific lot size or risk percentage settings. The Local Trade Copier does not depend on any web service and this makes the transfer of data extremely fast.

Aside from customizing trade filters, there are a lot of available settings and customizations for LTC. Each slave account can have a fixed lot size for each trade. A certain percentage of risk can also be adjusted which would vary from one account to another, based on the account size. This facilitates the copying of trades regardless of the individual balances of the different accounts. This means that it doesn't matter whether the master account size has a $1,000 equity balance while the slave account has $25,000... or the master has $25,000 and the slave has $500 in funds. The LTC will copy the trades correctly according to the settings. This flexibility is one of the most outstanding features of the Local Trade Copier.

Another advantage of LTC on the slave accounts is not having the need to open the same charts, time frame and currency pair on the platform as what displays on the master account. The slave MetaTrader must be running and only one chart (running the EA) needs to be opened in order to receive copied trades. For optimal performance, the chart should be any major currency pair in any time frame. It doesn't matter what currency pair is open—it will still receive trades of all pairs.

Disadvantage of Local Trade Copier

LTC is only available for the MetaTrader 4 platform. Although MT4 is the most common platform that is widely used by brokerages, other brokers are now trading with MT5 and other platforms such as Ninja Trader, and also other web-based platforms. Traders with these unsupported platforms will not be able to enjoy the benefits of LTC.

Local Trade Copier works like a plug-in for MT4. It is not a standalone software that can be installed on the computer. Thus, it requires manual installation and configuration in each individual MT4 account.

LTC is only compatible with Windows Operating Systems. This means that LTC cannot be installed on Mac OS and Linux computers. Additional system requirements include a Windows OS with versions of 2000, XP, Vista, and 7; one gigabyte RAM space; and a CPU running at 1.0GHz frequency. Virtually any modern computer will be able to run the LTC successfully. An internet connection is not required for the Local version, however it is obvious that internet connection is required for the MT4 platform to receive data.

This EA is not free, but for many people, a one-time fee payment for LTC may be a better choice than monthly payments with other trade copy services. A 30-day trial is available for each LTC, which makes it very easy for traders to test.

For whom Local Trade Copier is best

With the LTC software, you can become an independent account manager. LTC works great for traders who have a number of accounts that need to be managed. It eliminates the problem of individually managing and executing trades on each account. No human can ever duplicate trades between several managed accounts faster than the LTC. Just one account is needed for a start and the rest will follow in your business. It can also be used between different MT4 platforms.

Traders can make use of this software to make their business more professional and stress-free. Account managers will not need to bother in re-calculating the lot sizes for slave trades, as the software will calculate it automatically, following the risk percentage of the master account, if this option is utilized.

Use this simple trade copier to replicate trades to different accounts and form a trading signal business

If you're just starting your trading signals business and have only a few clients, you may want to consider the process of trade copying straight from your computer, without using any 3rd party website's services. In order to do this, you will need a trade copier for the MetaTrader 4 platform. Your customers' accounts must be on MT4 as well.

Let's assume that you have five customers. You will need to setup six MetaTrader 4 platforms on the same computer. The first MetaTrader account will be your master account. This is where you will open, close or modify your trades. The other five accounts will act as slave accounts, receiving the trades from the master account.

Next step is to use software like the Local Trade Copier to duplicate all trading actions from your master account to the slave accounts. Once you have everything set up correctly, the software will perform the trade copying automatically, without any additional input on your end.

You just need to focus on making good trades. You can even initiate trades from another computer or even a mobile device like an Android or an iPhone smartphone. If you have a robot that is performing well, you might even consider running this on one platform while the trades are automatically copied to the other accounts you manage.

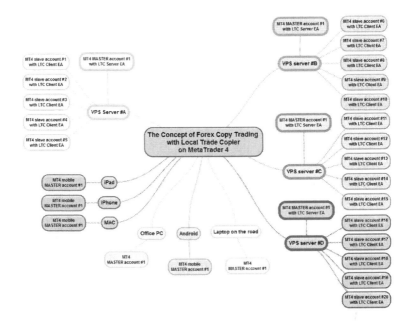

This is the simplest and most convenient way to deliver signals on your own without any 3rd party involvement. You can purchase a trade copier for a one-time fee and use it on your computer without any extra costs or monthly charges. It is up to you to pick how you'll be compensated for the signals. Will it be a fixed monthly fee or performance fee based on a high watermark? It's all up to you as the trading fund manager!

Beware of trade copying services and software that disrupt MetaQuotes policies

There are online trade copying services and trade copier software that will replicate your trading signals to your customers' accounts without the need to run a MetaTrader platform. This is easy and convenient because you and your customers don't need to run any software on your computers. These services are very similar to ZuluTrade, SimpleTrader and several of the other networks, but instead of getting paid based on the trading volume you generate, you can decide how you want to get paid.

These services have a monthly charge or even can be a onetime fee for the standalone software. The fee usually depends on the number of customers that receive your trading signals. The main disadvantage with this approach is that your trading signals get exposed to a 3rd party and some of these companies may use an unapproved MT4 Server API to connect to your customers' accounts. MetaQuotes (the creator of Meta-Trader) can, and has in the past, interpreted some of these actions as platform hacking.

This means that the services provided by these websites can be unreliable, if they are using an unofficial MT4 Server API. Because MetaQuotes doesn't support this activity, it can land these sites in hot water with future legal problems. In addition, MetaQuotes has, in the past, employed a heavy-handed approach of blocking the servers of these websites. They have also included the code for this block in an update to the MT4 platform itself. MetaQuotes does not mess around with services that use unofficial APIs to access their systems or data.

The creators of MetaTrader can repeat this action at any time if they want, and any 3rd party sites using unofficial APIs for the purpose of trade copying may encounter great difficulties. Then, those services or software can stop working until their programmers reverse-engineer the protocol and make the necessary changes to the software.

On the other hand, if you find out that such trade copier services use official API connections and they operate their business by using the MetaTrader platform according to MetaQuotes policies, you can better trust such a company.

Become a money manager at a Forex broker

If you have a profitable trading record that spans at least a few years, you can contact Forex brokers and ask to work as a money manager for their customers. Brokers like Sensus Capital Markets, FXOpen, Alpari UK and many others offer this type of service. If you get approved as a money manager, you will need to open a so called MAM, PAMM or LAMM account. Investors can then add money into your account and you can use these customer funds to trade currencies.

How these types of accounts work

Here's how this works… let's assume that you get 100 customers and each of them deposits $1,000 in your MAM account, bringing the total balance to $100,000. When you make a 10% profit, each of your customers will make the same 10% profit. Each is paid according to the size of capital they have placed into the account for management.

You will be paid a monthly performance fee which is automatically transferred from your customers' accounts to your personal account. This performance fee is usually based on a 'high watermark' principle and customers pay the fee only if you make money for them. Most money managers charge a fee in the 20 to 50 percent range.

Here is how it works: let's say that you decide to charge a 30% performance fee. Last month you made a 10% monthly gain on your $100,000 MAM account. In US dollars, this translates into a profit of $10,000. With a 30 percent fee, you will receive 30% of the profits, or 3,000 USD.

Note: Personally, I did not have to knock on the doors of Forex brokers and ask them to invite me to become a money manager for their customers. Several brokers noticed my trading signals website and some even gave me their live account for testing of my strategy. After several months they gave me a great deal and asked me to become a money manager for their customers.

I consider MAM and fund management to be a step forward from running a signal service and I believe that we all need to take small steps to get to the top in our businesses. I am glad that I started a signal service because that was the first step for me towards being a money manager. Now I see more and more opportunities opening for me after first starting a signal business, and it might happen in a similar way for you.

There are differences between MAM, PAMM and LAMM accounts and usually you need to be regulated by financial organizations to offer this kind of a service to customers. (I explain the difference between these account types in another chapter of this book.)

Remote Trade Copier or the All-in-one trading signals delivery software

This one is my favorite ideas in forex. I use it myself in my own trading signals business at www.vavatrade.com.

A few years ago, I developed software called the Remote Trade Copier. It's an all-in-one solution for any signal provider who wants to be independent and run their own Forex signal business. You can set the compensation scheme for your service at just about any level you choose. You can create your own rules, work with any Forex broker you choose and not be bound by the rules/broker selection of some 3rd party website. This freedom is the advantage, in my mind, over all the sites like Zulu, FX Copy, etc.

When selling signals on ZuluTrade or MyFXBook, you are limited to work only with those Forex brokers that support these platforms. If the Forex broker you are using is not on the list then you cannot use these platforms. Also, MyFXBook has strict limitations to how your trading strategy can perform.

The Remote Trade Copier delivers trading signals worldwide through an internet connection and does this automatically. It can deliver the signals in less than 1 second, even if you have hundreds of customers. Customers can configure their accounts individually and chose a risk profile that they want and is appropriate for the size of account they have.

Under the default setup, customers have to run the Client EA on their MT4 platforms. But you can decide to provide this service for them and run their EAs on your own VPS server. The usual cost to host 4-6 MetaTrader terminals is around $25 per month. If you consider this as a normal cost of running such a business then you will agree that this cost is next to nothing.

The RTC has extra plugins that can allow you to have multiple signal providers. Your customers can choose which one of them they will follow. Also, with the help of other plugins, you can connect the system to your PayPal or ClickBank account and have email notifications sent for each action. In other words, this software can pretty much do everything for you except trade currencies. In every other area, the Remote Trade Copier can make your entire signal business run without the need for human intervention.

As you can see, the Remote Trade Copier (RTC)is an absolute all-in-one trading signal delivery software. RTC is used to sell and manage trading signals to other traders who have limited time to manage their trading accounts manually. This software automatically delivers trades from a signal provider to the clients' MT4 accounts. It contains most of the features that every trader and signal provider needs. It has opened limitless doors for traders in the Forex signal service business. With a successful Forex trading strategy, you can become a Forex signal provider too with the help of this robust software.

How does RTC work?

RTC is very well designed trade copier software. It has a web based control panel and two MT4 Expert Advisors (Server EA and Client EA), one designed for the master account and the other for the slave(s) account(s). The RTC control panel is where you can manage clients' subscriptions. The Server EA is installed on your MT4 account (as the signal provider) which is referred to as the "master" account. This master account is where you manage the trades and will send trading signals to clients. Conversely, the client EA is installed to the client trader's account, known as the "slave" account. The slave account receives the same trades that the master account has executed.

It is best to run the MT4 terminals with the EA on a VPS server because it is best to have a stable internet connection 24/5. Also, slave accounts attached with the client EAs should also be on VPS servers ideally (but this is not an absolute requirement) to receive all the master signals without any interruption. RTC's control panel allows customers to submit their MT4 account password so that you, service provider, can host them on your VPS servers. This option gives your clients easier access your Forex signal business so they would not need purchase and configure their own VPS.

The master and slave account communicate with each other through the RTC's web based control panel. If the Server EA has executed a trade in the master account, the trade is sent to the RTC website. The website will then send the trade to all slave accounts that are running the Client EA. The server EA is capable of delivering trades to thousands of clients instantaneously and enables every slave account to receive the trade execution in a fraction of a second.

RTC efficiently copies exact trade parameters such as market order price, take profit, and stop loss levels. Any trade adjustments or modifications in the master account are automatically executed at the slave accounts in real-time. Client EAs automatically apply trade settings to trade signals it receives—money management, filter unwanted currency pairs, lot size per trade, and other settings within a second. RTC will execute both market orders and pending trade orders on any MT4 platform.

Note: With the Multiple Signal Provider (MSP) plug-in, RTC is capable of supporting an unlimited number of signal providers. Customers can then choose which provider to follow. This is a great upside for building a trading signals business.

Advantages of RTC

The Remote Trade Copier comes with a built-in control panel website which gives you, as the signal provider, the ability to manage your clients from anywhere in the world. You will have the ability to control and check client subscriptions, account information, as well as trade history of the master and slave accounts. Clients can also access the RTC control panel on which they can see their profile account information, as well as check the past and open trades of the master account.

Helping clients save on VPS fees and simplify signal delivery

Your clients don't necessarily need to subscribe to a VPS service to use your Forex signal services, because you, the vendor, can do this for them. The RTC control panel allows customers to provide their MT4 account login credentials so you could use them to run their MT4 on your server. This saves customers money from VPS monthly subscription fees. I do this on my trading signals website at www.vavatrade.com and people are more than satisfied with this option.

Remember, RTC copies trades in less than one second. Most of the available copiers have an average copy speed of 400 milliseconds. In most cases, the broker server delay is usually about 1 second but could be even more.

The Multiple Signal Provider (MSP) plug-in allows the RTC to manage multiple signal providers. Clients can now choose which signal provider to follow. They can set individual money management options for each signal provider they follow.

With an RTC license, you can brand your own Forex signal services with your company name. RTC can automatically manage your clients' payments by connecting the system to your payment processor by using the RTC payment plugin for PayPal, Clickbank or Click2Sell.

The web based RTC control panel is available in 9 languages including English, Spanish, Italian, French, Japanese, German, Hungarian, Lithuanian and Chinese.

Disadvantages of RTC

RTC software runs only on the MetaTrader 4 platform. Clients with other trading platforms will not be able to benefit from RTC. Although it is compatible with any MT4 platform, OANDA MT4 terminal is excluded for being used as a master account to send trades using Server EA. OANDA MT4 platform handles pending orders in different way. In MT4, a pending order has a unique ticket number that identifies the order. When the order is filled and it becomes a market order, most MT4 accounts retain its ticket number. But OANDA MT4 changes the ticket number into a different ticket number if the pending order is filled. This makes for a problem with RTC Server EA. However, RTC Client EA will work fine on the slave account from OANDA MT4.

Note: The RTC control panel must be hosted on a Linux based web server. The server must have Apache, PHP 5, MySQL 5, and SMTP software installed. Once you start with no or just a few customers, you can chose simple web hosting plans from LiquidWeb.com. However RTC will need much more powerful server to handle 100 and more clients and the price would start at ~$200 a month to rent such a dedicated server. Of course, having 100 clients would pay off this fee easily.

For whom RTC is best

If you are a profitable trader or have a proven profitable Forex robot, you can start your own Forex Signal business. With the Remote Trade Copier, your Forex trading signal business can run on autopilot. Remote Trade Copier handles almost all of the things needed for the business to operate. You will only need a few staff members to monitor the servers and to take care of the client account hosting.

You'll likely also want a staff member who can help with email or chat support. Traders will subscribe to your service with the hope of profiting from your trading methods/signals. You can even integrate multiple signal providers in your business. Clients then can have several choices on which signal provider to follow. In turn, signal providers and clients will pay you an amount you specify, which could range from a few dollars to a few hundred dollars per month. You could also charge a percentage of the monthly gains if you are inclined to bill in such a way. The options are manifold and the profit potential is very great!

Let's look at the income and expenses of a full trading signals business

For example, let's say that you get 100 subscribers paying you $100 each per month. A webserver for this amount of people would set you back around $250/month. With your income at 100 x $100 = $10,000 a month, it will more than cover your server costs and also pay for any support staff you might need to help answer customers' questions.

Now knowing the usual cost of $25 to host 4-6 MetaTrader terminals, let's assume that we will need 20 VPS servers to host these 100x MT4 platforms. This would set you back another $450/month. You could also then hire someone for about $500/month to monitor and manage these VPS servers and you have yourself a full-fledged trading signals business!

This adds up to about $1,200/month in expenses. But as you can see, the return is almost 10x times higher.

Before setting up the Remote Trade Copier you will need a domain name and web hosting account for the control panel website. I recommend using a dedicated server cloud hosting from LiquidWeb.com.

RTC is great for building a company brand

This method for delivering trading signals is popular among bigger companies because this software can be branded with a company name/logo. This presents a professional image and helps engender more trust with customers.

For bigger companies, using services like ZuluTrade or MyFXBook might look unprofessional. This branding idea came up so that they will have an effective trade copying solution incorporated with a complete business brand. It's an expensive software, but many signal providers already use it in their businesses and are doing quite well.

Be bold, build a trade signal business and test out as many options as you can

In the section above I went through a few different methods for selling signals. It's very important that you choose a method that fits your own needs. Start today and pick at least one of the presented options to begin growing your trading services business. Setup an account, or if the website/service offers it, go for a trial version.

Test out as many of the options as you can. For optimum results, try all of them. This will help you make a good decision when it comes time to settle down with one method. You might learn from all of these providers and then come up with a better idea than all of them together. Your idea might just be the next great idea that traders are looking for to build their portfolios and wealth.

Once you have chosen the system you will use, set it up and start testing with real and demo trading accounts. You can start by delivering the trading signals to your friends or even to your own auxiliary demo trading accounts. This will help you gain more experience and see how the software works inside and out. You will learn every detail of the software and will be able to teach your future customers how to use it as well.

After you setup the trade copier software (or service depending on which signal delivery method you picked) you can go live and start delivering the signals at any time. Your next assignment is to find a profitable trading strategy and start replicating its signals to your customers' accounts.

Remember, you learn to ride a bike by riding a bike. Consequently, you learn to use a trade copier software by using a trade copier software. You learn how to run a trading signals business by running a trading signals business. There is no substitute for real life experience. So start today and test as many solutions as possible or simply start with the simplest one. Build upon your experience as you go and don't look back.

Chapter 3 Takeaways

Chapter 3: Forex Trading Signals Delivery

Trading Signal Delivery Software

You need software that copies the trading actions from your account to the account of a client in real time. As soon as you make changes to a trading position, that same action will get replicated to your client's account.

Most popular methods of trading signal delivery

- ZuluTrade.com
  - One of the largest social trading networks.
  - You can use demo account to sell your trading signals.
  - ZuluTrade trader ranking boards help promote you to trade followers.
  - You and your copiers are not charged with any amount by using the ZuluTrade's service. ZuluTrade's commission is added from the spread of your copier's trades.
  - Your monthly compensation is calculated as 0.5 pips per lot per transaction from a live follower account.
  - No need to install any software on your computer in order to start sending or receiving trading signals.
- MetaTrader Signals Service
  - The MetaTrader Signals service is a simple and built-in solution for MT4 and MT5 platform. You can easily start sharing you signals to all MetaTrader users around the world.
  - MetaTrader Signals service is completely free for all traders
  - To sell your trading signals, register and activate an account at MT5.com as a signal provider.
  - You can price your trading signal from free to any amount.

- o Information about your signal will be available in all MetaTrader terminals around the world and each MetaTrader user can subscribe to your signal
- MT5 Marketplace
  - o A great Forex community wherein you can securely buy or sell MetaTrader 4 and MetaTrader 5 trading software.
  - o Best marketplace to promote your EAs and indicators if you are looking for feedback and testers.
  - o It has a wide variety of Forex mql5 programming articles for traders who desire to learn how to program and automate their trading strategy.
- MyFxBook.com
  - o Very similar to ZuluTrade
  - o Demo traders are not allowed to become signal providers.
  - o Only experienced traders are allowed to be an AutoTrade provider. The requirements are very strict and aim to protect traders from unreliable providers.
  - o Offers unparalleled metrics and account performance tracking
  - o It provides trading transparency and security to both AutoTrade providers and copy traders.
  - o It supports only a limited number of Forex brokerages.

- Tradeo Social Trading Network
  - You can sell trading signals through a live or demo trading account.
  - Traders can copy your trades for free
  - Tradeo pays you 1 to 5 USD per trade per lot traded in your copiers' accounts.
  - It operates on a broader scale. It runs across numerous trading platforms which include ActTrader, FXCM, MT4, and MT5. It integrates 60 of today's top Forex brokerages
  - Dynamic Leverage system allows the copiers to change the trade parameters set by you.
  - Few registered and active traders compared to other social trading networks.
- FX Copy
  - All registered traders must download and install the FX Copy EA into their MetaTrader 4 platform in order to transmit/receive trades.
  - Traders can follow, learn and copy trades from top performing traders for free
  - Traders can set to Auto-Copy or manually copy the trades
  - All copied trades are tracked by the system and kept synchronized with the signal provider's account.
  - You will earn a rebate from every FX Copy registered trader who copied your trade
  - You cannot use demo account to provide signals
  - In order for you to sell signals, your broker must be a platinum member of FX Copy.
- Currensee
  - Currensee doesn't offer demo accounts
  - To become a signal provider, you must have a minimum of one year trading history with a 10% ROI in a live Forex trading account, and also maintain a consistent track record of positive trading performance.

- o Becoming a signal provider is free of charge but must have a live account with one of the supported brokerages funded with 10, 000 or more
- o Money managers and fund managers with a real and proven history of positive performance and strong risk management are the only allowed to become signal providers
- o Retail traders will have no real possibility to sell their trade signals
- o Signal Providers are only paid each month by 20% of the profits they generated on the investors' accounts that copied their trades. Losing trades will not be paid
- SimpleTrader
  - o Web based trade copier which allows traders to sell trade signals through their Commercial Trade Copier or to manage private accounts through their Private Trade Copier
  - o You can be a commercial trade copier and create your own brand, and then impress clients and sell to them your trading services
  - o You can choose to be a Private Trade Copier and manage your clients' accounts directly
  - o You can build your own signals business where you manage both sides (recruiting successful traders and also signing up investors)
  - o The copier platform doesn't need to be installed on your client's MetaTrader 4 platforms and they don't have to worry about installing EA's onto their charts
  - o Your clients don't need to subscribe to a Virtual Private Server provider since SimpleTrader is directly connected to their brokers
  - o Your trades are directly executed with your clients' respective broker servers, bypassing

the need for the clients to run a MetaTrader
platform

- o The platform copies and executes trades
  with a very fast execution time of 10 to 50
  milliseconds
- o There is no upfront payment in subscribing to
  the commercial signal copier
- o Once you have attracted customers, you will
  be charged for $15 per month
- o ConnectForex, SimpleTrader VPS, and
  MyLiveAccount are powered by the SimpleTrader platform which provides VPS hosting, as well as a vehicle to sell your trading
  skills
- Local Trade Copier
  - o Used by traders to automatically duplicate
    trades of a signal provider's account (master)
    to several clients'MT4 accounts (slave)
  - o Comes in the form of an Expert Advisor in-
    stalled on any MT4 chart
  - o Designed to work for any accounts with an
    MT4 platform, with any Forex broker, and can
    copy trades on any currency pair
  - o Works regardless of how many master and
    slave accounts are connected
  - o Master and Slave accounts must be running
    on the same computer or VPS server
  - o There are many different options that can fil-
    ter trades, which is very useful for traders us-
    ing Forex robots and also for account
    managers managing several accounts
  - o MT4 indicators can be used by LTC as a
    trade filter indicator
  - o Trade filter indicators can be modified to only
    copy trades of certain currency pairs
  - o Can be configured so that both master and
    slave accounts will not send and receive any
    trades during a specified time period

    o Does not depend on any web service and this makes the transfer of data extremely fast

Become a money manager at a forex broker

- You must have a profitable trading record that spans at least a few years
- You will need to open a MAM, PAMM or LAMM account investors can then add money into your account and you can use these customer funds to trade currencies

Remote Trade Copier or the All-in-one trading signals delivery software

- An all-in-one solution for any signal provider who wants to be independent and run their own Forex signal business
- Used to sell and manage trading signals to other traders who have limited time to manage their trading accounts manually
- Automatically delivers trading signals to the clients' MT4 accounts worldwide through an internet connection
- It can deliver the signals in less than 1 second, even if you have hundreds of customers
- Customers can configure their accounts individually and chose a risk profile that they want and is appropriate for the size of account they have
- The RTC has extra plugins that can allow you to have multiple signal providers
- You can connect the system to your PayPal or ClickBank account
- Can make your entire signal business run without the need for human intervention
- RTC is great for building a company brand
- Before setting up the Remote Trade Copier, you will need a domain name and web hosting account for the control panel website
- Dedicated server cloud hosting from Liquid-Web.com is recommended

Income and Expenses of a Full Trading Signals Business

Let's say, You have 100 subscribers paying you $100 each per month:

Profit: 100 subscribers x $100 per month = $10,000 a month

Usual VPS cost of $25 per month to host 4-6 MetaTrader terminals

Therefore, you need 20 VPS servers to host these 100 customers:

20 VPS x $25 = $500 per month

Webserver would cost you around $250/month

You hired someone for about $500/month to monitor and manage VPS servers

Expenses: $500 + $250 + $500 = $1,250 per month

Total Net Profit: $10,000 - $1,250 = $8,750 per month

Understanding the Management Tools: MAM, PAMM and LAMM accounts

When a trader reaches the skill level that makes them confident enough to start trading with others' money, today's technological age provides a number of tools and systems that facilitate this process. Advancements in the Meta Trader systems, particularly MT4, have allowed brokers to provide money managers with accurate and streamlined software that allows trading over seemingly limitless accounts, all with the click of a button.

Here we look at the different options that are available to today's forex money managers and break down the pros and cons of using each. The three most commonly used and most effective tools used by forex money managers these days are Multi Account Management (MAM), Percentage/Profit Allocation Management Module(PAMM) and Lot Allocation Management Module (LAMM) accounts. While every regulated brokerage system offers both MAM and PAMM accounts, brokers that offer LAMM accounts are less ubiquitous.

Before a trader, who is moving into money management, can decide which management system is best for their needs, they must understand the basic functions of each as well as the rules and regulations applied to using them. The forex industry may be notoriously loosely regulated however there is a worldwide synergy among national financial authorities to take stricter approaches to both regulations and the powers to enforce them. While some brokers may seem relaxed about the rules applied to these money management tools, it may not be long before mandatory rulings step in to intervene. The chapter on Financial Regulation will look at this subject in further detail but it's vital for a money manager to seek legal advice on how their trading activity is regulated in their own country. Just because a brokerage firm hosts your MAM, PAMM or LAMM account in another jurisdiction, doesn't mean that you will be automatically exempt from your domestic regulations.

MAM: Multi Account Management

The definition of a MAM interface is quite simply and generically a program that allows one central or controlling account to place trades on behalf of other subsidiary accounts. It is the base of all money management tools and effectively any program that allows a money manager to guide the activity of other accounts can be classified under MAM. Because of this, there are a number of brokers who offer MAM services but are somewhat vague about how their system works. Money managers who are shopping around for the right broker need to be sure that they understand the operational and legislative parameters of any MAM account before committing their own and their clients' money to it.

Benefits

Multi Account Management tools, if offered by genuinely regulated brokers, offer a high level of convenience and security to both the money manager and their investors. The programs are the first line of protection for both parties because while the manager effectively has access to each investor's account, each investor has the control to opt out of a MAM link at any point. Equally from the other side, the best MAM software will have an integrated payment and commission system where investors automatically have the fees due to their manager deducted from their accounts. The manager does not need to get involved in chasing payments for their services. And then at the top of these is the fact that final liabilities for all traders are managed centrally by the broker. This is why it is so important to be operating a MAM account through a regulated broker. Those who don't will not be covered by the underwriting protection each regulated broker must have as standard.

Different types of MAM accounts will come with different rules on registration and regulation for money managers. The differences will come in the permissions and functions of the MAM account combined with the financial regulation in the manager's country of residence. Whatever the requirements, MAM interfaces will generally come with an administrative function which allows managers to create customized POA agreements, where necessary, and have them submitted to and approved by the clients/investors online in a matter of minutes.

The integration of either PAM or LAM modules to a MAM account will dictate how much regulation and authorization is needed by the money manager. Further detail will be given below but it is worth noting that in some jurisdictions simply running either of these modules with certain volumes of funds and clients will automatically require financial regulation or investment fund manager status.

The success of MT4 has revolutionized the MAM software industry and the top brokers, as well as several others; all offer systems that are completely integrated with the MT4 platform. Some brokers will offer completely web based platforms and while these may seem convenient and simpler, be careful to check the trading parameters of these programs. This becomes particularly important when using EA trading. Every MAM program on the market makes claims of almost zero delay in executing trades between the main account and slave accounts however the definition of almost zero varies between systems. Brokers will advise on the time lapses in their money manager terms and conditions so it's vital to be sure that you are not using a system that may cause delays in execution. For EA trading where everything is automated, the delays may not be picked up until much later down the line when significant profits have been missed out on.

That being said, it should be noted that the general integration of EA trading is well synchronized among the most popular MAM programs.

Things to Watch Out For

As mentioned above, the trading permissions and parameters of MAM accounts need to be scrutinized before committing both your and your investors' funds. Below is an overview of the two most popular types of MAM account and it will give a new money manager the information needed when shopping around for the best broker and best MAM system.

LAMM: Lot Allocation Management Module

The first innovation in multi account money management for forex traders came with the introduction of Lot Allocation Management Modules (LAMM). These software programs allowed money managers to execute trades over a multitude of accounts almost simultaneously. Every "slave" account is managed directly from a central account and the controlling trader need only submit the order on their own system to then have the exact trade copied to each account which was subscribed.

This is the first step up from signal selling where the balance of authority moves from the clients to the managing trader. In the above situations, the onus lay on followers to execute trades based on the activity of the expert they followed. Whereas in the signal selling scenario, there is no way to tell how much an expert is actually trading off the intelligence they are selling, for copy traders linked to a LAMM account there is the certainty that the person they are following is actually putting their own funds into each opened position.

A trader who controls the LAMM for several accounts is typically paid a percentage commission of profits from each following account. Since inception, LAMM software has automated this process so that on a monthly basis the required commission is automatically deducted from each follower account into the central trader's balance.

Lot Allocation Management was designed specifically to allow traders to profit by sharing their knowledge and expertise with lesser skilled traders while at the same time avoiding the extra regulation and financial requirements of an investment fund manager or mutual fund trader. However, the LAMM system is limited in so much as it is only really most effective when each following trader has the same or similar total funds and acceptable risk levels. LAMMs literally replicate the exact trade of the central trader irrespective of the balance and risk requirements of following accounts. If a following trader is insufficiently matched to the central trader in terms of trading funds and risk requirements it is likely that the trades they get linked into will not be in the best interest of their overall fund and trading strategy.

Consider the following example:

Master account opens a trade for 1.2 lots. All the slave accounts will open exactly the same trade as follows:

Client 1 – 1.2 lots
Client 2 – 1.2 lots
Client 3 – 1.2 lots

In the traditional LAMM account, the financial backing against each lot would be the same as the master account too. It means that in the predecessor LAMM accounts, each slave account would automatically put the same price per pip, stop loss and take profit levels as the master account.

PAMM: Percentage Allocation Management Module

Following the limitations created by the simplistic programming of the first LAMMs, the Percentage Allocation Management Module (PAMM) was created to allow a central trader to link up with several following traders irrespective of their balances and risk requirements. As the name suggests, instead of each trade being copied directly, a percentage of each of the central overall trader's opened positions are automatically executed on following accounts. The larger a following trader's balance, the greater the number of lots they were allocated and therefore the lower the balance of a following trader's account (in respect to the overall trading fund managed by the controlling trader account), the lesser the number of lots allocated to their account in each respective trade.

Consider the following example:

A Money Manager is running a PAMM account which has 5 "slave" accounts linked to it. Each of the clients owning these 5 accounts has the following breakdown of total fund ownership:

Client 1's account represents 25% of the total client fund
Client 2's account represents 15% of the total client fund
Client 3's account represents 20% of the total client fund
Client 4's account represents 10% of the total client fund
Client 5's account represents 30% of the total client fund

Each time the controlling trader opens a trade position, the representative percentages are reflected in each account's individual trade. So if the central trader takes a long position of 100 lots on the USD/GBP pair, the breakdown would be as follows:

Client 1's account would activate a long position for 25 lots
Client 2's account would activate a long position for 15 lots
Client 3's account would activate a long position for 20 lots
Client 4's account would activate a long position for 10 lots
Client 5's account would activate a long position for 30 lots

When the position is then closed, each client's account would reflect the profit or loss relevant to their share of the trade.

As an update to the older LAMM systems, PAMMs allows money managers to trade the accounts of clients from all backgrounds with all levels of funding and a wide range of risk level. Everyone from the lowest funded traders to the highest and most risk accepting can all benefit from the expertise of one trader.

As with the LAMM systems, commissions are paid automatically from each "slave" account into the controlling account on a monthly basis after the total accumulation of fees and commissions have been calculated.

Revamped LAMMs

Perhaps one of the biggest changes to the forex money management industry has come from the redesigned and newly coded LAMMs which some brokers are now offering to money managers. They take a big step in departing completely from the automated and blind access that money managers currently have, moving closer into the realms of investment manager and financial advisor.

Instead of operating like the old LAMMs and modern PAMMs where the money manager cannot control how much of a client's funds are traded, new LAMM accounts give the money manager the authority to tweak and tailor their trades to the specific needs of each and every one of their clients. This is a system which is not so much suited to the shorter time frame trading techniques because of the slightly more laborious set up but for those who do implement it, the money manager is able to select the number of lots applied to each account based on their central trade.

This revolution has thrown into question the ability of national financial authorities to use existing regulations to suitably control and police the market and so across several regions there have been calls for modernized and rewritten regulations.

Money managers need to be aware of the sizes of their clients' accounts when using more advanced systems though. Every broker has a minimum trade size and in the case that a slave or client account follows a trade that doesn't meet the minimum requirement, that account will not follow the trade.

Consider the following example:

Let's say we have 3 slaves with accounts:

Client 1 - $10,000 (16.4%)

Client 2 - $50,000 (82%)

Client 3 - $1,000 (1.6%)

Now if the master account opens a 1.2 lot and it tries to distribute it equally, the following will occur; so $50k is considered 82%, then $10k makes 16.4% and $1k makes only 1.6%.

Now lot 1.2 is distributed:

$10k gets 0.2

$50k gets 0.98
$1k gets 0.02. Now here 0.02 is too low if broker allows minimum of 0.1 lots only and this user does not get that trade. While it is the responsibility of each client or investor to check that a money manager's trading will match their needs, once a client invests, a professional money manager will monitor the number of instances where clients' accounts are not qualifying for trades. This will allow them to either amend their trading to meet the needs of all their clients, or suggest certain investors move their money to a more suitable manager.

Regulation

The following chapter on Financial Regulation will look at the country specific requirements for money managers in each country but for the purposes of this chapter, it should be noted that enforceable regulation for money managers using LAMMs and PAMMs is generally quite ambiguous. Where some countries will require regulation based on the total volume of funds traded, others may look at the number of clients being represented through a LAMM or PAMM account. Others still take the blanket view that any person who has control of another's money for investing purposes must be regulated by the local financial authority.

However further ambiguity comes when looking at the penalties involved in ignoring these rules. Where some countries have very strict rules and necessary judiciary power to enforce them, others have very comprehensive guidelines but no enforcement power. This effectively makes their regulatory requirements nothing more than strong recommendations.

For traders looking to move into money management and code their own LAMM or PAMM accounts for hosting through Meta Trader 4, they need to pay attention to the constantly changing rules surrounding money management because changes tend to be implemented quickly and often without much broadcasting. The penalties for operating in contravention of such regulations can be very costly.

However, for traders who wish to register as approved money managers through regulated forex brokers, they will find that the vast majority of brokers will insist on the applying money manager having the applicable regulation from their native country. This tends to be an obligatory requirement whether or not the relevant financial authority has enforcement powers or not. The next chapter on Financial Regulation will look at this matter in greater detail as well as discussing the potential changes that the industry anticipates over the next few years.

The Pros and Cons

If you find yourself in a position where you are looking to start managing the forex accounts of others, a MAM system is by far the most effective way to help others capitalize on your knowledge. And of course subsequently you will then reap the rewards through charging fees and performance commissions.

The smaller your number of followed accounts and the closer each of them is to your own trading volumes; the better it would be to adopt a simple traditional LAMM system. Each following account will effectively replicate all your trades and will subsequently provide you with the commission on each of their profits. You will not want to adopt a percentage system where following traders will only be executing a portion of each of your trades and therefore missing out on the higher levels of return. This of course then means you are missing out on the applicable higher commissions.

Alternatively, if you are looking to attract as many investors as possible to become followers to your account, then a PAMM system is much more flexible in allowing a wider range of potential client. You will not need to worry about any disparity between your own trading volume in regards to dollar value and that of your clients because of the way your trades are copied to each slave account. PAMM systems will automatically calculate what percentage of the total fund each of your clients' funds represent and set their lots accordingly. Fluctuations will of course occur as clients draw down funds or top up their balances but once again this is something that will automatically be calculated so your own personal trading activity can remain unchanged and you will not have to make amendments at any point to factor in changes to your clients' funds. Equally, when you attract new clients and the lots are split further, there will be no administration required on your part.

Some PAMM systems will allow you to treat your funds and your clients' collective funds as separate entities whereby each trade you place counts as 100% for your own fund and then the percentage of each of your client's funds will be calculated based on their whole.

For example:

You are trading an account balance of $10,000 and you have 5 clients each with the following funds:

Client A - $10,000
Client B - $2,000
Client C - $5,000
Client D - $2,000
Client E - $1,000

Instead of the standard PAMM calculation where your balance would count as 33% of the total fund and each of your clients making up the remaining 67%, your balance is counted as 100% of the controlling account and then your clients will have the following percentage for each of your copied trades:

Client A – 50%
Client B – 10%
Client C – 25%
Client D – 10%
Client E – 5%

The benefits of this second system become more apparent for your clients as you gain more and more slave accounts however as a relatively new system, very few brokers are offering at the time this is going to print. There may also be regulatory impacts that affect this separated MAM style that have less of an impact on the typical PAMM trading systems.

Fees

It is down to both you and your clients to negotiate and agree on the fees they pay you for your services. Brokers will not get involved beyond calculating the fees at the end of each month based on the figures you supply them in the MAM agreements that are filled in and submitted on account opening. However, brokers tend to be willing to offer both you and your clients advice on generally accepted industry standards and will allow fees to be calculated in a number of ways. This can include percentage fees, flat fees per month, pip and points based fees.

These fees are always calculated monthly and debited directly from clients' accounts to cut down on administration on both your and your clients' part. It also takes away the hassle of payment chasing for you.

High Water Mark

Most brokers these days will also offer what is known as a monthly corrective fee based system referred to as the "high water mark" calculation method. It is a transparent and comprehensive approach to fees that helps your clients feel assured that they will only be paying when you produce positive results for them over the long term. The details of each can fluctuate slightly but the general basis of the system is as follows. Imagine you have set your monthly management fee at 10% of total profits and in the first month you realize profits of $10,000 across all your clients' funds collectively. That would entitle you to a fee of $1,000 which would automatically be deducted from each of your clients' respective accounts. So using the split example above, each client would pay:

Client A - $500
Client B - $250
Client C - $100
Client D - $50
Client E - $100
TOTAL - $1000

However, if in the following month you affected losses of $5,000 across the whole account, of course you would not pay your clients for those. All standard MAM terms and conditions remove financial liability from the money manager with regards to fees and losses. Nevertheless, if in the following month you rallied the accounts back into a positive position and profited $15,000 across the portfolio, the system would not calculate your fees based on the $15,000 profited for that month, but rather $10,000 which is the total profit above and beyond the last recorded positive position, ie the end of the first month.

While this may seem unfair in times when profits are hit hard, the fact of the matter is that money managers have to be protected from being financially liable for losses. This then means in the case of losses, money managers cannot be paid a fee for simply returning a fund back to a previously positive point. Of course the slate is wiped clean in the instance that a client withdraws funds and profit calculation begins with the new balance as if the client had only just started with your services.

In the example above, if a new client is to deposit funds into a slave account in a month following a loss, their profits and therefore the money manager's commission is calculated from the new client's starting point. Their funds are not used to offset against a previous month's losses. One of the greatest benefits of any multi account management system is that the account manager's profit and loss sheet is calculated individually for each client "slave" account.

There is unfortunately fairly widespread malpractice in this industry, which fortunately has been significantly reduced in recent years, but this method of remuneration for money managers ensures a level of transparency and fairness in performance related pay and basically keeps clients assured that they will only have to pay when they benefit, not when they lose. In reality, this form of fee management is not a problem for career money managers as their fees tend to be a top up on the profits they make. Genuinely dedicated money managers are looking to grow accounts over the long term rather than simply make a quick buck at the end of each month.

Promotion and Solicitation

As is discussed in more detail in the financial regulation chapter, the amount of self-promotion and advertising that money managers can do is limited depending on the regional jurisdiction in which you are based. However, there is far less limitation for brokers and at the end of the day, once they have you registered as a money manager with a MAM account through them, it is in their benefit for you to be trading as much funds as possible.

Many brokers will have internal rating systems whereby they rank their money managers according to performance, volume, risk levels and many other matrices. You will rarely have to get involved in this process any more than opting in to be put forward for public clients and of course delivering figures that inspire people to want to trust you with their funds. However, the calculations by which these systems rank can vary and brokers may not necessarily be using a system of ranking that shows your trading in the best light. If you are actively looking to increase your portfolio you may want to take more control of your performance promotion outside of the brokering system. This is of course not against their rules. They will not be deliberately ranking you down, in the event that you do feel that your figures would be more appealing if displayed differently, it will just mean that the broker's standard ranking system doesn't fit yours. After all, these brokers have to use standardization otherwise they'd be spending far too much time just rating their money managers and not enough time focusing on their core business.

Sites like MyFXBook.com are highly respected independent sources of forex trading performance. Not everyone on there is a money manager looking to show off their performance, many retail traders using only their own money do so as a way to compare their performance with others and rate their performances based on what other people are achieving. It does however offer a unique opportunity for you to get your stats out in a way that offers the level of clarity that is most suited to your results. That is not to say that you should try to find a way to skew statistics in your favour. This is rarely possible in the long run and never beneficial for either you or potential clients. What it does do though is allow you to find a ranking system that suits your method of trading.

Investors who are looking for money managers all have different needs and risk levels. If you are a trader who consistently delivers high R multiple profits but when compared to an overall percentage growth of the account is low, you will not rank too favourably on a system that gives high value to overall growth. Independent sites like MyFXBook.com will allow you to display your trading activity to demonstrate this ability and therefore entice investors who are looking for precisely this kind of result.

A final thought

The decision to move into money management is not one that should be taken lightly. You may feel that you have already achieved the level of success required to take you to the next level and if you have then congratulations are in order. This is not an easy profession to master by any means and if you have attained the expertise required of a money manager then you will have clearly worked hard to get there. One thing to bear in mind though, take your money management career progress very much like the way you started with your real money trading account, whether that was 6 months or 6 years ago. Start small and build up both a strong portfolio and sturdy reputation. Begin trading only with slave accounts that belong to close friends and family, those who will trust you enough to believe in what you can do but also whom you will be able to reason with in the event that you come up against losses.

A successful career in money management is a marathon, not a sprint. Recovering from significant losses of your own money will not compare to having to come back from losses that were not only your own, but several others too. Grow slowly, build momentum gradually and pick a money management system and providing broker that supports your needs every step of the way. Don't be afraid to move on when your existing broker is no longer meeting your needs and always be ready to ask yourself the big questions before taking on more and more investors.

Chapter 4 Takeaways

Chapter 4: Understanding the Management Tools

MAM: Multi Account Management

- A program that allows only one central controlling account to place trades on behalf of other subsidiary accounts
- Allows a money manager to guide the activity of other accounts
- Offer a high level of convenience and security to both the money manager and their investors
- The best MAM software will have an integrated payment and commission system where investors automatically have the fees due to their manager deducted from their accounts
- Different types of MAM accounts will come with different rules on registration and regulation for money managers
- The integration of either PAM or LAM modules to a MAM account will dictate how much regulation and authorization is needed by the money manager
- Trading permissions and parameters of MAM accounts need to be scrutinized before committing both your and your investors' funds

Two Most Popular Types of MAM Account

- LAMM: Lot Allocation Management Module
    - Allows money managers to execute trades over a multitude of accounts almost simultaneously
    - Every "slave" account is managed directly from a central account and the controlling trader need only submit the order on their own system
    - A trader who controls the LAMM for several accounts is typically paid a percentage commission of profits from each following account

- o Designed specifically to allow traders to profit by sharing their knowledge and expertise with lesser skilled traders while at the same time avoiding the extra regulation and financial requirements of an investment fund manager or mutual fund trader
- o Literally replicate the exact trade of the central trader irrespective of the balance and risk requirements of following accounts
- PAMM: Percentage Allocation Management Module
  - o A percentage of each of the central overall trader's opened positions are automatically executed on following accounts
  - o The larger a following trader's balance, the greater the number of lots they were allocated
  - o The lower the balance of a following trader's account, the lesser the number of lots allocated to their account in each respective trade
  - o Commissions are paid automatically from each "slave" account into the controlling account on a monthly basis after the total accumulation of fees and commissions have been calculated
- Revamped LAMMs
  - o A new version of LAMM
  - o Give the money manager the authority to tweak and tailor their trades to the specific needs of each and every one of their clients
  - o In the case a trade doesn't meet the minimum trade size of a slave or client account, that account will not follow the trade
- Regulation
  - o Regulation for money managers using LAMMs and PAMMs is still unclear but there are penalties involved in ignoring these rules

Pros and Cons

- MAM system is the most effective way to help others capitalise on your knowledge while you're rewarded through charging fees and performance commissions
- LAMM system is much recommended for smaller number of follower accounts
- PAMM system is much recommended wider range of potential trade followers

Fees

- Only you and your clients negotiate and agree on the fees they pay for your services
- Brokers will only get involved by giving advice on the generally accepted industry standards
- Fees are always calculated monthly and debited directly from clients' accounts to cut down administration hassle on both your and your clients' part

High Water Mark

- A transparent and comprehensive approach to fees that helps your clients feel assured that they will only be paying when you produce positive results for them over the long term

Promotion and Solicitation

- Self-promotion and advertising depends on your regional
- Many brokers will have internal rating systems whereby they rank their money managers according to performance, volume, risk levels and many other matrices
- Brokers will benefit from you trading as much funds as possible
- Independent sites like MyFXBook.com will allow you to display your trading activity to demonstrate your trading performance and therefore entice investors

Global Financial Regulation for Forex Signal Vendors and Money Managers

As forex traders, we are accustomed to operating in a market that is unique to many other forms of financial trading. The global nature of foreign exchange and the individual way in which the market operates often sets it apart in a ball park of its own. With so much cross border interaction it has historically been exempt from much of the financial regulation by which other financial markets are controlled. However, following the global crash of 2008, the need for multinational regulation in finance has become a focal point and as forex brokers, traders or simply signal vendors, we need to be aware of the regulatory constraints which we are bound by. Irrespective of the country you operate from and the countries in which your clients are based, there are sets of regulations that will apply to you. Some are mandatory, many are optional, but all are vital in ensuring a high level of best-practice objectives are adhered to.

While it would be near impossible and in many ways unnecessary to cover the regulations that govern every country worldwide, below is a breakdown of the internationally recognized regulations and accreditations that are widely accepted by our industry. Further exploration and explanation is also detailed on 20 of the most important forex trading countries. There are many definitions by which to categorize such a list so for the purposes of this exercise the countries have been chosen based on their volume of Foreign Exchange reserves as documented by the International Monetary Fund (IMF) as of 2013 and the percentage each region's currency represents of the global forex market. There will also be a brief summary of famously unregulated regions like Cyprus and Malta.

While all the information and definitions below are correct and up to date at the time of publishing, it is important to remember that the industry is evolving on both global and regional levels all the time. In particular in the periods between 2013 and 2014 experts expect big moves from financial regulatory bodies in clamping down on regulations in all levels of money management. This chapter should be viewed only as a guide to regulatory interpretation and anyone looking to begin money management of any kind should consult with a lawyer and their country's financial authority before commencing the venture. This resource should not be seen as definitive legal guidance on the matter.

Classification of Traders

When a retail trader gains enough experience and success in managing their own funds, there are a number of development stages where such a trader can profit from offering their expertise to less experienced traders. As well as the level of financial regulation varying between countries, it also changes according to the level of control and influence it is deemed that an individual or company has over other traders' funds.

Copy Trading

If your forex expertise has reached the point where other traders are manually copying your trades through platforms like MetaTrader4, you are moving towards the point of money management. There is however no financial regulation that applies to your activity with your followers. The influence you are exercising over their trading accounts is entirely passive and therefore no accountability applies either in law or industry regulation. While many individual retail traders sell subscriptions to give copiers access to their trading activity, every copied trade is done so actively by the copier and therefore the level control is not enough to fall under industry regulation.

Selling Trading Signals

In a similar way to copy trading, there is a limited level of accountability placed on individuals or companies who sell trading signals. They do not have any direct control over their clients' funds and their influence is deemed to be limited. The difference arises when looking at the balance of profit for the Signal Vendor. While in the vast majority of cases the vendor will also be trading using their own signals, in the specific transaction of each signal sold, there is the potential for the vendor to be earning more revenue from their trading intelligence than from any trades they execute themselves.

A potential grey area for trading signal vendors comes with the specificity and bespoke nature of the signals provided in relation to each client's individual needs. At the point that a signal vendor is tailoring advice to the specific parameters of each of their clients, the vendor will be moving towards the point of becoming an entity that needs to be regulated and or accredited. The country specific sections below will go into further detail for each nation and its governing body.

Placing trades across a group of client accounts - general and non-specific to each account's equity or needs.

After the situation where a signal vendor is selling tailored advice to individual clients, the first significant step a retail trader will take towards falling under regulatory and accreditation guidelines is when the entity (individual or company) begins placing trades on behalf of clients. At this stage the entity is considered to be a money manager and will start to meet some criteria that require it to be awarded accreditation from the appropriate body and adhere to relevant guidelines. For the majority of countries insufficient criteria will be met where the Money Manager is placing trades on behalf of a small enough group of clients and is placing the same trades for each, irrespective of every client's fund availability and risk preferences. For many countries the definitions for a small group of clients is often vague. Governing bodies do not publish precise parameters and most of the time will only give rulings on a case by case basis. This is done to allow them to step in when they believe an entity (individual or company) is achieving profits which they wish to tax under financial institution and investment banking guidelines. The most concrete advice that can be given to money managers who are trading for a group of clients is to contact their respective governing body (see details in the country specific sections) to discuss the volumes they are trading and the number of clients they are representing. Most of the time anything less than 15 clients and total funds of less than $100,000 will be considered insufficient to need accreditation and many traders don't even bother to check. It is always best to check though as the penalties for not registering when required or not reporting revenue for tax purposes can be very steep.

On the subject of individual client consent, many countries will require Power Of Attorney (POA) contracts to be signed by both a Money Manager and each client prior to acting on clients' behalf. In some cases an individual POA agreement will need to be issued for each individual trade. There are several money management software tools that have streamlined this process through template agreements and online "signatures" of approval to speed up approval times. The individual country sections below detail the points at which a Money Manager qualifies for needing POA agreements with their clients and anyone entering into such agreements should either use templates from reputable brokerage firms which are registered as financial institutions or consult a lawyer for drafting.

In the same way as trading signal vending, a money manager will take further steps towards falling under regulatory control when the money management function is tailored to the needs and circumstances of individual clients. Further information on the boundaries for individual countries can be found below.

Tailored Trading and Pooled Funds

Specific definitions of tailoring trade decisions to individual needs varies between countries however the vast majority of countries will consider an entity to be required to gain accreditation and adhere to industry trading guidelines when a group of clients have their funds pooled into a single overall trading fund where all participants benefit from the total leverage of the collective fund. In these cases each participant will typically have a percentage or all of their money tied in to the pooled fund for predefined periods.

Most money managers will avoid taking the final step of pooling funds in order to prevent the need to gain accreditation and adhere to the financial regulation of their country of residence. Alternatively, some choose the option to register and operate their business in a country which has more relaxed guidelines to be met. The Low Regulation Locations section below will cover this in more detail.

The definition of tailored trading for clients has been considered as ambiguous by many traders so the following example shows the difference between a money manager who is placing tailored trades for clients versus one who is not:

Untailored Trading - every follower of your signals gets the same information, if you were running a MAM account every linked account would open and close the same trades - unless individuals chose not to.

Tailored Trading - a signal vendor gives advice to traders based on how much money they have and how much risk they are willing to take. A MAM operator is selective about which of his linked accounts place which of his central trades based on how much money they have and how much risk they are willing to take.

Multi Account Management

The next step up for a trader will come when they are exercising some control over their clients' accounts through MAM, PAMM or LAM functions. This area is under particular scrutiny at the moment from organizations like ESMA (The European Securities Market Authority) because of the wide expanse of grey areas that cover definitions. The current ruling over the EU (for example) is that while clients' funds remain separate and each client retains the ability to cease activity and withdraw their funds at any point, the controlling trader does not sufficiently fall under the requirement of regulation. This is mostly the case with automated trading accounts, although it should be noted that it is these forms of automated trading which are being analyzed very carefully by ESMA and the FCA in the United Kingdom in a move to bring stricter regulation in.

Solicitation

Among a spider's web of unclear, misleading and confused definitions for when money managers are required to register with their country's financial regulation body, the subject of marketing and solicitation is very clear. As soon as an entity (individual or company) is actively marketing their money management services or soliciting clients they will have to register with the relevant authority. This does not affect advertising the sale of signals in most cases (see below for exceptions to this rule) but anyone who is advertising the sale of trading signals will have to be very careful not to cross the barrier by placing trades in any way on behalf of their clients.

The various stages of money management, whose definitions vary between countries, come with different solicitation rights and often the lower levels of money management which do not require regulation from financial authorities have fewer rights when it comes to promoting their services. In all cases there are strict guidelines on the inclusion of risk warnings and disclaimers to any advertising and solicitation material.

Penalties and Fines

Because of the blurred line between entities who are obliged to be registered and those who are recommended to do so, the penalties and fines relating to these are also vague at times.

Any entity which is required to be regulated but fails to adhere to this will receive on the spot set fines and may also incur penalties which represent a percentage of profits made during the infraction period. Those who are not obliged to register with the appropriate authorities may not be liable to the same on the spot fines but in some cases the financial authority may bring a civil action against said entity if they are found to be acting in a manner which is in deliberate contravention of the general guideline codes of conduct for that organization.

Any entity which is not required to gain accreditation from their financial authority should be fully aware of the codes of conduct which govern their respective regions. It is possible to gain a copy of this document from the organization directly or alternatively legal advice can be sought to get a definitive interpretation and overview of codes of conduct.

Country Specific Regulations

1. The United States of America

Financial Regulatory Authority

The Securities and Exchange Commission (SEC) - www.sec.gov

The Commodity Futures Trading Commission (CFTC) - www.cftc.gov

The National Futures Association (NFA) - www.nfa.futures.org

Trading Activity Classification

In the US, forex money managers can fall into two categories, Commodity Trading Advisors (CTA) and Commodity Pool Operators (CPO). Both need to register with the Commodity Futures Trading Commission and the National Futures Association. The main difference between these is that a CTA can only advise individuals on their trades or place trades on behalf of one client at a time. CPOs have extended rights to trade the funds of a collective or "pool" to benefit from the leverage of all their clients' funds.

Generally speaking individuals will start by registering as a CTA and then at a later stage a CPO. To avoid needing to register as either, an individual or company must be able to show that they are not providing bespoke advice for 15 or more individuals within a 12 month period. This includes placing specific trades on a client's behalf however if the individual or company is placing trades using a collective pool of clients' funds, they will be considered a CPO even if the pool consists of less than 15 parties.

Taxes and Penalties

All individuals and companies who generate income/revenue from trading signal vending and money management are subject to standard income and corporation taxes.

CTAs and CPOs are subject to standard sole trader and corporation taxes. When a CTA or CPO fails to comply with the regulations and guidelines of the CFTC will be subject to legal actions and while there are no set penalties, voilations fall under civil law and fines can run into the tens and hundreds of thousands.

Refs.   http://www.cftc.gov/LawRegulation/CommodityExchangeAct/index.htm

2. China

Financial Regulatory Authority

China Securities Regulatory Commission (CSRC) - ww.csrc.gov.cn

Asset Management Association of China (AMAC)

Trading Activity Classification

Up until June 2013 there was no legal recognition of hedge funds in China. The CSRC defined the term "securities" as only applying to bonds, shares or stocks which were in a mutual fund. While the country is still very early in its stages of enacting legislation and governance regarding forex trading, it is expected that hedge funds will be required to register soon.

Because the country is so far behind other nations, money managers are likely to have a number of loopholes to avoid registration with the CSRC and at present there is no legal requirement. However, for a country whose currency may soon be evolving to become more openly regulated and traded on the open market anyone trading and using China as a base will need to be careful not to get caught out on sudden changes to regulation and governance.

The current benchmark set by the AMAC for fund managers is set at 100million RMB (about $16million dollars) of Assets Under Management (AUM) or when a manager has 50 or more investors.

http://www.risk.net/hedge-funds-review/news/2253614/china-introduces-registration-for-hedge-funds

---

3. Japan

Financial Regulatory Authority
Financial Services Agency (FSA) - www.fsa.go.jp
Trading Activity Classification
There are no regulations or licensing requirements for traders based in Japan while all their clients' funds are managed through multi-level accounts. The trader is only deemed to have sufficient control to require licensing once there is a single fund in place that clients need to request permission to withdraw fund. The rules and regulations governing this stage is the same as with mutual funds and typical hedge funds.

---

4. Saudi Arabia

Financial Regulatory Authority
Capital Market Authority (CMA) - www.cma.org.sa
Trading Activity Classification
The definitions of money management in Saudi Arabia are generally reserved for large sums of money and do not take into consideration the number of clients a manager may have. Any individual who is actively trading accounts which collectively exceed 500,000 dinar must be registered and regulated by the CMA. This also applies even in the case that the total fund only comes from one source.

5. Switzerland

Financial Regulatory Authority

Swiss Financial Market Supervisory Authority (SFMSA) - www.finma.ch

Trading Activity Classification

The SFMSA has very little information on the differentiation between fully fledged money management (mutual funds or pooled trading funds) because of the distinct lack of outfits which fall into the grey areas of this market. It loosely advises that "any individual or entity who controls private funds belonging to others must be regulated by the SFSMA and renew their regulatory application every 3 years." There is no definition as to what is meant by "control" but legal interpretations have generally set the precedent that a trader must be placing the trades manually from another person's account and specifically for that account (see the definition of tailored trades above) to qualify.

6. Russia

Financial Regulatory Authority

Federal Financial Markets Service (FFMS) - www.fcsm.ru

Trading Activity Classification

There have long been significant holes and absences in the FFMS regulatory guidelines for Forex Trading Management. Most noteworthy of which is the lack of any clear definition on the difference between a money manager and simple retail trader. While Russia is not bound by the ESMA guidelines (set to come into force soon – see the EuroZone) political pressure is expected to have significant influence over any decision made by the FFMS following ESMA and EU directives.

7. Turkey

Financial Regulatory Authority

Banking Regulation and Supervision Agency of Turkey (BRSA) - www.bddk.gov.tr

Trading Activity Classification

The BRSA requires all money managers to be regulated under their general guidelines however they are a relatively new arm of the Turkish Government and therefore do not have any enforcement powers as yet. Money managers of all levels, even pooled funds, in Turkey are able to operate without regulation at the time of printing but they are being strongly advised to gain accreditation and regulation before it becomes obligatory to avoid sudden penalties.

8. Brazil

Financial Regulatory Authority
Securities Commission of Brazil (CVM) - Comissão de Valores Mobiliários - www.cvm.gov.br
Trading Activity Classification
The CVM does not require individual money managers to be regulated until they are trading from one individual account that only the controlling trader has access to. There have been discussions between the CVM and the Central Bank of Brazil about setting stricter definitions and potentially introducing obligatory regulation for traders who manage multiple accounts with clients' consent but there have been no definitive guidelines laid out yet.

9. The Eurozone

Financial Regulatory Authority
European Securities and Markets Authority (ESMA) - www.esma.europa.eu
Trading Activity Classification
Early in 2013 the ESMA published guidelines for money management and copy trading which it is rumored to be pushing towards legislating. Individual member state countries each have their own financial authorities which must adhere to the EU directives enacted on behalf of the ESMA and the whole European Community is monitoring the progress of these guidelines with great interest.

Until the ESMA guidelines are enacted, there is no obligation for licensing if a money manager controls their portfolio

through Multi Account Managed accounts although some member states' governing bodies highly recommend licensing and accredited regulation. These countries are as follows:
France – Autorité des Marchés Financiers (AMF)- www.amf-france.org
Germany – Federal Financial Supervisory Authority (Bundesanstalt für Finanzdienstleistungsaufsicht, BAFIN) – www.bafin.de
Italy – Commissione Nazionale per le Società e la Borsa (CONSOB) – www.consob.it
Spain - Comisión Nacional del Mercado de Valores (CNMV.es)

---

10. Australia

Financial Regulatory Authority
Australia Securities and Investments Commission (ASIC) - www.asic.gov.au
Trading Activity Classification
Regulation for Money Managers in Australia is still very loose and open to interpretation. The ASIC has a published a set of guidelines for licensing managers who control collective funds of more than 10 investors but although stipulated as regulations, they are not legally enforceable and so therefore only considered to be a good practice guide.

There is however a growing trend for Money Managers to become licensed and gain ASIC accreditation which may have a catalytic effect in pushing through legislation to manage the whole industry.

---

11. Hong Kong

Financial Regulatory Authority
Hong Kong Monetary Authority (HKMA) - www.hkma.gov.hk
Trading Activity Classification
The Hong Kong Monetary Authority carried out extensive research into industry practices in 2012 with a view to tightening up regulations for Forex Markets. The project, carried out in combination with the Securities and Futures Ordinance (SFO)

put their findings in front of a panel of 12 companies who represented the leading organizations operating in Hong Kong. While the principles that were laid down did not form part of an enforceable initiative for money managers, the clearer definitions of futures contracts as well as redefined guidelines for what constituted a portfolio showed clear intention on the HKMAs behalf in taking steps toward regulating automated money management and low level tailored money management. As it stands at the moment, no entity must be regulated by the HKMA while their client count remains less than 25 individuals or companies and less than 1,000,000HKD in total funds.

---

12. Singapore

Financial Regulatory Authority
Monetary Authority of Singapore (MAS) - www.mas.gov.sg
Trading Activity Classification
Singapore is perhaps one of the strictest regions for forex money management. While Signal Vendors and money managers who do not tailor trading are not required to be regulated, those who fall under regulation requirements (mainly brokers) were subject to a ruling change at the end of 2012 that required them to double their security margins on FX trading from 2% to 5%. This came as a result of a continent wide crackdown in Asia and is threatening to trickle down to simple money managers and signal vendors in the form of introductory regulation. At the time of printing there were no regulatory requirements as yet.

---

13. India

Financial Regulatory Authority
Securities and Exchange Board of India (SEBI) - www.sebi.gov.in
Trading Activity Classification
As India moves towards becoming a more influential economic power, there has been a great deal of pressure on the government to carry out an overhaul of its financial regulation.

This is especially true with regards to forex money management. Currently unless trading a mutual fund, money managers are not required to gain regulatory approval and there is not currently a great deal of emphasis on encouraging entities to become regulated voluntarily.

14. Mexico

Financial Regulatory Authority
   Comisión Nacional Bancaria y de Valores (CNBV) www.cnbv.gob.mx
Trading Activity Classification
   There are no specific instructions for regulation of money managers who do not pool funds in Mexico. There is an optional regulatory accreditation that can be obtained but it is very much an exercise in futility as general industry opinion is that the accreditation does not hold any weight with potential investors.

15. Canada

Financial Regulatory Authority
   Investment Industry Regulatory Organization of Canada (IIROC), Organisme Canadien de réglementation du commerce des valeurs mobilières (OCRCVM) - www.iiorc.ca
Trading Activity Classification
   As one of the most financially regulated nations in the world, Canada takes much of its direction from the US. On the other hand, the overall understanding in Canada, contrary to the US, is that voluntarily signing up to regulation is a good practice which should be considered mandatory. In the majority of cases money managers who fall outside of the requirements to register as CFAs and CPOs (see The United States for definitions) still opt in to IIROC regulation.

16. Malaysia

Financial Regulatory Authority
   Securities Commission Malaysia (SC) - www.sc.gov.my
Trading Activity Classification

Although historically quite relaxed with financial regulation and legislation, the SC of Malaysia is starting to move towards taking direction from its neighbor and stronger financial authority, Singapore. At present no regulation is required until a money manager is pooling client funds but developments across Asia are likely to change this in the near future.

---

17. The United Kingdom

Financial Regulatory Authority

Financial Conduct Authority (FCA - previously FSA) - www.fca.org.uk

Trading Activity Classification

The FCA does not publish parameters or legal definitions for money managers who trade on behalf of clients without pooling funds. It is believed that the organization's limited detail on classification is such that there is not too much red tape and bureaucracy for individuals managing only a very small number of accounts or with insignificant volumes of money. At the same time though, it gives the organization a great deal of potential power when it comes to assessing entities when they begin to grow.

The UK is subject to EU Directives though and the recent announcements from the ESMA which address the potential for regulation to come into effect for copy trading and multi account management is likely to guide changes to the UK legislation. Progression of this is likely to be limited by the fact that there are still no clear instructions as to how regulation will work in the cases where a money manager is located in the UK but their clients are located outside of the UK and EU legislative jurisdiction.

---

18. Poland

Financial Regulatory Authority

Polish Financial Supervision Authority (KNF) - www.knf.gov.pl

Trading Activity Classification

Although not officially under the judiciary of the EU for financial regulations of this matter, Poland takes the majority of its instruction from the ESMA regarding regulation and rarely sets legislation or regulation which contradicts ESMA direction. See the EuroZone for more detail.

19. New Zealand

Financial Regulatory Authority
Financial Markets Authority - www.fma.govt.nz
Trading Activity Classification
The FMA in New Zealand is closely aligned to the ASIC (Australia) and although it is not officially linked to rulings and changes to policy, the organization has historically followed ASIC rulings and there is no expected change to this situation in the immediate future. Currently the FMA operates under the same guidelines as ASIC and is actively encouraging money managers with more than 10 clients to apply to become regulated.

20. Sweden

Financial Regulatory Authority
Financial Supervisory Authority - www.fi.se
Trading Activity Classification
The Swedish FSA only regulates the forex trading market in a supervisory capacity and does not hold any judicial power with regards to contravening its guidelines and codes of conduct. However, the industry within Sweden is very closely monitored by higher governmental departments and the majority of money managers based in Sweden go through the relatively simple process of gaining accreditation because of the widespread popular belief that unaccredited individuals or entities are not worth investing with.

Low Regulation Regions

Typically when a trader reaches the point when they are coming against too much regulation which is prohibitive to their services provision for clients, a common solution is to register the business in a region that has more relaxed rules and regulations governing the forex trading industry. In some cases the company need only be registered in the new location however for the vast majority of countries, they will not be considered as operating outside of the stricter jurisdiction unless the whole company and its staff are located in the low regulation region in which the company is registered.

Malta and Cyprus are two of the most popular destinations used by forex traders and money managers to avoid strict regulation and legal requirements. In both jurisdictions all levels of automated trading management is exempt from regulation. Equally managed accounts of pooled funds which fall under the 250,000EUR threshold are at liberty to register for regulation optionally. Everything above this threshold falls under regulatory control, however it is well documented that regulations for these entities are very relaxed.

Malta

Financial Regulatory Authority
Malta Financial Services Authority (MFSA)

Cyprus

Financial Regulatory Authority
Central Bank of Cyprus – www.centralbank.gov.cy
Cyprus Securities and Exchange Commission (CySEC)
www.cysec.gov.cy

Where Do Your Activities Fall?

In order to get the clearest picture of whether your trading activities for clients fall under the need for regulation, the best thing to do will always be to contact the financial authority in your country and get a specific ruling on your individual case. In some cases legal advice may need to be sought too. As this can all be a very expensive process, these are the things you need to check against before considering where you fall:

- Do you provide any advice to clients on an individual basis or are any of your automated trading systems set up based on a client's individual needs?
- Do you advertise your services in public forums? If so do these services include having access to a client's account and funds?
- Can your client's withdraw their funds at any time without your consent?
- Do you manage any accounts that have a collective of multiple client funds?

If you can answer "yes" to 2 or more of these questions, it is likely that you will need to speak to your financial authority about your specific case. Remember, whenever seeking specific advice, always get rulings in writing for future reference and make sure legal advice is obtained from officially certified legal sources.

Coming soon we'll be offering Country specific Forex Financial Regulation Reports for specific countries which will go into each country's rules in greater detail. We're reviewing which regions have the highest demand at the moment so get in touch with us if you'd be interested in obtaining a report specific to your country.

A Sensible Approach to EU Forex Regulation

Have you looked into how the European Markets Infrastructure Regulation (EMIR) is going to affect your trading?

There has been a great deal of talk in the Forex industry about regulation changes for some time now. The EMIR announced last year, a deadline of 12th February for the changes to reporting of derivative trading to come into effect. While the European Securities and Markets Authority (ESMA) has been warning companies to take the deadline seriously, the UK's Financial Conduct Authority (FCA) has reportedly been quoted as saying that a degree of leniency will be applied because they understand that the industry needs time to adjust and there will understandably be a learning period.

This is not only good news for the larger fund management firms but also smaller and individual money managers, many of whom are still coming to grips with how the regulatory changes will be affecting them. Historically the FCA (formerly Financial Services Authority – FSA) has taken a similarly consultative approach to enforcement of fines, but not always so much in favor of fund managers. It seems that as the likes of money managers and signal vendors come closer and closer to landing on the radar of stricter regulation globally, regionally based financial authorities are more willing to start treating them with a similarly consultative approach to that applied to traditional financial institutions. The extent that this will remain constant though is yet to be seen.

Independent Money Managers

While small firms and individual money managers familiarize themselves with the industry changes, it is encouraging to know that at least in the UK there will be support from the governing body to help everyone acclimatize to changes rather than taking a more draconian approach. For those traders whose activity falls outside of the FCAs remit, but still within that of the EMIR, it would be wise to get a familial understanding of how their financial authority intends to enforce EMIR. It is of course going to become obligatory for all member states, but the flexibility given to regional bodies in the application and enforcement of fines is where traders could stand to benefit or fall.

Many around the continent are hoping that other regulatory bodies will follow the lead of the FCA, a trend setter and opinion maker in EU trading matters, and elect to support traders of all level understand and conform to the new regulations rather than blindly handing out fines and penalties from day 1. It is, after all, in everyone's best interests to allow all levels of the industry to gradually adjust to new regulations, rather than taking too hard a line too soon. If a level of fear is injected into markets at independent money manager level, it would have a knock on effect that would not be beneficial to anyone.

Irrespective of how governing bodies around the EU act, the message is coming across loud and clear to those involved in any level of money management. The seed of fear planted during the crash of 2008 is finally starting to bloom within Forex trading regulation and looks set only to grow in application and enforcement as time goes on. This is not so much to say that the industry is at threat, more that a firm understanding of how the regulations apply to each individual is becoming more and more important every day. The sooner that MAM trading managers and signal vendors take it upon themselves to understand regulation before it becomes globally mandatory, the smoother that transition will be, if and when it is implemented.

Don't Avoid Regulation, Understand It

Delving into the labyrinth of financial regulation is often a factor that dissuades talented traders from going out on their own, or getting involved in trading money on behalf of others. Even those who are already doing so, but on a low scale, could be getting worried about what EMIR is going to mean for their businesses. There is no need for there to be such concern, and despite ESMAs loud bark when talking about overhauling the money management industry in Forex, these regulations are in place to protect all levels of trader and investor.

The problem then becomes accessing detailed, accurate and concise interpretation of how the regulations will affect you as a money manager, or even personal trader. Those who do not have the resources and backing of large funds don't always have the time and money to take on the mammoth task of disseminating the new EU regulation. There is good news though in emerging forex money management resources which go further than just generic summary. Consultation with leading fund managers, EU finance law specialists and top billing brokers is going into building the resources that money managers will need to circumnavigate any problems which may seem to occur with the new regulation.

There will undoubtedly be a lot of free information on this subject floating around the internet, but when it comes to such an important and potentially costly issue, traders would be wise to seek out the professional advice and resource which can ensure that the clearest picture possible is found. Preparation is the best defense against the impact of change and this principle has never been more important in forex trading than now. Those who are on the cusp of regulatory control can take comfort in the knowledge that they still currently have time, and an element of leniency from the authorities, on their side. Neither of these will last forever though. Now is the time to be seeking out authoritative information which can be relied upon to guide you through a potentially difficult period. It would be far better to be over prepared than get caught off guard and face the challenge of having to play catch up while trying not to let your business and trading activity suffer.

Whether you're trading for yourself, a few mates or a spread of anonymous investors, can you afford not to fully understand how regulation change will affect your business?

Chapter 5 Takeaways

Chapter 5: Global Financial Regulation for Forex Signal Vendors and Money Managers

Classification of Traders

- Copy Trading
  - other traders are manually copying your trades through platforms like MetaTrader4
  - no financial regulation that applies to your activity with your followers
- Selling Trading Signals
  - Individuals or companies who sell trading signals
  - Same as Copy Trading, there is a limited level of accountability
- Tailored Trading and Pooled Funds
  - clients have their funds pooled into a single overall trading fund where all participants benefit from the total leverage of the collective fund
  - required for accreditation and must adhere to industry trading guidelines
- Multi Account Management
  - Under particular scrutiny at the moment from organizations like ESMA (The European Securities Market Authority) because of the wide expanse of grey areas that cover definitions

Penalties and Fines

- Because of the blurred line between entities who are obliged to be registered and those who are recommended to do so, the penalties and fines relating to these are also vague
- Any entity which is not required to gain accreditation from their financial authority should be fully aware of the codes of conduct which govern their respective regions

Country Specific Regulations

- The United States of America
  - Financial Regulatory Authority
    - The Securities and Exchange Commission (SEC)
    - The Commodity Futures Trading Commission (CFTC)
    - The National Futures Association (NFA)
  - Trading Activity Classification
    - Commodity Trading Advisors (CTA) - can only advise individuals on their trades or place trades on behalf of one client at a time
    - Commodity Pool Operators (CPO) - have extended rights to trade the funds of a collective or "pool" to benefit from the leverage of all their clients' funds
  - Taxes and Penalties
    - CTAs and CPOs are subject to standard sole trader and corporation taxes
    - Failure to comply with the regulations and guidelines of the CFTC will be subject to legal actions which fall under civil law and fines can run into the tens and hundreds of thousands
- China
  - Financial Regulatory Authority
    - China Securities Regulatory Commission (CSRC)
    - Asset Management Association of China (AMAC)
  - Trading Activity Classification
    - There's still no legal recognition of hedge funds
  - Still very early in its stages of enacting legislation and governance regarding forex trading

- Japan
  - Financial Regulatory Authority
    - Financial Services Agency (FSA)
  - Trading Activity Classification
    - There are no regulations or licensing requirements for funds that are managed through multi-level accounts
- Saudi Arabia
  - Financial Regulatory Authority
    - Capital Market Authority (CMA)
  - Trading Activity Classification
    - Any individual who is actively trading accounts which collectively exceed 500,000 dinar must be registered and regulated by the CMA
- Switzerland
  - Financial Regulatory Authority
    - Swiss Financial Market Supervisory Authority (SFMSA)
  - Trading Activity Classification
    - Any individual or entity who controls private funds belonging to others must be regulated by the SFSMA and renew their regulatory application every 3 years
- Russia
  - Financial Regulatory Authority
    - Federal Financial Markets Service (FFMS)
  - Trading Activity Classification
    - Lack of any clear definition on the difference between a money manager and simple retail trader

- Turkey
  - o Financial Regulatory Authority
    - Banking Regulation and Supervision Agency of Turkey (BRSA)
  - o Trading Activity Classification
    - BRSA requires all money managers to be regulated under their general guidelines
- Brazil
  - o Financial Regulatory Authority
    - Securities Commission of Brazil (CVM) - Comissão de Valores Mobiliários
  - o Trading Activity Classification
    - CVM does not require individual money managers to be regulated until they are trading from one individual account that only the controlling trader has the access
- The Eurozone
  - o Financial Regulatory Authority
    - European Securities and Markets Authority (ESMA)
      - France : Autorité des Marchés Financiers (AMF)
      - Germany : Federal Financial Supervisory Authority
      - Italy : Commissione Nazionale per le Società e la Borsa
      - Spain :Comisión Nacional del Mercado de Valores
  - o Trading Activity Classification
    - ESMA published guidelines for money management and copy trading
    - Each member state country have its own financial authority which must adhere to the EU directives enacted

on behalf of the ESMA and the whole European Community

- Australia
  - o Financial Regulatory Authority
    - Australia Securities and Investments Commission (ASIC)
  - o Trading Activity Classification
    - ASIC has a published a set of guidelines for licensing managers who control collective funds of more than 10 investors
- Hong Kong
  - o Financial Regulatory Authority
    - Hong Kong Monetary Authority (HKMA)
  - o Trading Activity Classification
    - No entity must be regulated by the HKMA while their client count remains less than 25 individuals or companies and less than 1,000,000HKD in total funds
- Singapore
  - o Financial Regulatory Authority
    - Monetary Authority of Singapore (MAS)
  - o Trading Activity Classification
    - Brokers are required to double their security margins on FX trading from 2% to 5%
- India
  - o Financial Regulatory Authority
    - Securities and Exchange Board of India (SEBI)
  - o Trading Activity Classification
    - Unless trading a mutual fund, money managers are not required to gain regulatory approval
- Mexico
  - o Financial Regulatory Authority
    - Comisión Nacional Bancaria y de Valores (CNBV)
  - o Trading Activity Classification

- - No specific instructions for regulation of money managers who do not pool funds
- Canada
  - o Financial Regulatory Authority
    - Investment Industry Regulatory Organization of Canada (IIROC)
    - Organisme Canadien de réglementation du commerce des valeurs mobilières (OCRCVM)
  - o Trading Activity Classification
    - Mandatory signing up of regulation
    - One of the most financially regulated nations in the world
- Malaysia
  - o Financial Regulatory Authority
    - Securities Commission Malaysia (SC)
  - o Trading Activity Classification
    - No regulation is required until a money manager is pooling client funds
- The United Kingdom
  - o Financial Regulatory Authority
    - Financial Conduct Authority (FCA - previously FSA)
  - o Trading Activity Classification
    - FCA has no legal definitions for money managers who trade on behalf of clients without pooling funds
    - Subjected to EU Directives
- Poland
  - o Financial Regulatory Authority
    - Polish Financial Supervision Authority (KNF)
  - o Trading Activity Classification
    - Poland takes the majority of its instruction from the ESMA regarding regulation and rarely sets legislation or regulation which contradicts ESMA direction
- New Zealand
  - o Financial Regulatory Authority

- ▪ Financial Markets Authority
  - o Trading Activity Classification
    - ▪ FMA operates under the same guidelines as ASIC and is actively encouraging money managers with more than 10 clients to become regulated
- Sweden
  - o Financial Regulatory Authority
    - ▪ Financial Supervisory Authority
  - o Trading Activity Classification
    - ▪ FSA only regulates the forex trading market in a supervisory capacity and does not hold any judicial power with regards to contravening its guidelines and codes of conduct

Low Regulation Regions
- Malta
  - o Financial Regulatory Authority
    - ▪ Malta Financial Services Authority (MFSA)
- Cyprus
  - o Financial Regulatory Authority
    - ▪ Central Bank of Cyprus
    - ▪ Cyprus Securities and Exchange Commission (CySEC)

Finding a Source of Profitable Trading Signals

"Do what you know and you will know what you are doing."

- Rimantas Petrauskas

The next obvious step before you can start delivering signals is to find a profitable source. This can be a lot harder than it seems at first glance. Someone (this can be you if you're a profitable trader) or something (an EA or a trading robot) has to generate the signals that you are going to send to subscribers.

Let's take a look at several options you have for supplying your trading signals.

Are you a trader yourself?

If you are a profitable forex trader, you can just attach a trade copying software to your account and you're ready to go. Now you can trade your own account as you usually do and send those same trading actions to your subscribers.

You can setup your master MetaTrader 4 account on a VPS server, where it will run 24 hours a day and send signals. At the same time you can open that MT4 account on any other computer and trade from it. This gives you the freedom to travel the world and initiate trades on your master account from an airport, an airplane or any other place on Earth.

You don't need any additional software running on your computer. A single MetaTrader platform will do. The copier is already running on your VPS server. Now you simply turn on your laptop or smartphone, open the MetaTrader 4 platform and place a trade. The trade will be copied to your customers' accounts as soon as possible, usually in under a second.

Hire a forex trader

If you're not a currency trader yourself, you can hire one or partner up. You can meet traders at live Forex events, at seminars or online. Talk to the profitable traders at signal delivery websites like zulutrade.com. Offer them a partnership, you will handle the signal delivery business and he will take care of the trading.

It could be a real challenge to partner up with someone who is managing funds for some major broker. Do not expect that everyone will reply to your offer. But keep reaching out, and if there is one great trader out of 30 you contact, it will be worth it. Give him this book so that he can learn what the potential of a trading signals service is. You can help him do the math to know the potential income you might be able to earn together.

Find a profitable trading robot

Another solution is to find or build a profitable trading robot also known as Expert Advisor (EA). It can even be a combination of a few trading robots. Any EA that places trades on a MT4 account can be used as a signals source. This is what I'm doing to generate my trading signals and it allows me to fully automate my business.

Even if you won't be using a trading robot or maybe you even hate this idea, I encourage you to read this chapter anyways. Robots for me are nothing but a solution to replace me sitting in front of the computer all day. It does the job for me when I sleep, when I am in my car driving to the office, when I am in the office working on my book and other projects, when I am answering emails, when I am with my family, when I learn, you name it. It is there to do the job that I have learned, mastered, broke down into steps and then automated.

When you have a lot of things to do in life, and usually that is the case, you want to put everything that works into a strategy and automate it or outsource it. Don't let your strategy become a tragedy.

I have created my own trading robot according to my trading strategy and I sell the trading signals instead of selling the EA itself. This way I can be 100% sure that no one will steal my intellectual property. Only authorized customers that know the password can get access to my signals.

You can create your own EA. If you're not a programmer, hire one that is capable of building an EA for your trading strategy. When ordering a trading robot to be programmed, make sure to write down all your trading rules in a document, include pictures with trade examples. Try to explain everything as clearly as possible. This will help the programmer understand exactly what you need.

Advantages of using a Forex robot to trade currencies

- Robots don't have the emotions and just do what they are "told" to do.
- Robots can be programmed to trade currencies based on economic news releases. Yes, in this case you would "give the robot advice" for the day or week at a specific time and it will follow your rules.
- The robot is suitable for both Forex novices and experts.
- It can trade any number of currencies at the same and analyze multiple timeframes in just a few seconds.
- The robot can keep you regularly updated. A lot of trading robots are programmed to trade automatically without any input from the user. This gives a trader the option to take some time off. Almost all traders have jobs and the robot helps them keep their day job, get

some extra sleep as well as generate a profit for their account in the process.

- Much more reliable trading process. A person who is new to Forex trading is very likely to make mistakes due to his inexperience. A trading robot however, is not subject to miscalculations or guesswork.
- A robot will always stick to the rules, no matter what, and we all know well that this is not possible for humans—in Forex and in life in general.
- And finally, you get a chance to run your trading signals business on autopilot.

Many of the paid robots or Forex signal providers offer free trial runs. This means that you can get an insider's tour into the performance of a particular trader or a robot without any initial investment on your part. You can use a trial (demo) account to subscribe to the signals and judge the performance without losing real money.

Subscribe to a few signal providers or trading robots. Give them some time and see how they perform. There are a lot of virtual dollars that you can use to test out different signals out there. In the meantime, hone your own trading skills and try to learn everything you can from the software or the trader you are following.

Sometimes it becomes very hard to decide which trading robot to use. Forex trading is an expanding market, there are many who claim to offer the best software and many more join in every single day. Here's a tip, choose the robot or signal provider that you would recommend to others, like your customers for example.

5 Step Proven Process to Selecting a Winning Forex Robot

Now if you are looking for a trading robot to buy, make sure you follow these simple 5 steps to evaluate if it's worth your money. Do not buy any trading robot or signal provider's subscription before you complete these steps: find, verify, review, contact and test.

1. Find the trading robot.

Start by looking at sites like ForexVerified.com which measures different EA's. These websites help track the performance of different systems. There is also a site known as MyFXBook.com, which you should become familiar with. They also have very good resources for tracking the performance of different trading systems.

ROI (return-on-investment) is just one number that you should be looking at to judge the performance of a system. You will also want to keep in mind the historical drawdown of the systems you are researching. It is said that the higher and faster something soars the quicker its flight down can be also.

Imagine if your system is on a list together with 1000 other systems. How would yours stand out? You want the most important numbers to be displayed that will help the potential investors judge the performance of your signals. Shouting out loud that you have made 10,000 pips in the last 12 months does not explain that well if you were not profitable during that time. Maybe you have the same amount of pips of floating loss? It is best to give at least 3 numbers to accurately demonstrate your gains in pips. If you don't include all the facts, bigger investors will go elsewhere, though newbies may still be convinced to join.

If you show a ROI number for past performance and let's say it's 2.5, people will know that when they put in $1, they are eligible for a $2.5 return. Of course, past performance does not indicate future results, but with good past performance you have a greater chance to make money than you would following a system with no or with bad past trading record.

2. Verify trading history with the MyFXBook.com or an investor password.

Only buy a trading robot if the vendor shows the past trading record in a trustworthy format. I prefer MyFXBook.com, as it is a better solution and it will give you ability to analyze the trading history by month, week, hour, pair, etc. With investor password you just get the list of trades and it's kind of old school thing.

If they do not share history, move further and keep looking; do not waste time on those who hide information. If they are on MyFXBook.com and some of the data is private, they are probably hiding huge drawdowns. Steer clear.

If the past performance is displayed in a simple table where the number of pips is reported for the months, be aware that anyone can write anything in such table when they own a website. Results should always be verified by a 3rd party.

---

3. Review on ForexPeaceArmy.com

Go to ForexPeaceArmy.com and read reviews about the robot/strategy-copier service to see what people say. It is difficult to get a review on that site, even from a satisfied customer! This is because there are good spam enforcement policies in place and several hoops to jump through before anyone can place a review. You can find my profile on FPA too. It took me more than a year to get those reviews. Each of those people are my customers and I had to deliver superb services to them to get them post a review. If you did not posted a review about my software or services there yet, please do now.

Because ForexPeaceArmy.com has this high security filter against spam reviews and only genuine reviews are posted it is a site that can be trusted. It is an excellent site that can help you see 'under the covers' of different trading strategies. It will help you evaluate the returns, the past trades taken, the drawdowns and a large number of other metrics. When they see some trading robot or signal service that has a potential, they ask for investor password and store genuine trading results on their website directly from the MT4 account. This makes it impossible to fake any trading results.

They are hosting trading history of my Vavatrade signal service too.

Do yourself a favor and get to know this site very well.

---

4. Contact the robot's owner and ask intelligent questions.

If they begin to respond harshly to your initial questions then you may not wish to do business with them. Contact them for initial questions. Ask several intelligent questions about the ideal settings that should be used and how it might perform on different brokers. You can ask about the success that others have had and then also about their recommendations for the account size you have (if you decide to share such information). If they offer very vague answers or seem misleading in any way, run! There are great opportunities out there with legitimate and respectable robots/trade copiers.

I personally like to ask simple questions that are usually answered on their website and easily visible to everyone. This is a great test to see if they treat customers well.

Remember also that it is best to test everything on a small account first, or even better yet, a demo account.

5. Test on a demo account first. Ask for a trial period

Don't repeat the mistake of thousands other traders and ask for trial period, or at least make sure there is a rock-solid money back guarantee. That's just common sense. Many EA/Robot owners do not give a trial because they're afraid that you will decompile the system and put it for sale online or share it with others. But they who give a trial are much more likely to be genuine. It is understandable if they will not do this, but better if they will. It only serves to increase confidence.

Another reason why robot owners will not allow for a trial is because they know that the robot will not work well for others. Sometimes broker spreads can have a lot to do with the situation and scalping-style EA's will not fare well when the spreads are high.

But yet another reason why most 'marketers' who sell trading robots will not allow for a trial is that they know deep down that the robot will lose money for the purchaser, but yet many people will not ask for a refund if things don't go as planned.

Common sense and patience are your two most valuable assets when it comes to evaluating opportunities to purchase or subscript to a trading robot. Make sure that when you find a good one and purchase it that you exercise and equal amount of diligence in selecting the risk level that you will use.

Resell trading signals from another website

If the previous three options don't work for you, you can try reselling the signals from a 3rd party website. There are a lot of signal providers' websites out there. Many of them are probably struggling to find customers because of poor marketing, for example. They would be happy to let you resell their signals under your brand name in exchange for 30% or 40% profit per customer. Make sure that you get the website's permission before you begin reselling their signals. It is their intellectual property, please respect that.

If you just resell trading signals from a 3rd party without their permission you will get in trouble for sure. You may hide this for a month or two or maybe even a year, but eventually you will be revealed and people on forums will not go short on bad words about your service. This is the easiest way to get enemies and ruin your reputation.

Furthermore, if you just resell signals from someone who is actually struggling to get customers, they could close their business and you will end up with a number of customers that do not receive trading signals anymore. I am sure they will get mad, start to ask for refunds, and maybe then you will plug in the very first strategy you find, just to not leave them without signals. But don't think that this will end well because the chances are slim.

People will spot that your new system is using different stops and trade entries are made at different times. They will spot the differences, and in case your new system is a losing one, you will end up losing your customers and receiving dozens of bad reviews on ForexPeaceArmy.com.

So be smart from the start. Do not cheat, but rather operate your business with integrity.

MAM, PAMM, LAMM

Look for PAMM, MAM or LAMM account traders on FXOpen, Alpari UK and other Forex broker's websites. You will find good traders that can become your partners at these websites. If you're unfamiliar with MAM, PAMM and LAMM accounts, I describe them and provide some advantages and disadvantages of each account type in chapter 4.

Look for good performing systems on myfxbook.com

Websites like myfxbook.com have a verification process that is hard to cheat. You can more or less trust the trading results posted on this website. Make sure that the account is not private and that all statistics are available for public viewing. If there is anything private about the account, the trader may be hiding something. A large open losing position is just one of the possibilities. They might be hidden a huge floating loss in open trades which simply tells you that the vendor is showing only the better side of his strategy. You do not want to mess around with such providers.

If you happen to find a 3rd party website verified by myfxbook.com and with a profitable trading history, don't assume that "it's the one." Make sure that the performance graph leads do a myfxbook.com website itself. If it's just the image of a graph I give you 99% chance that the seller is trying to cheat you.

Think it this way—if you have a profitable MyFXBook trading history, would you add image + link to your MyFXBook profile to prove it's genuine, or you just put an image with no link to prove it? Of course you would add both the image and a link to its MyFXBook profile. In fact, that is what MyFXBook gives you by default for sharing a profile with an image.

If you want just an image, you need to put that on the website in a completely different way. MyFXBook gives you a simple HTML code, so it's totally easy to add that to the website. Now if you want to cheat and add just an image, you need to save it to your computer first and then upload to the website.

Another thing you should be aware of is that the vendor can put someone else's MyFXBook performance graph on his website and that way convince you that it's created by the software he is trying to sell you. So keep in mind that as well. On each MyFXBook profile page, there is a tab labeled "General" on the left side of the graph. Usually it holds the link to the original website. Make sure it points to the same website you are trying to purchase from.

If there is a link pointing to the website you are purchasing from, it is likely that those stats are genuine. However, if you find a link pointing to another website, I encourage you to do more research and find out who the actual owner of that performance record is.

Test any signal thoroughly to make sure it is error free

Incorrectly programmed trading robots can initiate unwanted trades or fail to set stop loss or take profit values. You need to test any software thoroughly before you use it on your customers' accounts. Forward testing is the best way to evaluate any trading robot. A test can be on a demo account or a small real money account.

Also, to show a good trading record, traders or robots can use the temporary gains provided by ultimately losing strategies like the martingale to scam prospective customers. The martingale strategy requires the doubling of trading size after each loss. By using this betting system, traders can show steady profits for weeks even months, but eventually a big enough losing streak will bust their account.

Analyze the trading history carefully to make sure that there were no trades with bigger than normal trading size. Also check for doubling up of trading size after a loss. If anything looks even slightly out of the ordinary, double check and triple check. Make sure to choose the best signal provider you can find.

Ask yourself this question: If I was a customer, would I want to invest my own money into these signals?

Consider copying the signals to your real money account. This is a good step to gain a customer's trust in both you and your signals. As your real money account grows you can show its performance as proof that your signals are profitable.

If you start only on a demo account, let the real money account be your next goal so you could follow your own signals. Focus on earning the customers' trust and their money will follow. By using this strategy you can make sure that your business will be around for a long time.

Verify any trading signals source on FPA

Check any system or trading robot on the Forex Peace Army website. Reviews posted there are genuine. You can check one of my FPA profiles here:

http://www.forexpeacearmy.com/public/review/www.ea-coder.com.

I had to deliver a superb service to my customers to get those reviews.

Many signal providers fail to take care of these reviews. What I mean is that you need to ask your customers to post a review there. It will become easier and easier to get a review when you deliver good service and fabulous customer support.

If you leave these reviews to be posted only for those who refund and leave your service, you will likely end up with dozens of bad reviews posted. Of course, there will be negative reviews as it is impossible to please everybody on this earth, but once you start asking and encouraging people to post a comment on FPA, they will likely post a positive one.

Experiment with the trade copier by reversing trades

Discover something new and unique. Experiment with the "Reverse Trades" feature in the trade copier software. The idea is rather simple in concept: find a system that loses money consistently and reverse the trades so that it becomes profitable instead. You can do this with the help of my Local Trade

Copier software. Now do not feel that I am selling this to you, there are dozens of other trade copier apps out there. But since I have one created by myself it is obvious that I am more familiar with it and use as an example here.

So how does the trade copier software reverse trades?

You can set the trade copier Client EA to reverse every trade it receives from the Server EA. So when you open BUY trade on the master MT4 account, a SELL trade will be opened on the slave MT4. And when you open SELL trade on the master MT4, a BUY trade will be opened on the slave MT4. Pending orders are reversed as well.

Did you noticed that most Expert Advisors and trading systems can make profits for some time, but then suddenly lose it all in a few days? Or have you ever tried to trade Forex manually and almost every single trade you enter turned out to be a loss?

With the trade copier that has a "Reverse Trading" feature you can have these trades reversed so they now become winners on the slave account! Think for a moment about the possibilities.

If you are interested in this type of experimental trading, you may find more information in *The Definitive Guide to Forex Trade Copying* that I have written. There you will find a step-by-step guide on how to use my Local Trade Copier software, reverse trades and learn various other trade copying scenarios. Find that guide at www.mt4copier.com.

Chapter 6 Takeaways

Chapter 6: Finding a source of profitable trading signals

Options:

- You can trade your own account as you usually do and send the same trading actions to your subscribers
- Hire or partner up with a forex trader
  - You will handle the signal delivery business and he will take care of the trading
- Find or build a profitable trading robot or Expert Advisor (EA)
  - Advantages of using a Forex robot to trade currencies
    - Robots don't have the emotions and just do what they are "told" to do.
    - Robots can be programmed to trade currencies based on economic news releases.
    - The robot is suitable for both Forex novices and experts.
    - It can trade any number of currencies at the same and analyse multiple timeframes in just a few seconds.
    - The robot can keep you regularly updated.
    - A robot will always stick to the rules, no matter what
    - You can run your trading signals business on autopilot.
  - Five Simple Steps to Evaluate a Forex Robot
    - Find the trading robot

- Verify trading history with the MyFXBook.com or an investor password
- Review on ForexPeaceArmy.com
- Contact the robot's owner and ask intelligent questions
- Test on a demo account first. Ask for a trial period
  - Resell trading signals from another website
    - Get the website's permission before you begin reselling their signals
  - Look for PAMM, MAM or LAMM account traders on FXOpen, Alpari UK and other Forex brokers' websites
  - Look for good performing systems on myfxbook.com

Test any signal source thoroughly to make sure it is error free

Verify any trading signals source on FPA

Experiment with the trade copier software by reversing trades

CHAPTER 7

Setting up Your Forex Signal Service Website

"You can fool some of the people all of the time, and all of the people some of the time, but you cannot fool all of the people all of the time." - Abraham Lincoln

It's now time to create a sales website for your trading signals service. A sales website is an online site where you will offer your services. It's the place where potential customers will be reading about your services and it needs to be done in a professional manner.

The website should include all relevant information about your business and the products you've created. It should display your trading record and a description of what is your service is all about.

This will make it easier for prospective customers to find your website. Include enough information so that visitors to the site get to know something about you and the services you're offering before subscribing.

The biggest mistake people make in this business is that they create a service for Forex traders. This means that if someone who is just starting to learn about currency trading, or even heard the word Forex from a friend yesterday, (s)he will likely not understand what your service is about. Of course, you can sell trading signals for Forex traders only, but you should present them in such a way that everyone understands what it is that you offer.

Have you ever visited a forex signals website and seen a poorly designed website that seemed to date back to 1995? Or have you read a forex article recently just to find that it does not talk about anything that is common sense and rather just talks about useless information or the same stuff you can find on Google? Have you ever found a signal service that shows their performance table on a site in a simple format with no concrete proof? Anyone could have created that table with random data just to look profitable. And if you ask them to post their trading stats on MyFXBook or similar website they say they are busy trading currencies and won't waste their time on that.

If you do not want to be like those sites, you should spend time and add the most important things to your website. I will explain these for you in detail below. I am teaching you all of this, having in mind that you will operate your business from the point of integrity, and that you will run a truly honest business. I am not about creating a website just to make some sales by convincing people using some marketing tricks and then not delivering what was promised. When you offer a genuine and honest service, this is what makes you different from the majority of other trading signals or software vendors in Forex market. You, like me, should be interested in doing good for people, not just to make your bank account bigger. Although money is very important, as with it we can reach more people and do better, I still value relationships more than money and care about each customer.

It is easy to lose trust in something when you get cheated few times and often it is enough even just one time for many of us. A lot of people got cheated online, especially in the Forex market, and many of them then see Forex as a scam. I think it's a global problem and the first thing that ruins the Forex market's reputation is cheap software and training where the vendor's goal is to sell something—only to then pass the trader to his recommended broker just to earn breadcrumbs when the inexperienced trader loses money.

People are barely educated on the forex market and programmed to believe that it's how professional traders make millions. When inexperienced traders learn only 10% of what the Forex market is and how it actually works, and then start trading with real money, they are left to act with emotions and basically to gamble money away. This is how people lose in forex and then lose belief. Now those who do not stop find a new training course or coach and start the whole process over. This continues until the individual loses faith or finds a reputable trading coach.

In my belief the coach is not someone who just shows what indicators to use, but also he explains what to expect in the markets. If someone looking at a 5 year trading history chart that goes up thinks that this is a Holy Grail system, they can be very wrong. They try to use the same trading rules and follow the same trading style, but later are surprised to have the first 10 trades to be losses.

When people find a signals website, all of them promise that no knowledge is required to trade forex and even that everything is done automatically for them. When people start to follow such signals they see it's not giving the results they saw promised on the sales page. People are not made aware that there can be losing months and if you happen to join during the "losing period" you will see a drawdown on your account.

Things to explain to your customers before they join:

- **Past performance does not indicate future results**. Yes, that's what every risk disclaimer tells you. However, no one reads them. We, as vendors, have it on the websites to avoid legal problems. But I bet that even you yourself have never read what it says, at least before you start selling signals. We should let people know that the past performance we show is genuine, and we did that in the past, and it is likely it will happen again and again. We have the potential. However, they should know that there is a very real possibility of losing their investment, and if they do, then most likely the vendor's account will lose money too. Other vendors make a huge mistake by not explaining this and then later creating unhappy customers. Do not try convince people to buy your product just to have better sales numbers. Instead, offer people your service honestly by letting them know the risk and then you will have low refund rates.

- **Explain the risk.** Yes, that's boring and probably will lower sales rates, but if those sales end up as a refund and unhappy customers then why would you want to sell them in the first place. Aim for customers that are informed and are serious about investing. Tell them what is the maximum risk per trade and the maximum drawdown expected. We can predict estimated drawdown based on past performance, but be sure to explain that it's just a prediction. At some time you may get a new high drawdown.

- **Explain your refund policy**. It is best if you offer a refund for at least 30 days, but if don't do that, be sure to give a trial period for the first month. On Vavatrade, I offer a refund only if the user decides to cancel their subscription and the last month was a loss. A refund is available only for the last month. Even though it may not sound fair for some customers, it's actually a fair enough offer because I give 30-day trial to try my service.

The most important things to add to your signals website

The majority of potential customers that land on my website start with a question like this:

"I just came across your site and I am interested in subscribing. I have 5000 euros to invest. I want a full automated system hosted by you. Is this possible? Please advise sign up details. I don't know anything about Forex so I would need a broker recommendation as well."

I get lots of emails asking the same information over and over again and once I answered those questions on my website they stopped and then I saw an increase in people signing up for my service. This explains that if people do not find answers to their questions when they visit your site, they will end up leaving your website. Only some of them will spend a couple of minutes to contact you and ask for the answers. And if you fail to add a contact form on your site, this will basically mean that you won't get anyone interested in your service at all.

This is why I have made a list of the most important things you should add on your website. If you add them you will definitely see more engagement from your prospects.

A logo or a banner with your logo at the top of the page. It is very important to start with this, because it adds a professional look. Think of this as a book cover for your site.

An eye-catching headline that will help visitors understand what this site is about. Example: "Forex Trading Signals via MT4 trade copier". Well, you should be more creative, but that was just an example.

A sub-title that will tell customers what problem they will solve with this website. It can also explain what this website is about, what results you have achieved or what customers are eligible to receive from your website. Example: "Raking in 200 pips on average every month since 2011".

Video presentation. Whether it will be you talking on camera or it will be a screencast from a Power Point presentation, you need to put up a video on your website. Video marketing is the future and it is the best way to demonstrate your authority and build trust. People are tired of those websites with a bunch of numbers and screen shots of perfectly profitable trading records. When you show your face on video and demonstrate your honesty and credibility, people will be more likely to subscribe.

3rd party verified trading record. Make sure it is simple and easy to understand. Your best choice is MyFxBook.com as it is very trusted and reliable.

Testimonials. Make sure they are genuine and you get them from your real customers. Make sure you do not violate U.S. rules that do not allow money figures in testimonials. Do not buy testimonials under any circumstances. The best way to get testimonials is to ask your customers to write one. Consider having beta testers for your system who can test it for free.

Later, after few weeks of testing, they can write testimonials for you.

Display the most important numbers in a picture or table to explain how your system works. Add numbers like maximum drawdown, maximum stop loss and minimum take profit size used, the number of months/weeks your system has been running, total profit in pips gained, and average number of pips gained monthly. A very important number that I haven't seen elsewhere before is a number of maximum hours/days between the trades. I have seen a lot of trading systems that show good trading records, but when I started to analyze the trading record, trade-by-trade, I soon realized that there were several weeks, or even months, of no activity whatsoever. You can only imagine the dissatisfaction of a customer who follows your signals and there are no trades for 2 months and he still has to pay the monthly fee.

ROI number. Imagine if your system is on the list together with 1000 other systems. How would yours stand out? You want the most important numbers to be displayed that will help potential investors judge the performance of your signals. Raving about how you have made 10,000 pips in the last 12 months does not explain if you are were profitable or not. Maybe you have the same amount of pips of floating loss. So this requires that you give at least 3 numbers for an accurate picture (profit made, floating profit/loss, time period in months) to demonstrate your gain in pips in such a way that it can reflect the true picture. If you don't show the full picture, bigger investors will go elsewhere—only newbies with smaller accounts may be convinced to join your signal service. If you show an ROI number for past performance and let's say it is 2.5%, people will know that when they put $1 they may receive a $2.5 return. Of course, past performance does not indicate future results, but with good past performance you have a better chance to make money than you would following a system with no record, or even worse, one with a poor trading record.

Brief description about your trading style and main rules you are trading by. This helps to remove the fear from potential customers. For example: "Maximum 1 open position per currency pair. Always using stop loss and maximum allowed size is 100 pips. NFA compatible. No hedge positions, no martingale trading. Works with all MetaTrader 4 accounts at any Forex broker". If you illustrate some or all of these rules in a graphic or picture it will be even better. Additionally, you can add a list of currency pairs your system trades.

Good price offer with a trial period of at least 30-days. A lot of providers make the mistake of not providing a trial period. For those who feel this is a bad idea, think of it this way: You are seeking to get a customer that will stick with you for years, thereby earning you money. Do you want a customer for 5 years, 10 years, or more? 10 years is 120 months, so don't be cheeky and give at least 1-2 months for free. You know yourself that when testing any trading system, you need at least 3-6 months to decide if it's worth to continue using it. So even that single month you are giving for free is not enough, but it will build more trust to your company. My customer list doubled when I started to give away trial periods. It is great proof that it is working.

Contact information. If you are a real business, then act like one, and list your company name, business postal address and a phone number on your website. If you do not have a company, then put your real name and your address on it. Do not hide yourself because anonymous signal providers look very suspicious and people usually do not trust them. Adding a contact form is the best way to go, because when you add an email address, it will be found by spammers, and your inbox will be full of junk emails in no time.

Risk disclaimers and terms of conditions documents at the bottom of the page. You should require that customers check a few boxes, before subscribing, to make sure they agree with your service rules and understand the risk of Forex investment. Many marketers will tell you that these things will lower conversion rates, means less people will subscribe, but actually, that is a good thing. It will also lower your refund rate. Think it this way: If a potential customer who read the risk disclaimers decided that your service is not right for him, it means that your service is not right for him. Why do you want someone to buy your product if they do not want it, or it is not right for them? And what if this customer loses his money? If you haven't explained to him about the risk and responsibilities, he may take a legal action against you. When you have a risk disclaimer, and make people agree with the risks before joining your service, you make them aware about the potential hazards. Do not convince people to buy your product, just to earn money. Let them buy your product so you can help them earn money in Forex trading.

All of these things listed above will make your website look professional and complete. This information should be clearly visible on your website at all times. Customers should be able to find this info easily. Make your website simple and easy to use. Avoid using a website design that will have your visitors browsing from one page to another in order to find relevant information.

Now you might think that when people use this all the websites will be the same. Well, in that case all Facebook profiles would be the same. We all use the same outline, it's the same for everyone, but we all put different information, and that is what makes our profiles unique. The same is true for book writing. Many of the books may use the same outline, but all of them have different information and this makes them unique. So this means that even if 100 signal providers use the same outline for their websites, they all will end up having different sites because of the unique and different content they upload.

But even before you start putting these things up, you need to learn how to set up a website in the first place.

Steps to complete in order to start a website

Here are the steps you need to complete in order to have your website up and running as fast as possible:

1. Buy a domain name.
2. Rent a web server to host your website or get a simple hosting solution.
3. Create a sales website using WordPress.
4. Collect names and emails to create a list of prospects.

5. Market your website on Forex forums, trading robot verification sites and general forex websites.
6. Don't anger the Search Engines! Follow white hat SEO practices.

If you follow these six simple steps, you will have your website online faster than you can imagine. Actually, to begin with, need to complete only the first three steps to have a website, while the next three are required to make it complete.

Let's take a closer look at each of these steps.

Buying a domain name

Your business needs a domain name. The domain that you buy can affect your signal service in all sorts of different ways. I recommend choosing a short, easy to remember domain name. I know that most of you will want to get a domain name with the word "Forex" in it.

You've probably heard that this is good for SEO and that search engines will give you a better position in their rankings, but this is an old myth. It doesn't work that way anymore. Don't let this myth influence you into choosing a boring domain name. Choose a domain name that can later also be your brand name. Or maybe you already have a brand name, so it's wise to use it for a domain name as well.

Another common mistake people make at this stage is choosing a domain name that has "4x" in the address. When you pronounce 4x it sounds a lot like "Forex". Although most of the services behind domains like these are likely genuine and probably doing a fine job (never tested them personally), their domain names make it hard to stand out from the competition.

4xservices.com
4xsolutions.com
4xsignal.com
4xsignals.com
4xtradingcoach.com

I don't have anything against these websites and I have no idea who's behind them, but I'm sure you get my point. They all look very similar and are very easy to mix up. When people want to share a 4x website with their friends they probably say something like this:

"Today I went to this great website about forex called 4x ... what a minute....4x something dot com....4xsignal.com? Or was it 4xservice.com? ... I completely forgot, let me look at my browsing history, mmm, never mind".

Meanwhile their friend is already bored and doesn't care what the website is called anymore.

This is only my personal opinion and some of my websites also have really bad domain names. However, if I could start from the beginning, I would choose a domain that is easy to remember and could become a brand one day.

You need to pick a domain name that your customers can easily remember and relate to your business. This will be your web identity from now on. Take your time on this step, think hard and come up with a short, engaging and relevant domain name.

Choose the Right Domain Extension

What extension will you use? What sounds better – "yourbusiness.com" or "yourbusiness.net"? How about "yourbusiness.org"? Different extensions can denote different things. Choose the right suffix and try to make the most of it.

Some of the suffixes have been around for a very long period of time. When you associate your forex trading enterprise with one of these extensions, it can signal to your customers that you are a reliable business that will be around for a long time.

Sometimes it's better to register your domain name using all the different suffixes that you can think of. Then, if you happen to change your mind in the future and want to use a different extension, your registered domains will be there waiting for you. You can buy "yourbusiness.com", "yourbusiness.biz" as well as "yourbusiness.net".

This can also be used as a defensive move, to prevent someone else from usurping your domain name. For example, you setup a successful forex business with "your business.net" but you choose not to purchase "yourbusiness.com" because it was costing more. Now someone can coattail on your success, buy "yourbusiness.com" and start their own signal delivery service there. Unsuspecting customers will never know what hit them when they arrive at "yourbusiness.com" instead of "yourbusiness.net".

Another good practice is to purchase common misspellings of your domain name. A lot of times people make typing errors online. How many times have you typed in "bussiness" or "busines" instead of "business"? Buying these misspelled domain names can bring back all that traffic that was initially intended to visit your site anyway.

Let me give you a few more tips for choosing a domain name.

Most people prefer using their business name as their domain name. This is a practical and common sense business decision. However, only the early bird registers the domain worm. Chances are high that your business name will already be taken.

So you'll need to think up your own domain name. You can use online domain naming tools for inspiration. You can also ask friends and family for their suggestions. Try to limit the length of the domain name to 10 characters or less. The shorter the name is, the easier it will be to remember.

Try not to get overwhelmed by too much information. You can return to this guide later if you want to. Right now, just choose a domain name. I recommend you only buy one with a ".com" extension.

As soon as you decide on the name, make sure to register it right away. The availability of domain names is decreasing at an alarming rate and you must reserve yours before someone else does. Registering is easy and not nearly as expensive as it used to be few years ago.

Avoid going for copyrighted names as it can land your business in a legal soup.

It's also important to remember that domain names can only be alphanumeric. You can't include symbols or special characters. You are allowed to use dashes in a domain name, but I wouldn't recommend doing this. According to SEO experts, search engines favor domain names without dashes over domains that have dashes.

I made a similar mistake several years ago when I registered ea-coder.com. There is a website version without the dash that belongs to someone else. This can potentially be very confusing for some of my customers.

If you still want to use a domain name with dashes in it, my advice would be to purchase the name without dashes as well and have it redirect to your main website. By doing this you will make sure that no one will profit from your website's popularity.

Where can you buy domain names?

I recommend purchasing all your domains at the same place but not having them with your server provider. I personally use www.namecheap.com. I'm not getting paid for mentioning them in my book, I'm just sharing what works for me. You could also try the most popular domain register, GoDaddy.com, or give some of the smaller registrants a shot.

Having all of your domains and websites with the same hosting provider is better than having different websites scattered around on multiple hosting accounts. If you host your domain name at the same provider where you rent out your dedicated or VPS servers, you won't have much difficulty with managing the domains because they all are in the same place.

If you ever decide to shut down your server with hosting provider #1 and move everything to a new server hosted at another hosting provider. The simplest way to do this would be to get a new server, transfer all of your content to the new host, then change the DNS "A" record to forward all visitors to the new server's IP address.

The website at the old hosting provider may show a "maintenance" message to all visitors while the transfer is in progress. When the DNS data is updated in different countries they will be forwarding visitors to the new server automatically. After a few days the old server will stop getting visitors.

At this point you can simply transfer domain names to your new hosting provider as well and shut down the old server. This is how you can transfer websites without interruptions in the service.

Ordering a Web-Server

When it comes to ordering a web-server I always recommend getting a dedicated server in a cloud. A dedicated server is your own personal web server hosted in a reliable data center. Make sure that your hosting provider offers the option to upgrade at a later date by adding more RAM, CPU power or storage WITHOUT having to restart the system.

These servers are not cheap, pricing usually starts at ~200 USD per month. But trust me, if your goal is to have a reliable service, you will need a hosting provider that has a good server. Keep in mind that this option is more for someone who has dozens of websites, or will need to host a trade copier control panel.

I completely understand that many of you will want a cheaper and simpler solution. Maybe you're just starting out and if you go for the expensive servers with no paying customers you may end up with a big loss.

I remember several years ago when I was living on a salary, paycheque to paycheque, $200 was a huge amount of money for me. It took me a week to earn that much at my job. But as luck would have it, I was working as an IT Admin in a company that had a web-server, so I managed to get free hosting for my website. I still use that hosting account for testing purposes, but the majority of my websites are now hosted with a lot more reliable provider called LiquidWeb.com.

A cheap and simple solution for hosting a website is to get an account with a popular web provider. This way you don't need to worry about servers and other geeky stuff. But with thousands, if not tens of thousands of hosting providers on the market, choosing the correct one can be a daunting task.

Below I give you a list of popular hosting providers. As you start to try out these hosting solutions you will notice that most of them have similar web interfaces for the online management of your account. The most popular system that hosting providers offer is cPanel. This program is very easy to use.

I always use WordPress for my websites. WordPress is a great platform for creating professionally looking websites. The platform offers a plethora of themes and different features that can help you build an appealing and secure website. It is the simplest way to create and manage a website.

The easiest way to setup a WordPress website is by using an app called Fantastico. This app is usually included in the cPanel of most popular website hosting providers.

After you create your account with your hosting provider, login to your cPanel interface (or whatever platform they use) and look for an icon that reads "Fantastico". This is the app that will help you setup a WordPress website in a few easy steps.

Setting up a website with WordPress and Fantastico (or some other 1-click installation tool) makes the whole process much easier. Fantastico was created especially for non-techie customers who are not very familiar with confusing installations over FTP or SSH protocols.

List of Top 10 Web Hosting Service Providers

Here are the few that I recommend. Note that I don't get paid for these recommendations. I included them in my book so that you could learn more about your options and have an easier time choosing a hosting provider.

In the list below, I provide pro/con comments regarding the top Web Hosting Service Providers at the end of 2013. If you plan to have a sales web site, the primary take-away from this analysis is to avoid the lowest-level plan in favor of the next level up. A good plan for a sales site will fall in the range of $6.00 to $8.00 a month based on a 2 to 3 year contract. Such a plan should easily support a sales web site with up to 1,000 shoppers/visitors per day. If you expect more traffic than that, you should consider a managed WordPress hosting platform such as Page.ly or WP Engine.

Perhaps your favorite site is not listed; this may be why I haven't listed it. If you have searched the Internet for web hosting service providers, you have found that there are many "web hosting service provider" reviews. Many of those reviewers have a hidden agenda which makes their ratings suspect. I like to call it "Affiliate Bias". Many of the "more popular" web hosting service providers have an affiliate program that pays affiliates very well for referring potential clients to their sites. As a result of that incentive, many review sites are built to exploit that revenue-earning potential. With that thought in mind, I scanned several review sites to get a sense of who is considered a top provider. I also reviewed publication sites that can't, by their very nature, be affiliates. The compilation of the names on my list draws heavily from those reviewers; however, my research and the conclusions drawn are based on direct contact with the Web Hosting Service Providers.

---

1. Arvixe, http://arvixe.com

Pros
Typical "unlimited" features are more than average.
Guaranteed 99.9% uptime.
Help and support group is rated very highly.
Full-featured cPanel-accelerated plus Softaculous 1-click script installer.
Shopping carts and SSL Certificates are available.
There are Windows and Linux servers on this site, Windows ASP.net is supported.

Arvixe is a highly-regarded Web Hosting Service Provider with unlimited bandwidth, disc space, domains and email accounts at the PersonalClass Pro level. Arvixe Guarantees a 99.9% up-time. This up-time rate is standard for the better providers. Their Help and Support group prides itself on being developer-friendly and is perceived to be one of the best of its kind. Their full-featured cPanel-accelerated is exceptional, making the management of a web site as easy as can be. The Softaculous auto-installer provides 337 scripts many of them 1-click options, including the 1-click option to install WordPress.

There are extensive options regarding shopping carts, supported by Softaculous or you can use WordPress plugins to accomplish the same purpose. SSL Certificates are also available if needed. With the latest .net framework and best ASP web hosting components, this site features one of the best ASP hosting capabilities around. This is one of the few sites where you can actually review/explore both cPanel and Softaculous on their website before buying. Go have a look by clicking on the corresponding links on this page: http://www.arvixe.com/Linux_web_hosting

Cons

A little more expensive.

There is not very much about this service provider that is negative. If you go for the lowest hosting price, you are limited to 6 domains. To get unlimited domains, you will have to go with the $7.00/month option.

---

2. Just Host, http://justhost.com

Pros

Typical "unlimited" features are more than average.

Guaranteed 99.9% uptime.

Help and support group is rated very highly.

Full-featured cPanel gives you one-click options as well as custom-build capabilities.

Shopping carts and SSL Certificates are available.

Just Host is a highly-regarded Web Hosting Service Provider with unlimited bandwidth, disc space, domains and email accounts. Just Host Guarantees a 99.9% up-time. This up-time rate is standard for the better providers. Consistent with their up-time guarantee, their Help and Support group is comparable. Their full-featured cPanel includes many 1-click options, including the 1-click option to install WordPress. cPanel support also simplifies the installation of shopping carts. Their featured WordPress plugin cart is WooCommerce, from WooThemes. You can also get premium themes from WooThemes that are specifically designed to work with WooCommerce. SSL Certificates are also available if needed.

Cons

This is a Linux servers only site, Windows ASP.net is not supported.

There is not very much about this service provider that is negative. If your programmers have a bias for Windows, you should know that this is a Linux servers only site, Windows ASP.net is not supported.

---

3. Go Daddy, http://godaddy.com

Pros

Guaranteed 99.9% uptime.

Help and support group is rated very highly.

Full-featured cPanel gives you one-click options as well as custom-build capabilities.

Shopping carts and SSL Certificates are available.

Linux and Windows servers on site.

Go Daddy started out as a registrar and expanded into hosting. They have made the transition very successfully, with a guaranteed up-time of 99.9% and a help and support group that is much better than the industry average. Their cPanel has many features and 1-click-type options, including the 1-click option to install WordPress. Their shopping carts, for the most part, are proprietary, but they allow some WordPress plugins if the plugins are not resource-hogs. SSL Certificates are also available if needed.

Cons

Typical "unlimited" features are few.

Many options are at additional prices.

While Bandwidth and Disc Space are unlimited, other features may not be. If you are a typical smaller business, you probably won't be affected that much, but as your demand for features and/or services gets larger, you may find yourself paying more for those.

---

4. iPage, http://ipage.com

Pros

Typical "unlimited" features are more than average.

Help and support group is rated very highly.

Shopping carts and SSL Certificates are available.
Linux and Windows servers on site.

iPage is highly regarded, providing unlimited bandwidth, disc space, domains and mySQL databases; however, this comes with a qualifier, see con below. Help and support group is rated very high. While iPage supports 1-click installation of WordPress, it does so through vDeck (see con below). Shopping carts and SSL Certificates are provided, however, the variety of carts is limited and most are at additional cost. If you are a Windows ASP.net user, you will find support for it here.

Cons

Typical "unlimited" features are qualified.
Many options are at additional prices.
Guaranteed up-time.
Web site management is through vDeck, not cPanel.

While unlimited is the term used, this comes with a qualifier, defining usage as "normal usage". With web hosting priced so low, you should expect that many options will only be available at additional prices. iPage doesn't quote a guaranteed up-time, but indicates that other third-party users have measured their up-time in the range of 99.1 to 99.5. With no guarantee, I would not expect a consistent up-time at that level. While vDeck is a very good webhosting control panel, it is perceived to be less user-friendly and more limited than cPanel.

5. MidPhase, http://midphase.com and

6. ANHosting, http://anhosting.com and

7. WestHost, http://westhost.com

All three of these Web Hosting Service Providers are part of the UK2 Group and all are well-regarded as Web Hosting Service Providers. Midphase and WestHost provides more options and flexibility than ANHosting. For a sales website, the Midphase business plan would be the one to use since it is less expensive than the similar plan at WestHost. Pros and Cons below are based on the business plan level.

Pros

Typical "unlimited" features are more than average.

Guaranteed 99.9% uptime.

Help and support group is highly rated.

Full-featured cPanel includes Softaculous, a 1-click script installer.

Shopping carts and SSL Certificates are available.

Midphase, WestHost and ANHosting are highly-regarded Web Hosting Service Providers with unlimited bandwidth, disc space, domains and email accounts at the business plan level in Midphase and WestHost, plus a variety of other products and services that would typically not be unlimited for other service providers. All three guarantee a 99.9% up-time. Their Help and Support groups are highly rated and easy to contact.. Their full-featured cPanels include a Softaculous auto-installer for many 1-click options, including the 1-click option to install WordPress. There are extensive options regarding shopping carts, supported by Softaculous or you can use WordPress plugins to accomplish the same purpose. SSL Certificates are also available and are free in the Midphase and WestHost business plan (which also includes a free dedicated IP address at Midphase). Don't be fooled by the simplistic unappealing websites at Midphase and ANHosting, behind the sales scene they know what they are doing.

Cons

A little more expensive.

Windows ASP.net is not supported.

The business plan level is a little more expensive, but a free dedicated IP address and a free SSL certificate at Midphase more than offset this. If you need to develop with Windows ASP.net, you can't do so on any of these sites.

---

8. HostGator, http://hostgator.com

HostGator provides a very large Reseller Hosting service which makes them seem to be larger than the typical Web

Hosting Service Provider. Pros and cons are for their web hosting service.

Pros

Typical array of unlimited features.

Guaranteed 99.9% uptime.

cPanel with 1-click capability.

Shopping carts and SSL Certificates are available.

HostGator provides the typical array of unlimited features including domains, emails, disc space and bandwidth along with guaranteed 99.9% uptime. The HostGator configuration of cPanel is not as clean as the better sites, but does provide 1-click installation of 75 of the most common open source applications including the 1-click installation of WordPress. A free eCommerce platform, Magento, is available plus the typical WordPress plugins for eCommerce. SSL certificates are available.

Cons

Help and support group is average.

Windows ASP.net is not supported.

HostGator is challenged in their help and support group, providing only average quality support. Part of this challenge may be the heavier workload caused by the cPanel configuration that is somewhat less than user-friendly. Their Customer Satisfaction Survey is dated 2008. The servers are all Linux, making Windows ASP.net support impossible.

---

9. BlueHost, http://bluehost.com

Pros

Typical array of unlimited features

Guaranteed 99.99% uptime.

Help and support group is above average.

cPanel with 1-click capability

Shopping carts and SSL Certificates are available.

BlueHost is a highly-regarded Web Hosting Service Provider with unlimited bandwidth, disc space, domains and email accounts. BlueHost Guarantees a 99.9% up-time, made possible by an above average help and support group. Their full-featured cPanel includes many 1-click options, provided through the MOJO Marketplace, including the 1-click option to install WordPress. SSL Certificates are also available if needed.

Cons

Windows ASP.net is not supported.

The servers are all Linux, making Windows ASP.net support impossible.

---

10. Network Solutions, http://networksolutions.com

Pros

Guaranteed 99.99% uptime.

Help and support group provides award-winning customer service.

Network Solutions is included in this review because it is highly regarded in the Web Hosting Service Provider community as an "a la carte" provider with an amazing guaranteed uptime, 99.99%, and an award-winning help desk. If you want to customize your domain and get extremely high performance out of it, Network Solutions can do it, but it comes with a price. You pay individually for almost all features.

Cons

Windows ASP.net is not supported.

No cPanel and limited 1-click install capability.

Only unlimited feature is bandwidth.

While Network Solutions does provide a WordPress blogging capability and a 1-click install, you are expected to use it as a blog. If you want to use it as a sales site, you must buy a website package and install WordPress in the package. You can then add WordPress plugins for eCommerce. The website package must be enriched with features that are usually free on other Web Hosting Service Providers. This probably prices most small businesses out of their marketplace.

Creating a website using a 1-click WordPress installer script

Here are main steps you have to complete to create a Word-Press website using a 1-click WordPress installer script. Start by logging into your web host cPanel. Not all web hosts will use this process, but it is quite common. Once you are logged into your cPanel look for the Fantastico section. Some hosting accounts will offer something like QuickInstall or "1-click Word-Press install", which will help you easily install a WordPress platform.

After you click on the Fantastico icon you will see an option for installing WordPress, as well as a number of other tools. You will select the WordPress option, and then select "New Installation".

At this point you will be given some options to complete information on where you would like to install the WordPress (if you have multiple domains on the same hosting account, for example). The install process will walk you through the different options. Most hosting providers have live chat or phone technical support if you would like someone to walk you through the process. Alternatively, there are many videos on YouTube that can also walk you through this install process.

A professional website design in minutes for the price of a bottle of wine

Most people think that website design is very expensive. This was true several years ago. Even today, some companies are still paying thousands of dollars to web-designers. If you are a big company then there is nothing wrong with spending a lot on website design. But if you're just starting out, then you will definitely not want to spend a few grand on website design alone.

In the steps below, I'll show you how it's possible to get an exceptional and professionally looking web design for less than

$50 dollars. I'll also go over how to apply this design to your website in mere minutes.

How to choose a website template

These are the steps I recommend you to complete before you buy a website template. Remember that most of them will look very professional with fine graphics on their sales pages, but once you install it on your server/domain you will need to replace all the text and images with your own. You can see all the sample text on these templates and all these nice images, but you won't want them to be on your site when your customers visit it. So prepare yourself with your own content and only then buy a website template.

- Test in multiple internet browsers like Firefox, Internet Explorer, Chrome, and Opera. Make sure the website looks the same in all of these applications.
- Test loading speed using this free tool from Google. http://developers.google.com/speed/pagespeed/insights/
- Go through all the pages and make a list of all the images and videos it has. Keep in mind that you will need to replace them with your own content. This means you will need images and videos of the exact same size to make your new template look good. Don't buy a template just to remove most of the features it has and then upload a few pictures. Make good use of a template you buy.
- Have a list of things you want to add to your website and see if your new template has for it all. Check where the main page headers appear and where you will add charts/images like MyFXBook trading record, etc.
- There are many places where you can purchase a website theme. Some sites that come to mind are ThemeForest.net, TemplateMonster.com, ElegantThemes.com and WooThemes.com. Some are more expensive than others. With WooThemes and ElegantThemes, you can join their membership and receive all of the themes for one price. With ThemeForest and TemplateMonster you will need to pay for each

theme individually. All of these sites support Word-Press themes.

Once you get your theme, you will need to install it onto the WordPress you have already installed using Fantastico/your hosting account.

Installing Your Template

You will generally download your theme template, once purchased, to a spot on your computer. It will come in a zipped folder, and just leave it in this zipped format. Your next step is to go into your WordPress admin area (typically http://YOUR-SITE.com/wp-admin) and then click on the APPEARANCE and then THEMES links (generally found on the left hand side of the screen, inside your WordPress admin area).

From the THEMES page, click on the ADD button at the top of the page. Next, click on the link that says UPLOAD. You will then hit the CHOOSE FILE button, select the zipped folder of your theme, and then hit OPEN. Once the file uploads, it will give you options to PREVIEW the new theme, and also to AC-TIVATE the new theme. You can first preview the new theme if you choose, and then activate your new theme.

Your new theme design should now be live on your website and ready for more advanced customizations (depending on the theme you have chosen).

Integrating Your Website with a Payment Processor

Obviously, you will be charging customers a monthly fee, so you will need a Payment Processor, also known as Payment Gateway. I think this step should be completed after you have your website in place, and have also completed all the information and the design. Usually, website designs already come with "Buy now" or "Add to cart" buttons, so after you register with a Payment Processor, you will just need to link those buttons to a special payment link generated for you.

Payment processors like PayPal, ClickBank and Click2Sell, make the managing of your online business easier, faster and more accurate. It is quite easy to sign up for an account with any of these payment services and create special payment links to include on your website. It may be difficult for Forex related products to get approved by ClickBank, but if you do get approved, your product will be listed in their marketplace and accessible to thousands of affiliates who can promote you. Personally, I use PayPal and the whole world knows that you can trust it. PayPal has been around for years and it's only getting bigger and better. You can definitely use another payment gateway/service, or maybe you are already using one in your other online business, but I will use PayPal as the example here in my book.

There are many other payment processing solutions, but PayPal remaints the easiest option. I have heard that people are afraid of using this payment processor because of the many horror stories about them blocking people's accounts or not releasing payments on time. But from my own personal experience with using a PayPal business account in Europe, I can tell that I have not had any major problems.

To understand those horror stories, I personally spent a few hours of my time reading many of them on a few websites, and I have found out that most of them were about the situations on eBay or associated with eBay purchases or selling on eBay. It's a known fact that there are a lot of scammers on eBay who try to cheat people in any way possible, and if you become a victim of such a scam it certainly is not fun.

Also, most of those stories about PayPal accounts being blocked are very old, sometimes posted even years ago when eBay and PayPal did not have the high level of security and protection they have now.

If you run a legit and honest business, you definitely won't have trouble with PayPal. And if this is still a roadblock for you, then you can always chose to use other payment processors. There are many available online.

What should you look for in a payment processor?

Choosing the right processor or payment gateway is an important financial decision. Here are a few things you should look for in a payment processor:

Secure online transactions. This is the No. 1 concern your customers will have when paying for your service. Make sure you are using a reliable payment processor. Do thorough research. Your processor should have all the necessary security checks in place. These include verifying the customer's billing address, their shipping details and confirming the credit card's security code. All these safeguards should be in place to protect your business from scams and frauds.

Recurring payments. This is an essential part of the payment gateway you will need. You will definitely want to charge monthly, weekly or even annually for payments.

Reasonable fees for processing. Different gateways charge different processing fees. Also, make sure to check out all the other fees they have. There can be additional charges for discounts, subscriptions, refunds, charge backs, minimums, per-transaction charges and other fees.

Invoices and bills. Invoicing can be easier through payment gateways. Though, if you are a big company, you definitely don't need this feature because your accountant probably takes care of the invoicing anyway.

Regular updates. Make sure that the system is interactive and provides updates continuously and for all transactions. If you refund a payment that was done last month, or even 2 months ago, you want to see its status change to "Refunded" in your monthly and annual reports from the payment processor. It sounds like a silly thing to consider, but a few years earlier I had similar problem with PayPal, believe it or not. Good thing they fixed that pretty soon.

24 x 7 customer support. Choose a checkout system that offers 24 x 7 customer support to you as a user. You should be able to contact the payment gateway's support team whenever you suspect errors in processing.

Choose a reputable payment processor and configure it according to the needs of your website. Getting a payment gateway is a cost effective investment that will pay for itself.

Creating a PayPal subscription button

Here is how to create a payment button on PayPal and put it on your website.

Login to your PayPal account. Next you need to create (or update existing) PayPal subscription buttons. If you are using a special software to automatically charge recurring or one-time payments, you may need to setup a PayPal button with your unique **notify_url**, which is the URL of the 3rd party script.

Once you are inside your PayPal account proceed with the next steps:

1) Go to "Profile" in the top menu.
2) Go to "My selling tools" in the left menu.
3) Click "update" next to "PayPal buttons".
4) Click "Create new button" in the right menu.
5) Choose button type "Subscriptions".
6) Enter your item name (example: Forex Trading Signals).
7) Enter unique "Subscription ID". This number is usually used by trading signal delivery software to know which PayPal subscriptions are used for trade copier.
8) Choose "Currency", enter "Billing amount" and choose "Billing cycle" you want to use.
9) You would want to say "Yes" next to the "Do you need your customer's shipping address?" PayPal will include shipping address of your clients which can be used later to print invoice.
10) Next you can set URL that points to your sales website pages when client cancel their checkout or finish it successfully.
11) If you are using a special software to automatically take actions on recurring or one-time payments, you need to setup a **notify_url** in the "Add advanced variables" text

area. When subscription is created, extended on recurring billing, canceled or refunded, PayPal will call this URL. This is where you need to enter notification URL for your PayPal subscription button to use. This URL usually provided by your trading signals delivery software if it supports this feature. Note that you need to add "notify_url=" before the URL in the "Add advanced variables" text field like in the example above. My Remote Trade Copier supports PayPal IPN calls for automatic creation of new usernames upon payment/subscription.

12) Click "Create button" to finish

Note that you do not need to use PayPal IPN (step 11) if you just want to receive payment. PayPal will email you new subscriber information anyway and then you can setup his account manually.

Now that you have your PayPal subscription button created you need to add its HTML code to your sales website. Follow PayPal on screen instructions to do this.

When client subscribes to your services using this PayPal button and that button is connected with Remote Trade Copier, PayPal will call special plug-in and it will do one of the following actions:

If payer email address does not exist in your users list, plug-in will create new username using payer's email. A welcome email message will be sent to the same email address that contains login info and other info (it depends what welcome email you have created in the "Settings" page on the RTC management website).

If payer email address exists in your users list, plug-in will set new expiry date (renew) the subscription.

If the subscription was canceled, PayPal simply will not call the plug-in with this user info and expiry date will not be expanded. This means that user will have access to your services until expiry date.

If the subscription was refunded, user access will be disabled immediately after PayPal calls the plug-in.

You can have multiple subscriptions with different prices, billing cycles and signal providers.

Chapter 7 Takeaways

Chapter 7: Setting up Your Forex Signal Service Website

Important things to add to your website

- Your logo or banner at the top of the page
- Eye-catching headline that will help visitors understand what your site is about
- A sub-title that will tell customers what problem they will solve with your website
- Video presentation - best way to demonstrate your authority and build trust
- 3rd party verified trading record
- Testimonials from real customers
- Display the maximum drawdown, maximum stop loss and minimum take profit size used, the number or months/weeks your system has been running, total profit in pips gained, and average number of pips gained monthly
- Show the ROI from past performance
- Brief description about your trading style and main rules you are trading by
- Good price offer with a trial period of at least 30-days
- Contact information
- Risk disclaimers and terms of conditions documents at the bottom of the page

Steps to start a website

- Buy a domain name
  - o Choose a domain name that can later also be your brand name
  - o Choose the right domain extension
  - o Having all of your domains and websites with the same hosting provider is better than having different websites scattered around on multiple hosting accounts
  - o You can buy from www.namecheap.com, GoDaddy.com, etc

- Rent a web server to host your website or get a simple hosting solution
  - Get a dedicated server in a cloud
  - Make sure that your hosting provider offers the option to upgrade at a later date by adding more RAM, CPU power or storage without having to restart the system
  - pricing usually starts at 200 USD per month
- Web Hosting Service Providers
  - Arvixe, http://arvixe.com
  - Just Host, http://justhost.com
  - Go Daddy, http://godaddy.com
  - iPage, http://ipage.com
  - MidPhase, http://midphase.com
  - ANHosting, http://anhosting.com
  - WestHost, http://westhost.com
  - HostGator, http://hostgator.com
  - BlueHost, http://bluehost.com
  - Network Solutions, http://networksolutions.com
- Create a sales website using WordPress
  - You can create a website using a 1-click WordPress installer script
  - You can have a professional website design at 50 USD or less
  - You can ownload and install your template once you have purchased it
  - You can integrate your website with a payment processor
    - PayPal
    - ClickBank
    - Click2Sell
- Collect names and emails to create a list of prospects
- Market your website on Forex forums, trading robot verification sites and general forex websites
- SEO your website

Tips and Tricks for Forex Trading Signal Providers

"If you tell the truth you don't have to remember anything."

- Mark Twain

If you're a skilled enough trader who has moved up the ranks to the point of providing trading signals to other less skilled traders, there are a few key things you need to bear in mind when you're building your website to attract new followers for your trading signal business. Don't be fooled into think that simply being successful at trading will automatically translate into hundreds of people following you. For every real trader out there offering genuine tips, there is at least one or two who don't really have anything to offer but still purvey the impression that they have valuable information.

10 Tips and Tricks for Forex Trading Signal Providers

Follow these 10 simple steps to ensure your site is giving out the right impression and winning over the trust and loyalty of potential followers:

1. Avoid anything on your site that will make it look spammy.

Images are very important for any site, but particularly with one that is asking visitors to trust it with their money. The wrong image can give all kinds of negative impressions leaving users feeling like they are not on a credible site. One common mistake is the use those images that seem to appear on any website that just use bad selling practices or even scam and lie to people.

Some people seem to think those are great images but believe me, it is anything but professional. Not just that, but if many sites use them so they has no real unique feeling. It just comes across as a generic repeat and if you use it your site will inherit that same impression. A simple Google images search for this particular one will throw up a lot of sites, many of which are just scams.

I myself have even been scammed by a site that had this image that seems to be added on any sales website where people creating them are just too lazy to do the work and just copy what other already have done. Separate yourself from the crowd and avoid over used images. If you go to Google and switch to "image search" you can try to find similar websites that use the same image. You need to click the "camera icon" in the image search bar and upload one of the images or just copy/paste its URL. You will find a lot of scam and fraud websites using the same image over and over again. Pretty good BS detector.

You should be sourcing unique images from sites like Photodune which is cheap at $1 per picture and it will give your site that unique feel. There are even sites that offer images for free like SXC.hu or this site at http://www.pixeden.com/free-graphics.

2. Post your trading history on MyFXBook.com.

This is a great site as it is well respected in the industry and it will give you an automatic way for your site visitors to verify that the profits you are claiming are indeed genuine. There are too many traders out there who do not bother to post up on here and as a result there are not that many people who feel they can rely on their reported trading history.

Of course posting on MyFXBook won't automatically translate to visitors joining your services but it will take a big step in winning over their trust in your claims. If you really are seeing genuine profits with Forex then there is no reason not to be using a verifying site like this.

3. Make things personal.

There's an old adage in sales that says people don't buy products and services, they buy people. Take the time to introduce yourself on your website. Write a detailed bio and let your visitors know a little more about you and your history. Using your real name and adding a picture are a great way of breaking down barriers and encouraging people to buy from you. They are much more likely to do this than if they are just on a generic site that is anonymous.

After all, you are asking them to put their financial future into your hands so they are likely to want to know a bit more about the person they intend to put so much trust in. Share your background and even go into detail about your own vision for Forex trading. The more users can connect with you and agree with your outlook, the more likely they are to place their money where your mouth is.

4. Don't confuse people, explain to them.

While you won't want to give away every ounce of your trading secrets, it is important that you go into a little detail about your trading system.

- How many trades you open at one time?
- How many pairs you trade in?
- What your maximum draw down record is?

A few sentences like this would cover the basics and give them an insight into the system they will be following. It will give them a sense of security when you show your authority on the subject and the more they understand what you are saying, the more likely they are to buy into using that same system. People feel empowered when they believe they understand something. They don't have to become experts, but if they don't understand anything at all, they will be far less likely to want to get involved.

Other things that are worth mentioning include:

- How many years you've been trading for and how long you have been turning a profit.
- Your monthly profit percentage for the past 12 months.
- Whether you use hedging techniques.
- Whether your system is NFA compatible or not.

5. Set and manage their expectations.

Make sure that you explain how you will deliver signals to followers. If you deliver through SMS or email, show an example on the screen of what they will receive. If you are using a trade copier, take them through the system you use and go into a little detail about its reliability and how it works. They will want to know what they are getting from you before they sign up.

It doesn't hurt also to have a section that explains how visitors go about signing up to your services. It only has to be a few bullet points but it will prevent losing potential followers who might struggle to get through the signing up process.

When you send trading signals by email or SMS, always include stop loss and take profit points together with the currency pair name and entry price.

6. Advertising, don't bother.

Generally speaking, people accept that advertising is an essential part of making a site profitable. But for a signals site, the money should be coming from profitable trading. Never put Google AdSense or any other form of advertisement on your signals site. It's not the right place for it and people will wonder why you need advertising on this site if you're really making profit from trading. Save any advertisements for your blog.

7. Look professional from the start.

There is no point in pinching pennies when it comes to design. You need users to feel like they are in a professional environment from the moment they enter your site. Either employ a professional designer or buy a professional template from the likes of ThemeForest.

The same thing goes for your domain name. Make sure you have your own. Anything like forexsignals.web.com doesn't leave a good impression and just makes your site look rooky at worst and unprofessional at best. A domain name can be as little as $10 on NameCheap so you'll find it difficult to justify claiming 100's of pips in positive movement if you can't even afford $10!

8. Show confidence in your services.

Offering a trial period for free, or perhaps a nominal fee of $1, is the best way to show potential clients that you believe in what you have to offer. It's good practice to have the small fee for the trial simply to verify that the person has a working payment source and it means you can collect their email address at the same time for mailings.

Customers who have used a trial period at first are much less likely to cancel their subscription at any point or ask for a refund. At the end of the day it is better to have 100 followers who will stay with you for years than 1000 followers who cancel after the first month and ask a refund.

9. Be realistic.

There is no need to claim that you are the No.1 signal service, unless of course you can prove that you are. The chances are you can't, but that doesn't mean that you won't get followers. Leave the grand claims for the big companies like ZuluTrade and MyFXBook and focus on your boutique or bespoke trading signals that offer a more personal service and are less anonymous than the big boys.

If you focus on what you truly have to offer rather than trying to be something you are not, customers will value that and are more likely to stay loyal to you.

10. Use bells and whistles sparingly.

Image sliders are a wonderful tool for adding depth and dimension to your site, but they don't need to appear everywhere. The homepage is the only real place that fancy elements like this should be used. I've seen far too many sites that go crazy with image sliders and have them all over the place. Not only do they slow your site down if you have too many, but they clutter up pages that really don't need them at all. You might be able to make the case for placing a slider on one other page on your site but for certain they don't need to appear on the Terms of Service or Risk Disclaimer pages.

Conclusion

All in all, you need to approach the construction of a trading signal services site like any commercial venture. It must appeal to the users in the same way as if you were selling them a mortgage or a new bank account. You need to remember that there are many other similar services on offer so just making big money claims isn't enough to convert customers.

If you stick to the core disciplines of creating an engaging and user friendly site, and go through the steps to verify and prove your credibility as a trading guru, you will reap the rewards of regular and loyal customers who will not only stay with you for a long time but will also take on your marketing for you by referring the service onto their friends, family and colleagues.

Put yourself in the shoes of a completely new visitor coming to your site and use your objective feedback to help improve your site.

If you already have a website, how does your site compare to the kinds of sites that you buy services from? If you were someone coming to your site for the first time, what would your first impressions be? Take this step seriously and be honest with yourself when judging your site's quality.

And if you do not have a website yet, make sure you follow these tips and tricks outlined above. They will help you start everything off on the right foot.

---

20 recommendations of how your trading system should look like to capture the imagination of a currency trader

If you only just try to sell trading signals then you may end up frustrated that no one buys your service. You need to know what types of signals are the most attractive to traders and big investors. In other words, let me give you 20 ideas on what most of the customers expect trading signals to be.

---

1. Customers will expect that you will trade signals on a real account,

but even with a demo it's possible to run this business too. However, if you use a demo to provide the signals, people will ask you why you do this so be prepared to answer this question for them.

Many customers would rather trade with someone that is investing 5k of his money rather than someone who is using a 100k demo account. Real funds above 5000 is best, sometimes you may need to start out with a smaller master account if that is all you have. Try to start with as much as possible (within reason and without crippling your finances—remember, the more you have at risk, the more emotionally involved you will likely be.)

As a signal provider, your clients expect that your trading account is funded with thousands of dollars and you are profiting like the 'big boys' of forex trading. This is a myth in our trading world that millions of traders keep on believing. This is why only a few stand out and create their companies to sell signals. It is an interesting fact that on the top 100 list of ZuluTrade's best signal providers, for example, only 4 signal providers are using live accounts/trading on real money. This, again, proves that you can use demo account to sell trading signals.

Getting your strategy published with a real money account that can attract lots of followers should be your goal. However, it can be a good option to sell signals using a demo account (so long as you're treating it like you are trading your own real money.) As your demo account prospers, you can then fund a live account from your followers' subscription fees. This will ensure that you are growing your business.

Make sure to never mention to your potential followers that you are using a demo account mainly because you can't afford to open a live account. This may be the case, but you do not need to emphasize this fact as it will reduce your clients' confidence in you. There are positive reasons why using a demo account to provide trading signals is better than a live account anyway, so focus on these instead. A demo account often provides better execution than live trading with no re-quotes, which is highly advantageous when using a trade copier. When a market order is placed in a live account, it is subjected to slippage as well. Thus, the entry price is not the exact entry price that you are expecting. In cases of a large sized order, your entry price may be too far from your expected entry price. Your exact entry price would be reflected to your followers' trading accounts. Therefore, the profitability of your system may be affected with a live account. In fact, many traders are profitable on demo accounts but experience successive losses with a live account sometimes because of price slippage and re-quotes.

---

2. People will want as low of drawdowns as possible.

Some will be okay with a max DD of 30% while others will start to panic with only a 10% DD. Keep the drawdowns as low as possible obviously (you need to consider this with money management, gain and risk factors). If you allow this kind of trader then you had better choose lower risk and potential drawdown settings, though the monthly gain is less usually with such settings.

Newbie traders take a general view of the market from the perspective of how much they will gain, disregarding the inherent trading risk. That's why they keep on searching for the trading system that will give them almost no losing trades. Most of your signal service subscribers are traders with little trading experience, and some with no trading experience whatsoever. These followers demand a maximum drawdown of the lowest percentage as possible, however unrealistic this may be in the real world.

Money management is very important. Experienced traders know that losses and drawdowns are part of profitable trading. No matter what system you use to provide signals, you will eventually have a losing trade. Thus, you should only risk a small percentage of your trading account so that you can survive the losing streaks. Most trading specialists preach that your risk per trade must be kept at most 2% of your account balance. That is, if you start with $10000, your single trade losses should not go beyond $200 on any given trade. You wouldn't expect to make a lot of money with a very small account and at the same time have a very minimal drawdown. Capital preservation is essential for a long-term success.

The table below illustrates 10 successive losing trades of two traders using 2% risk and 10% risk model.

Trade #	Account Balance	2% Risk on Each Trade	Account Balance	10% Risk on Each Trade
1	$10,000	$200	$10,000	$1,000
2	$9,800	$196	$9,000	$900
3	$9,604	$192	$8,100	$810
4	$9,412	$188	$7,290	$729
5	$9,224	$184	$6,561	$656
6	$9,040	$180	$5,904	$590
7	$8,860	$176	$5,313	$531
8	$8,684	$172	$4,782	$478
9	$8,512	$168	$4,304	$430
10	$8,344	$164	$3,874	$387

If you happened to go through a losing streak and lost 10 trades in a row, and you are risking 2% of your account on each trade, you would have lost only 17% of your initial account balance. If you are risking 10% on each trade, you would have lost 62% of your initial account balance. Trading at 10% per trade often represents extreme risk to most accounts.

Even if you lost more than 10 trades in a row, with a consistent 2% risk model, you can still end up profitable. That is, if you only take trade setups with a decent risk reward ratio of at least 2:1. Meaning, you only look for quality trades that can potentially give you at least two times more than you are risking.

3. Investors will want to know the Monthly return that you

have achieved in the past, and more importantly what you expect the monthly return to be in the future. Even if it is impossible to predict you will still need to give numbers. Taking last year's profit and dividing by 12 will give you average monthly income for last year. Although this does not guarantee it will repeat (and you should be clear explaining that), you still can show this to people. They can expect the same average monthly results. Also people will consider this relative to the potential drawdowns.)

To a professional trader, having a profit target every month is not a realistic thing to do since the market is going to produce a variable number of trades and your risk reward is always a random outcome on every trade. Some trades would give you 2:1, others would be greater than 3:1, and some are breakeven and loses. You never know what exactly your monthly profit since a trader just works with the market as opportunities unfold. Having a target is not necessarily a bad idea, but it can work against some traders. For others, the targets help them to focus and get more out of themselves.

Psychological pressure can affect your performance when you have a profit target every month. The pressure to make money increases as you lose since the target level is being missed. Having a constant weekly or monthly profit is terribly dangerous because it increases the chances of failure. Pushing the market to give you the monthly profit target under circumstances where there is no statistical edge in your favor is a recipe for disaster. You need to only work with the market as the market allows.

Achieving a certain profit target every month may be possible, but the possibility may be extremely low. However, to attract more followers to subscribe to your signals service, you need to track and publish your average monthly return. But you must warn your followers that your published monthly return is not a guarantee. Your previous performance will never be exactly the same to your future performance.

4. Your MyFXBook trading history should be at least a few months

long before you can gain interest from more experienced traders. For history, anything more than 6 months and 1 year is good. The more the better when it comes to your trading track record.

The performance record of your trading signals is extremely important to attract more followers. You must aim to build a performance graph that goes up from left to right because this is your main marketing tool to sell your trading signals. It is vital to verify your trading performance by posting your trading history on a third party website. MyFXBook is recommended since it is a very reliable and trusted verification site that provides authenticity and credibility. It offers unparalleled metrics and performance tracking that forex traders have come to trust.

When posting your performance record on third party websites, include your website address on the description or simply make your website address as your username. Traders can check on your website once they see you on the list of signal providers.

A longer performance record period is better. Experienced traders know that trading performance is measured over a long series of trades, not just one month or two. It's not a guarantee that a month of profitable trading performance will be the same on the succeeding months. In fact, market conditions are unique for each month. Cases of seasonality are found on major forex pairs (USD-paired currency pairs). January is generally an unprofitable month for these pairs because many investors withdraw all their profits at the end of the year and the Christmas holiday time causes many bankers and traders to go on vacation. At the beginning of the year, most investors would start with a blank slate. September is generally a busy and active month in the financial markets because of many expected economic new releases and political events, as well as ends the typical summer vacation time in the Northern Hemisphere. Traders anticipate a greater activity that could lead to breakout moves in currencies.

Thus, a performance record for one month is not as credible compared to one year of trading performance. This means that you can usually only attract followers after months of maintaining a positive trading performance. Building a reputable signals service business doesn't happen overnight. It takes months and even years. But after your business is already set up, you might possibly reap all the fruits of your efforts for decades.

5. People will question your trading methods.

Manual or EA based trading is what people will want to know. Others will be more comfortable to invest in EAs, as a robot removes emotions and will not start to freak out opening martingale positions to cover losses when 100 clients start to email their dissatisfaction messages, etc, for example.

Many traders are sceptical about trading robots simply because there are hundreds of them that do not work. Other traders have fear of losing their trading capital on trading robots because it may initiate unwanted trades or fail to set stop loss or take profit values. The feel a robot does not have the power of the human mind. It is not flexible, and will not allow the trader to take advantage of profitable short term positions if it is not configured to do so.

Many traders tend to invest more in manual signal providers despite the risk of emotional trading mistakes. Manual signal providers, though they are experienced traders, are still subjected to emotional trading caused by fear, greed, hope, and regret. They are always pressured to open less profitable positions just to send signals to subscribers. They are prone to over-trading and over-analyzing the market which often leads to account destruction.

There is also a rumour that signal providers start to lose money once they get few dozens or a few hundred followers. Although I do not have any data to back up this statement, it sure sounds true because when traders know that hundreds of people are relying on them to trade their hard-earned money, it creates this tension and fear of losing. This is where traders get emotional too and start to fail.

A correctly programmed trading robot behaves consistently in the market regardless of market conditions. It will never commit emotional trading mistakes and does only what it is programmed to do. It is not subject to miscalculations or guesswork. Thus, it is a much more reliable than most trading signal providers. An automated signal provider with at least 6 months of consistent profitability can surely capture the attention of traders, and even the interest of EA sceptical traders. As a signal provider, a trading robot will run your trading signals business on autopilot. This gives you the option to take some time off and will definitely remove some, if not all, of that tension, knowing that hundreds of traders are relying on you. You can get some extra sleep while your robot generates profitable signals on your followers' accounts. Smart subscribers know they can increase their edge by investing in both manual and automated signal providers.

Whether you are going to provide signals through manual trading or automated trading, show confidence in your service by giving your prospect subscribers a free trial period of at least a 30-days and/or a money-back guarantee.

6. Trading multiple pairs can often provide diversification.

While some pairs lose money on certain months, the other pairs may be profitable. That is how my trading robot, Vavatrade, often stays in profit, even when few pairs lose for 2 or 3 months in a row while eventually they give good profit.

Diversification is a very important aspect of forex trading that can potentially increase your chances of long term survival. Generally, every trading system has the possibility to reach drawdown periods during unfavorable market conditions. In the forex market, it is nearly impossible to predict future prices because markets are often driven by human emotion and unexpected events. That's why forex trading is very risky and not suitable for all investors. Without trading strategies, money management, and trading tactics, you could lose all your trading capital. Coming up with several trading tactics like portfolio diversification will minimize catastrophic losses.

Currency diversification between unrelated currency pairs is a key to a balanced portfolio. As a signal provider, trading at least four uncorrelated currency pairs makes for good diversification and can produce decent amounts of quality trade signals every month. Although you can trade as many currency pairs you want, it is also important to consider the correlation among currencies to avoid doubling your risks. There are certain currencies that move in tandem with each other. For instance, GBP/USD tends to mirror the price movements of EUR/USD, while USD/CHF moves exactly at the opposite direction of EUR/USD. The Yen pairs will often move at the same time and in similar ways (AUDJPY, EURJPY, GBPJPY, CADJPY, and other yen pairs, for example.

If you plan to offer several trading strategies as trading signals, your trade copier software must also be able to support multiple signal providers so that your signal subscribers can also diversify their trading portfolios by following several signal providers. Subscribers could profit from the combination of top trading strategies and reduce the risk of a single strategy. Of course, you should allow traders to undertake measures to limit their risk from each provider. In fact, true diversification is achieved through subscribing to various trading strategies. A portion of a subscriber's trading account can be allocated to copy the signals of a certain trading robot, while another portion of the capital can be allocated to copy certain manual trades. Having more than one trader to handle your subscriber's account may decrease some of the volatility within a trading portfolio.

7. People will question whether or not your monthly fee is worth paying.

If you charge too high a price then smaller traders will not be able to join. Explain how much they should putting in to invest to cover expenses and earn a profit. There really is no point if you are using $1000 to invest and the copier costs $100, while the monthly gain is 10% on average! You may as well put the money in the bank instead. Also, note that people will need to pay taxes on profits and some countries may charge their citizens 50% or more on such income. Your trade copier should be viable for people and their finances if you hope to have long term clients.

If your trading system can generate a profit every month, it's possible to charge your subscribers for a monthly subscription fee. The usual monthly subscription fee ranges from $25 - $100 - $200 per customer. Having just 100 subscribers could generate close to $10,000 monthly income.

Specify a monthly subscription fee that is based on the minimum deposit amount and the profitability of your trading system. It's important to require a minimum deposit amount according on your trading strategy and risk management methods. Make sure that subscription fees can be covered up by the profit you generate, and the subscriber can still earn more than his expenses.

You must also consider the forex trading taxation laws in other countries. Traders from these countries may be left with very little profits after your subscription fee and taxes are deducted from their trading profits. Countries like the United States of America impose taxes on forex trading profits, wherein U.S. traders who are trading with US brokerage firm are subjected to up to 60% of taxes on total trade incomes. Traders of a U.S. brokerage firm that are not U.S residents or citizens do not have to pay any taxes on foreign exchange profit. Some other brokers do not accept traders from U.S.A., Cuba, Nigeria, Lebanon, North Korea, Iran, Iraq, and Afghanistan because of forex trading taxation laws. These are not your responsibility as a signal provider, but it helps you to understand where your clients are coming from and what they have to deal with. And if you happen to be a US Citizen yourself and are going to offer signal services then you have much more to deal with to register and follow CFTC/government regulations.

8. Boast about your good client customer service.

Do you respond quickly when your customers or potential clients write to you for support or with questions? Do you respond quickly only before they are clients and then slowly once they join your service? Always do your best to respond quickly to inquiries and support issues if you want to have a business with a good reputation.

Customer service is paramount when it comes to dealing with potential and existing signal subscribers. Subscribers need your assistance and support at any given time. There must be several different ways to contact you including phone, email, live chat, and many other ways. If a subscriber runs into a problem with your signal service, the only thing they can do is to contact you in order to fix it. If you allot enough time for customer service, you could easily build a great business relationship with your subscribers.

Having a 24/7 customer service would be the best thing to do, if possible. You should be able to answer your subscriber's concern immediately no matter what time it is. However, a 24/7 customer support would be impossible if you are just alone running your business. A better approach is to add an email support for your subscribers to leave their messages. Be sure to check and reply all their messages by the time you are available. Subscribers have entrusted to you their money, so you need to give them the best possible customer service. Make them feel absolutely comfortable that all their needs will be addressed promptly. Another consideration is the ease of speaking with a live person rather than a time consuming, and often frustrating, auto attendant.

A great customer service is measured by your responsiveness, your ability to provide concisely answers to questions, and how you respect and treat your customers. Would-be subscribers may try to give you a quick call to gauge your responsiveness in answering their needs in a real situation. Be sure to always check the quality and efficiency of any service that your customer needs. If you outsource your support service, make sure that you are regularly testing it yourself to make sure it is serving people well.

9. People love free trials and sometimes even that is not enough to convince people to buy.

If you have less than 6 months of live results and trading history then it is a good idea to give a trial. I personally think it is always a good idea, and a good service to people, to offer free trials to your signals.

A free trial is a great marketing strategy for your signals service. Because trading signals are an intangible product, you need to give your customers a chance to see the real value of your signals service so they will be willing to subscribe to it. Giving customers a free trial of your service actually increases the chance that they will purchase it/subscribe to it in the future. You may offer free trials for a limited period or of a limited quantity of currency pairs and capitalize on the leads you get. By taking advantage of MyFxBook.com for some free marketing and exposure, you can give free trials from one of the currency pairs you trade at no cost. This strategy really works and it shows your confidence about the quality of your signals service.

A free trial makes an impression that your service can be trusted. It helps a potential subscriber learn the ins and outs of your service before making a final purchasing decision. It provides an opportunity for traders to compare your service with that of others. Most traders utilize free trading signals to get the most out of them which will create a routine in their trading activities and eventually make your service a necessity for them. Traders are more likely to subscribe once they have a good idea of where they will spend their money. If you are able to grow their trading account, or if they have developed a taste or preference for your signal service, they will surely subscribe month after month. Through offering free signals for trial, loyal repeat subscribers can be gained.

In addition to cutting down on refund request, giving potential subscribers a free trial period will cut down on your customer service calls. If subscribers have already more than 30 days of free trial with your signals and they subscribe to the paid signals, it means they are comfortable with the service. Free trials eliminate the stressful consequence of customers calling up with tons of questions. Don't think about your free signals as a free giveaway and wasted revenue, but rather think about it as an investment in your future revenue that will bring and keep more customers.

---

10. An important part of your trade signals business is what platform you are using to deliver your signals.

It also matters how well and how fast the trades are being copied.

Trading platform, market condition, and copier speed may adversely affect trade executions. Compared to other platforms, MT4 is the most popular, advanced and easily accessible trading platform. Some brokers offer completely web based platforms, and while these may seem convenient and simple, it will likely not be compatible with a trade copier software. Supported trading platforms become extremely important when you use an Expert Advisor to generate trading signals since most EAs are programmed using MetaQuotes Language and are only supported by MetaTrader platforms.

Every trade copier software on the market claims an almost zero delay in executing trades between the master account and slave accounts (subscriber's account). Most of the available copiers have an average copy speed of 400 milliseconds. However, the broker server delay is usually about 1 second and could be even more. To avoid too much delay, be sure that your trade copier software and your broker server must copy trades as quickly as possible. In other words, the trade copier software is not the only part of the system responsible for the speed of execution.

The trade copier software may also experience problems in copying trades between different brokers. Sometimes the difference in broker spreads and execution time alone is enough to put your trade copying software in trouble. No two traders from different brokers will have 100% identical entry and exit points due to varying broker spreads and speeds of execution. Thus, Subscribers should be advised to subscribe to the free trial first to see if trades are copied with minimal delays, and only after solid testing that a subscriber can proceed to a paid subscription. In my opinion it does not matter if there is a differ-ence in open price by 2 or so pips when you aim for 100 pips profit per trade for example. For trades with take profit levels of 5 pips, it is obviously that there will be bad results when having different entry prices.

---

11. People are concerned with how many trades might be open at any one time.

Most will expect no more than 1-3 trades per day. Again it depends on trading style. Scalpers may find it not enough to have only 3 trades a day, though scalping is not the best style for a signals business anyway. A manual trader with less than 5 trades max per day is good.

Traders are likely to subscribe to a signals service that pro-vides an average of 1 – 3 profitable trades per week. The num-ber of trades per day or week depends on the strategy, as every trader has a different trading approach. A pure scalper can make a number of trades in a day, from 5 to 10 or even more. Automatic and instant execution of trade orders between sub-scriber platforms is crucial with a scalping strategy. That is why it is not the best trading style and not recommended for a sig-nals service business where simple broker spread differences can mean the difference between winning and losing trades.

Day traders may make 1 to 5 manual trades in a day. This depends on trading strategy and average hold time. Trade vol-ume is dependent on the markets that the trader is monitoring. In contrast to a day trader, a swing trader doesn't place trades daily. Generally the trader places trades every few days or up to 2 - 3 weeks. Most trade copiers or subscribers choose to have at least 10 profitable trades in a month to compensate for the subscription fee, but really this is more due to account size and overall return than anything. Thus, a swing trading strategy may not the best strategy in this business. But in the end, a profitable strategy is a profitable strategy and that is what you want in your business.

12. Make sure that you, as a trader, walk the talk!

If you say max drawdown is 15%, make sure it is 15%. Some traders may just average their losses and are not willing to cut a loss. Rather they hold onto the trade and hope, sometimes even carrying losing positions for months at a time! Good traders cut losses. You will be on the right track even if you have less winning trades but the losing trades follow very strict SL and your winners are often rockets. If customers see that your statements do not match the MyFXBook reports they will be suspicious and look elsewhere. Some providers will mask their open trades on myfxbook.com because they are embarrassed by the large losing equity position they are holding. Be transparent with your reporting at all times and you will gain favor and trust with people.

As a trader, stick to your trading rules and never deviate from it since all your subscribers are depending on it. Follow a complete trading strategy with defined stop loss and take profit level. Always stick with the rule "Cut your losses short and let your profits run". Any statements you have in your website or on a third party website must be accurate and true.

Keeping your statements builds trust and client loyalty. Clients evaluate your service based on how you walk the talk. Satisfied clients pass positive feedback about your signals service along to other traders, who may then try to subscribe to your signals. Reliability of your service is one of the keys to your success so make sure you give accurate statements to your subscribers. If the expectations aren't aligned with your ability to provide them, your business will suffer.

13. Risk and money management are of utmost importance.

For example, the one I use on Vavatrade, at the moment of writing this book, is not the best money management style. I use fixed lots and variable stops with a fixed take profit level. This makes every trade risk different amounts of money/percentage. Not all traders love this but it works for me for now. I am looking to improve this as my money management style does not square up with many prospects. So my point with this is that you should not repeat this mistake.

Money management is the most important skill you should have. It's the core ingredient of trading success. Failure to fully understand the implications of money management as well as actually implementing money management techniques in your trading signals service is a recipe for disaster. Money/risk management allows you to deal with your performance downturns and preserve your trading capital.

You may have the best trading strategy in world but it will still fail without proper money management. Even if you are generating trade signals through a demo account, you should strictly follow a sound money management plan to avoid large drawdowns. Cut your losses by setting stop loss at a certain level as you initiate your trade. It should reasonably limit your risk on the trade and make good sense with regards to market swing points. Once your stop loss is set, stick with it. Just let the market prove you're either right or wrong with your analysis. Moving your stop loss farther and farther out will only ruin your trading account, as well as your business in the end. People do not like to see stop loss levels moved further away, although it is a good idea to move the stop loss closer to the open price if that is a part of your strategy and the market has moved accordingly.

While risking only a less than 2% on every trade you take, the lot size should adjust to meet your predetermined risk amount and stop loss distance. This means that lot sizes are variable depending on the distance of stop loss price from the entry price. Tight stop losses will have larger lot size while wide stop loss will have a smaller lot size. For example, your risk amount is $100 and you have a stop loss distance of 50 pips, then you need to trade 2 mini-lots. One mini-lot is usually about $1 per pip. So 2 mini-lots is $2 per pip, multiplied by 50 pips stop loss distance, is equivalent to $100 risked.

The most important point is to never adjust your stop loss to meet your desired position size. Instead, adjust your position size to meet your predefined and logical stop loss distance.

It is also important to understand the correlations between currency pairs. For instance, EUR/USD is inversely correlated to USD/CHF. If you go long on EUR/USD and short on USD/CHF, you are doubling your risk on USD since your trade is equivalent to two short orders on USD.

14. Make sure your risk is less than returns.

I failed with this and it has lost me a lot of clients. Drawdowns will depend on the strategy employed. If its swing trading, it's unavoidable sometimes to hit 20-30% max DD before the swing moves in favor. However, if on a scalper with mere few pips take profit but with a drawdown of more than 25-40%, it is not a good thing. For instance, if its swing trading, tanking 400-500 pips in red, but then swings back with 200-400 or more pips, its fine. You can also use partial position closes at every 50-100 pips to lock in some profits.

The most essential aspect of money management is that risk must be less than returns. In other words, maximize your rewards and minimize your risk on any given trade. This is the basic building block of becoming a consistently profitable trader. The more consistent you are in trading, the more clients will subscribe to your business/signals.

Risk reward doesn't only mean calculating the risk and re-ward of a trade. It means that by achieving a reward of 2 to 3 times or more of your risked amount, you can make you money and your subscribers too. When you combine your trading strategy with a consistent risk reward of 1:2 or larger, you can still make money over a series of trades even if you lose most of the trades.

15. If your equity curve is too smooth then it might appear too good to be true.

Novice traders may fall for this, but more experienced investors will avoid it for sure. For me it indicates two things: a martingale or grid style trading system or that the trader is unable to accept a losing day. Sometimes its better just to turn off the screen, cut the losses, accept it and go plant flowers in the garden and wait for another chance in the market. Sure, it requires very good mental skills. But systems that "hold and hope" will end up in the same way sooner or later. For me, this is a very risky approach for long-term trading.

Your trading system's equity curve mirrors how much money your strategy is making. It has ups and downs, and hopefully your equity curve has more ups than downs. The goal for your signals service is to create a smooth equity curve which gradually increases from left to right. A natural tendency among traders who are looking for a signals service is to avoid an ugly equity curve. Thus, you should be consistent and disciplined in following your trading system to maintain how your equity curve grows. Again though, there is no such thing as perfection so just always do your best and if you are profitable at the end of the year then you are profitable at the end of the year!

Some signal providers use a martingale trading system to trap novice traders into seeing a smooth equity curve. A martingale system can be detected through the equity curve since it has a very smooth slope but with many saw tooth-like dents underneath. Martingale or d'Alembert system may seem to be in high favour with some traders but eventually it will blow out your account. Through the system, your equity curve increases for sure because you would double your contracts when the equity curve shows a decline. In theory, you will not lose because you will eventually win and get back your money in a single winning trade. However, you need unlimited funds to survive doubling the losses. Practically speaking, not all traders have unlimited funds to copy your trade signals with such a system.

A nice equity curve can be achieved not through martingale type of system but by cutting losses short. As a trader, you should accept losing trades. You're not going to win on every trade every day. It's better to cut your losses and patiently wait for the next profitable trade signal. Holding a losing position and hoping it will go in your favor will only end up in a larger loss.

---

16. A too-high, unrealistic winning ratio is another factor that will make your prospects run away.

Anything over 80% just looks too unrealistic.

Never try to appeal to everyone's desire to win by advertising that your trading system has an 80% or higher winning ratio. If you use a high winning percentage as a sales pitch to advertise your product, you may appear that you know very little about what it truly takes to be a successful and profitable trader.

Even though you have that winning percentage, the truth is that high winning percentages has nothing to do with being a profitable trader. In reality, even a strategy with a 90% win rate can still lose money. Most often, amateur traders go bankrupt by taking larger loses and smaller profits. These traders take losses that are too large relative to their winning trades. A winning percentage doesn't mean that you are a successful trader. It's not how often you win, but how much you win when you win that counts.

To illustrate further, imagine that you take 10 trades in a month with a 90% win rate. Nine trades are profitable for $1 per winning trade. Thus, you have made $9 in profit. Out of 10 trades, you have only 1 losing trade (10% losing rate) in which you lose $10 on that one losing trade. Among your 10 trades, you have lost $1 with your 90% winning ratio. This illustrates that winning percentage is irrelevant in trading success when not measured against risk/reward.

In reality, some professional traders are not winning more than 50% of the time. However, because they apply efficient money management and risk reward, they still make a shocking amount of money in the markets. As Bill Lipschutz stated from the New Market Wizzards, "I don't think you can consistently be a winning trader if you're banking on being right more than 50 percent of the time. You have to figure out how to make money being right only 20 to 30 percent of the time".

17 Avoid REMOVING STOP LOSS/Change SL and DO NOT EVER TRADE WITHOUT A STOP LOSS!

However, some copiers do have hidden stop loss levels to prevent broker stop-loss hunting, and this is okay so long as your customers know what you are doing. There is an inherent danger, however, in the event that a connection is broken between the copier accounts and a hard stop loss has not been entered on the client's end. This could possibly lead to large losses should the worst happen. Believe me, people do not like trading strategies that have no stop loss, because this basically means there is no limit how much money is risked on that position.

The success of your signals service business as well as your success as a trader depends upon your ability to consistently make decisions that are completely based on logical reasons and uninfluenced by emotion. When interacting with the market, most traders like you and I, are influenced by how we feel.

Since the market goes up and down, in favor of you or against you, you should always be defensive by placing stop loss and target profits based on your trading strategy and market structure. Your greatest battle once you enter a trade is not to allow yourself to be influenced by market movement. Even if you risk a very tiny portion of your account, trade with the least micro-lot position size available and manage your risk extremely, if you sit in front of your screen and watch your open position play out, your emotions will begin to cloud up your judgment and may lead you to make stupid decisions such as removing the stop loss or changing the stop loss based on emotional reasons.

Sometimes, you're not aware that you are being controlled by greed. You still keep your profitable trade open and thinking about the profit you have made and how much more you can make by keeping the trade open without securing any of the profit and moving your profit target further away as the price approaches it. As a result, the market will often revert back and you'll be forced to take much smaller profit than the original profit target or no profit at all.

---

18. If you are a trader who is delivering trading signals by email only, you better have myfxbook.com live results to back up your stated results.

If not, is a waste of time for almost everyone who lands on your page. There is little to NO point in using an Excel sheet and telling everyone how good you are because anyone can create an Excel sheet with made-up numbers!

There are numerous ways that you can use to sell your trade signals. You can send trade signals for the subscriber to place the trade themselves through SMS, email, online alerts, phone, or you can do it in a more automated method by sending electronic signals straight into the subscriber's MT4 account.

Sending trade signals through email and SMS is very inconvenient since the subscriber must have access to his MT4 platform every time you send a signal. He needs to be always online to be able to receive the notification immediately and manually places the trade quickly. If you choose to use the old method, be sure to have a MyFXBook live account to back up your performance claims. Of course, this is the best practice when delivering trading signals by trade copier software as well, but in this case, usually you already have an MT4 account with a trading history to show to your customers.

A completely automated signals service is what traders are looking for these days. They want a fully automated system that can work with as little human intervention as possible, and make them money on autopilot. The more you offer this solution to your clients, the better your business will do.

19. Give the most attractive strategy to subscribers.

I know it's a hard thing to do, but you should do your best to fall into this category if you want to make your business a high success. Nick McDonald from SimpleTrader.net gives good advice on what people are attracted to. It is to have 5-10 trades per week, fixed stop levels, primarily trade the majors (EURUSD, GPBUSD, USDJPY, and AUDUSD), and have profit targets of 10-30 pips and risk/reward of at least 1:1. Follow at least a few of these notes and you will sure be on the successful side.

If you are a trader yourself with a profitable trading method, then generating trade signals would be easy. It is good for a signals service business to trade only the most liquid forex pairs, primarily the EUR/USD, GPB/USD, USD/JPY, and AUD/USD. You can always trade other pairs when lucrative opportunities present themselves. Trading the majors helps lessen the risk of large whiplash during market swings and increased spread during volatility.

Your trading strategy must have a high probability for success. It must be able to identify the most likely movements in a particular pair through technical indicators along with other variables such as the relationship between price in the recent past and the current price. Remember that capital preservation and risk management are paramount to your strategy. Thus, risk must be extremely well calculated. Most importantly, the drawdown must be managed and controlled effectively. Of course, losses are expected, and are part of any trading strategy. They cannot be avoided but you can employ a hedging technique when needed because it has an ability to cut down losses.

20. When every month is a winner it will look suspicious for some.

Sure this might be a great start for every system and business, but admit that it is not possible to stay profitable each month for 1, 2 or more years. If you are truly profitable for 2+ years in a row every month, be sure to give more proof than just MyFXBook and make sure the record happens on a reputable forex broker.

Being consistently profitable every single month without fail for two years is surely impossible. The market produces variable numbers of trades every month, and your risk reward on every trade is always a random outcome. You can't force the market to make up losing trades at the end of the month because trading is solely a game of probabilities and capital management. Professional traders concentrate on the risk reward ratio of each trade, and not on unrealistic monthly returns and always needing to win every trade.

It's a good practice to track your monthly profitability, however, keep it as a separate thing from your trading. Once you start worrying about a losing month or not reaching your monthly profit target, you are not looking for the best market opportunities to trade; instead you are forcing yourself to take less profitable and higher-risk trade setups. It's better to eliminate monthly expectations and focus on trading the price movements or sticking with the rules of your robot.

To be able to maintain a consistently profitable month without fail, you need to have a trading edge. Monthly profitability depends on strategy, how much you are willing to risk, and most importantly whether you can constantly make and keep pips. If you can do this, you will have many happy and satisfied clients for years to come.

Following all of these rules won't guarantee you success, but it will sure make you 20 steps closer to being spotted by bigger investors, as well as more currency traders and forex brokers who might want to bring you on to help manage their money. The income potential of this kind of business is truly staggering and into the millions of dollars for those who do it right.

Chapter 8 Takeaways

Chapter 8: 10 Tips and Tricks for Forex Trading Signal Providers

Avoid anything on your site that will make it look spammy.

Post your trading history on MyFXBook.com.

Make things personal.

Don't confuse people, explain to them.

- How many trades you open at one time?
- How many pairs you trade?
- What is your maximum draw down record?
- How many years you've been trading and how long you have been turning a profit?
- Your monthly profit percentage for the past 12 months.
- Whether you use hedging techniques.
- Whether your system is NFA compatible or not.

Set and manage their expectations.

- Make sure that you explain how you will deliver signals to followers.

Advertising, don't bother.

- Never put Google AdSense or any other form of advertisement on your signals site

Look professional from the start.

Show confidence in your services.

- Offer a trial period for free, or perhaps a nominal fee of $1
- Customers who have used a trial period at first are much less likely to cancel their subscription

Be realistic.

Use bells and whistles sparingly.

Customers will expect that you will trade signals on a real account, but even with a demo it's possible to run this business too.

People will want as low of drawdowns as possible.

- Investors will want to know the Monthly return that you have achieved in the past, and more importantly what you expect the monthly return to be in the future.

- Your MyFXBook trading history should be at least a few months long before you can gain interest from more experienced traders.
- People will question your trading methods.
- Trading multiple pairs can often provide diversification.
- People will question whether or not your monthly fee is worth paying.
- Boast about your good client customer service.
- People love free trials and sometimes even that is not enough to convince people to buy.
- An important part of your trade signals business is what platform you are using to deliver your signals.
- People are concerned with how many trades might be open at any one time.
- Make sure that you, as a trader, walk the talk! If you say max drawdown is 15%, make sure it is 15%.
- Risk and money management are of utmost importance.
- Make sure your risk is less than returns.
- If your equity curve is too smooth then it might appear too good to be true.
- A too-high, unrealistic winning ratio is another factor that will make your prospects run away.
- Avoid REMOVING STOP LOSS/Change SL and DO NOT EVER TRADE WITHOUT A STOP LOSS!
- If you are a trader who is delivering trading signals by email only, you better have myfxbook.com live results to back up your stated results.
- Give the most attractive strategy to subscribers.
- When every month is a winner it will look suspicious for some.

Build a Customer Base with Free Forex Signals

"There is no such thing as a stupid question--only arrogant and angry people who get mad answering them."

- Rimantas Petrauskas

In the previous chapters I wrote about how and where to get Forex trading signals and a signal copying software. I also gave you some tips on picking a good domain name and building a website.

Now it's time to start the work of building a customer base. Before you invest any more money into your business venture, you must make sure that there are people out there who are eager to buy your products and services, or at least willing to give them a try.

The free trading signals might be delivered by special software directly to a customer's MT4 account or the delivery may take place by using older methods like email and SMS messages. Consider Push Notifications, they are widely popular nowadays among smartphone users. Or maybe you want to expose some of your signals on the huge trading signal networks. Choose a delivery method that you think will suit your customers best.

How do free trading signals benefit your customers and your business?

Offering free signals is a good way for your potential customers to try and test out the signals. This step is a way to increase awareness about your business and products. Make sure that potential clients leave their email addresses with you before they can receive the free signals.

You can use the free signals as a way to build your email contacts list. In the future, whenever you create a new product or a service, you can use these email addresses to market the new offering to an already receptive customer base.

Make sure that the signals are reaching your customers in a timely fashion. You also need to test and find out if the signals are replicated correctly to their trading accounts.

People who leave their contact details with you will likely want to continue the communication further. They are your targeted, prospective customers and they are already half sold on your service. Now all you need to do is follow up with them.

A successful sales cycle requires you to be proactive and take the lead in maintaining a regular contact with clients. You must come up with feasible solutions to their Forex trading problems.

If you teach someone to do the stuff they are interested in, and you do this for free, you have a good chance to get a customer.

When customers receive the free signals, they can apply them to their trading accounts. They can also choose to just try them out on a demo account. Demos will mostly be used by beginners, new to the market, who are just starting to learn how to trade. Free signals do not require any financial investment and they are completely non-obligatory on the customer's part.

In addition, by going through the process, beginners can learn about concepts, forex terminologies, software, trading platform and trading strategies. For example, it could help them differentiate between a "stop loss" and a "take profit" market order. They will learn how to operate MT4 platform and more.

For an experienced Forex trader, free trading signals will mean the chance to evaluate your business. A chance to see when, how, and what trades are placed on customers' accounts. Some may follow free signals for only few weeks just to get confidence that it works as you described, and promised it will, while others may follow free signals for months before they are comfortable enough to follow your full signals package on their live account.

And even when people switch from free signals to paid signals, they will definitely still want a trial period. That is to try if your paid signals, which will usually be generated on multiple pairs, are performing the same way they were used to with the free service.

Free Forex Signals on 3rd party websites

One of the best ways to lure trading enthusiasts is to offer free trading signals. Now, giving away all that you have may be a bad idea, but giving away only some of the trading signals may become a good teaser and introduction to your service. This method works if you start an independent trading signals service, have your own website, deliver signals to customers using a special software and charge customers monthly. If you are providing signals on myfxbook.com or ZuluTrade, then providing free signals is not an option. In this case, they are "already free" from the customer's point of view. In fact, those two websites are good places to give your signals for free.

You could offer as much as 20 percent of your Forex signals free of charge to prospective customers. What I mean to say is that, if you trade five currency pairs in total, for example, then give away signals from one of those pairs.

Here's a simple model you can use to do this. You start with your signals service website where you sell signals for a monthly fee. For the people that want to try your service, you give them a free trial period of at least 30 days. Now on Zulu-Trade or myfxbook.com you can give signals from one of the pairs you trade at no cost. This is not something you need to advertise on your website, but the goal of this is that you can add your website address in the description of your trading strategy on ZuluTrade and MyFXBook or even the MT5 marketplace.

So this functions as an advertisement for you and gives you more exposure to the people interested in trading signals. At first you won't get spotted on those giant websites, but once you build your trading record over several months, this technique will payoff for sure. People will notice your system if it's making profits and will connect their accounts to try your signals. Once they get interested in your system, they will see your website address, get to know your service, subscribe for a trial and then become your long time customers.

A wise move here would be to use your website address as a username on those websites. This will give you even more exposure and people may even check your website once they see you on the list of providers. Imagine your website address listed among thousands of others. People look through that list very often in search of something to follow. Once they spot a trading performance graph that goes up and there is a username that says your-website-address.com, most of people will visit the in a new browser window.

It is important to note that many trading signal networks will not allow you to use a domain name as a username, but you should be okay to use your brand name. Be creative, read the guidelines of the website you are submitting your signals to, and try to use all the available benefits.

Your trading system description should use all of the available space and include a link to your main website, if that is allowed. Otherwise, maybe you can post a comment under your system which will have a link to your site. This will likely not break any rules, as the link is actually not in the description field.

Free content in exchange for email address

One of the most effective practices in online marketing at the moment is to give away high value content for free in exchange for a person's name and an email address. Later on, you will use the prospects that you get in this step to sell them your products or services. Thus, the content you give out should be relevant to the services you offer.

Maybe a small eBook about forex or a free course on the topic of trading signals? No point in trying to sell signals or a managed account to prospects gained by publishing a book on gardening. So you could write a 20-50 page eBook and give it away for free. This is how you get emails of people interested in Forex on your mailing list. Later you can reach them anytime and send them your trading results for the past month. It can be a good teaser and you will remind your prospects about the service you are running.

You can also offer a case study with examples of how your customers made profit by following your trading signals. The content should be well written and contain charts illustrating monthly income in terms of percentage or pips. Additionally, you could add a chart that shows the monthly income in terms of US dollars. But be careful with this one because U.S. laws do not allow websites to show such information to prospects about the exact amounts of money you or any other customer have made. It is obvious that no one will make the exact same amount of money because of different price feeds, spreads, delays, slippage and many other factors that will occur in any type of copy trading, especially between different brokers, but regardless, you cannot post any income claims or testimonials that tell about people making specific amounts of money.

I recommend telling the story about how it was done. Go into the specifics, talk about how easy or how hard it was to accomplish. People love reading personal success stories.

At the end of the document offer a monthly subscription to your trading signals service. Or better yet, hold off on selling anything at this point. Just mention your name or a website address and people will come looking for you if they are interested. The bonus of doing "soft sales" like these is that the customer doesn't feel the pressure of a salesperson pushing a product on them.

Put a lot of effort into creating this example write-up. The content quality should be on par with the quality of your trading signals service. Make sure that the free content doesn't look like advertising. People are not stupid. They will run away the second they see that you're trying to sell them something. That's why it's more effective to use stories as a selling method instead of listing the long line of features a product has.

An example story for a case study with an indirect sale would be: "Customer X decided to open an account with the minimum required amount of $5,000. X was excited to see 10 currency pairs being traded automatically with no human input. There was no need to install any software, Vavatrade signal service hosted his MetaTrader 4 platform on their server and he didn't even need to learn how to operate it, all he had to do was submit his login credentials in the website's member area".

Here is the same example as direct sale, a bad practice these days: "Subscribe to www.vavatrade.com forex trading signals and earn money. The minimum required amount to open an account is $5,000. We deliver signals on 10 currency pairs. As an added bonus, we can host your MT4 platform on our server for free".

Can you feel the pressure? I lost interest after reading the first word "Subscribe". People feel the sale coming. Most of us will skip a paragraph that is trying to sell us something. A lot will simply stop reading what you have to say altogether.

Using the indirect sale technique is a lot more effective. If you are not yet convinced, try both. Test them out and see which one converts better.

If you have an impressive case study of a customer that made a lot of profit by using your services, advertise it on social networks like Facebook, Twitter and StumbleUpon. You can also try Google AdWords. In the marketing for your case study, make sure to include a free trial offer for your service. If you did a good job soft selling, people will give your signals a try. This will be your chance to prove that your signals will make them money.

Offer a trial period

You should always offer a trial period for your service. When I first started doing this my customer base grew by 400%. This was just from my own mailing list. I offer a trial period for 1 EUR and it lasts for 30 days. After that customers are charged the full amount for the next month if they want to continue using my signals.

You can offer a free trial, but let me explain why it's better to charge a small amount like $1. When you give away a free trial you can't be sure if customer gives you his primary email address or if they have a valid credit card at all.

When you offer a $1 trial through a PayPal subscription, or some other reliable payment processor, you are sure that the customer at least has a working PayPal account, possibly tied with a credit card. Charging this small symbolic amount will keep out a lot of the people who weren't really serious about your offer in the first place. This filtering process will leave you with higher quality subscribers. You will experience less cancellations and refund requests later down the line from these customers.

Another great practice is to get in touch with your customers all the time, especially during their trial periods. People often subscribe to a trial period thinking that this is something they can try, but maybe they already have too much on their plate and will forget to use your system. Or maybe they do not have enough time for testing your system. Even the simplest objections may stop them from using your system.

That is why you may want to contact them by email twice a week or so and ask if everything is clear or see if they need help. Keep in touch with them, send the latest news about your trading and help show them that there is a real person on the other end of your website.

Work hard for your customers. If anything is unclear to your customers, do your best to help them. Make them feel important, make them truly important. I often get emails from customers that begin with a statement like this "sorry, this might be a stupid question to ask, but...". Now how in the world can the question be stupid? It may seem stupid for you because you learned the answer many years ago, and it's something you have been doing for the last 10 years. But for someone who just came into the Forex world two weeks ago, it might be a huge puzzle. So be sure to answer every question like it is the most important thing you have to do, and you will notice how people will compliment your support service and want to stay with you for years to come.

It's sad, but true, that many services fail to communicate with their customers and that becomes one of the first reasons why their customers quit.

Give away signals on the MT5 marketplace

If you trade multiple currency pairs, you can give away the signals from one pair on the MT5 marketplace. This will get you noticed by prospective customers, people who are already highly interested in trading signals. If they like your trading record they may give the 30-day trial offer a go. Next thing you know, you have a new subscriber.

Make sure you don't give away too much free stuff. People may not take you or your business seriously if you do this. Personally I've never made money by following free signals. The subscribers to your free trading signals might be not serious either. Well, I was not serious either when I followed someone's free trading signals for a few weeks, and later I just forget about them, as I had other work to do.

Keep your customers up to date about the profit or loss made during the last month. Do this at least one or two times a month. It's important not to be afraid of losses, openly share this info with everyone who is interested in your service.

Letting the customers know that there will be some losing months beforehand will save you a lot of grief later on. Showing a past trading record that has both losing and winning trades is something that not many traders do, but doing this would give your credibility a boost.

The MT5 marketplace shows the list of available signal providers directly on the MT4 or MT5 platforms, so it is extremely easy for clients to spot them and follow different providers. It is truly one of the easiest ways to go public. It is one place where everyone is looking for the service you are providing.

Beta testers are potential customers

Invite software beta testers and let them use your service for free for 6 months or so. You won't get any money from this bunch, but they will give you something that is much more important than money. After a few weeks of using your software ask the Beta testers for an honest testimonial.

Here are some example questions of what a good testimonial should include:

- Was it easy to start using the product? How did the installation process go?
- What obstacle would prevent you from buying this software?
- What happened as a result of you buying this product?
- What specific feature did you like the most and why?
- Can you list three benefits that this product offers?
- Would you recommend this software to your friends? If so, why?
- Is there anything you would like to add?

Don't simply ask for a testimonial without providing the testers with guidance about what areas you need their input on. If you do this, most of them will just write a few sentences about how the product is awesome. This won't help your future customers make a decision about buying the software.

A testimonial that talks about a specific problem a subscriber had and how using the product helped to solve it is much better than a "satisfaction testimonial".

On the other hand, if a testimonial mentions money, and specifically, the profit amount made, the U.S. laws may get you in trouble. It is obvious to you and I that if one of your customers says they have made $1554.56, no other customer will make the same amount of money. This is because of different spreads, price feeds and account types among different brokers and customers. There are a lot of factors that will stand in the way of making the same exact amount of money. Ideally, it will be close, but it will never be exactly the same.

An important thing to note is that the testimonials shouldn't say how much money other people made with your service. This may fool prospective customers into thinking that they will achieve the same results. This is a wrong practice. You shouldn't give out guarantees or claims like these to anybody, directly or through testimonials. For example, an investor made a $10,000 profit on a $100,000 account in one month. Other subscribers won't be able to replicate those monetary gains with a small $1,000 account.

After a few more weeks of Beta testing you should also ask the following questions:

- What was the most confusing part about using this software?
- Name a feature or an option that you feel is missing in this product.
- What would you change about this product?
- Have you encountered any issues while testing the software?

The things you will learn from these answers will be priceless. They will help make your service much better and put it light years ahead of the competition.

You can use the answers to these questions in your blog posts. People love to read detailed testimonials especially if they're interested in purchasing a product. As an added benefit, the new content may lead to improved search engine rankings for your blog.

After two or three months ask your testers if their accounts turned a profit by following your trading signals. If they did, use this information to create a case study. I would offer another 6 months for free if they agree to have their trading account info, real name and photo published in the case study.

An example testimonial that contains a real person's name with a photograph and a detailed trading record can have a powerful impact on prospective customers. Make sure that everything is genuine, use great care while making the case study and most important of all, be honest.

ForexPeaceArmy.com Reviews

Ask beta testers and customers to post a review on Forex-PeaceArmy.com. This is very reputable website and they have a good system in place to filter out fake reviews. It is close to impossible to post a review for yourself or slander a competitor with a fake review.

I'm not exactly sure how they filter out the fake reviews, but I have proven for myself that their system is very effective. I asked a friend of mine to post a review on the FPA website. He lives in another country and posted the review from his home. Still, the website somehow found out that the review was fake and didn't publish it.

Another time I tried to post a review for myself. I used a completely new VPS server located in another country but my post was also filtered out. You can try different IP addresses, you can delete cookies or even clear your entire browsing history. It will not do any good. Don't try to do this yourself or you risk getting on FPA's list of dishonest websites.

It is truly difficult to get your customers posting reviews about your service. Here is my trading signals website review page on Forex Peace Army.

http://www.forexpeacearmy.com/public/review/www.vav-atrade.com

I know everyone would say that a few dozen of reviews are no big deal, but once you will try to get reviews for your site you will understand how hard it may be to get them.

Chapter 9 Takeaways

Chapter 9: Build a Customer Base with Free Forex Signals

- Free signals do not require any financial investment
- Completely non-obligatory on the customer's part

Benefits from offering free signals

- Offering free signals is a good way for your potential customers to try and test out the signals
- Increase awareness about your business and products
- A way to build your email contacts list
- A way to find out if the signals are replicated correctly to their trading accounts

Free Forex Signals on 3rd party websites

- Giving away only some of the trading signals on 3rd party websites is a good teaser and introduction to your service
- Give away some free signals at any social trading network websites like ZuluTrade and link your username on those sites to your own website

Free content in exchange for email address

- One of the most effective practices in online marketing
- use the prospects that you get to sell your products or services
- the content you give out should be relevant to the services you offer

Offer a trial period for a free or a nominal fee of 1 USD

- If you give away a free trial, you can't be sure if customer gives you his primary email address or if they have a valid credit card

- By offering a $1 trial through PayPal or any reliable payment processor, you are sure that the customer has at least a working PayPal account, possibly tied with a credit card
- Get in touch with your customers all the time, not only during their trial periods but after they had subscribe

Give away signals on the MT5 marketplace

- Give away the signals from one pair on the MT5 marketplace
- Don't give away too much free stuff

Beta testers are potential customers

- Invite software beta testers and let them use your service for free for 6 months or so and ask honest testimonials
- A testimonial that talks about a specific problem a subscriber had and how using the product helped to solve it is much better than a "satisfaction testimonial"
- Testimonials shouldn't say how much money other people made with your service
- A testimonial that contains a real person's name with a photograph and a detailed trading record can have a powerful impact on prospective customers

ForexPeaceArmy.com Reviews

- This is very reputable website and they have a good system in place to filter out fake reviews
- It is close to impossible to post a review for yourself or slander a competitor with a fake review

CHAPTER 10

Interview with the Trading Signal Provider

Aforex.com is one of my customers who use Remote Trade Copier to deliver trading signals to their customers. I interviewed Ben Lewis, the founder of this company and forexsignal.com, and let me share this with you.

Ben and his team were the first ones in the industry to start sending Forex signals, so you can be sure they have tons of expertise in this field. Below are several questions answered personally by Ben for my book.

Q: How did you get started in this field, and what do you think has made you successful throughout your career?

A: I was always fascinated by the dynamics and the possibilities of the stock market as early on as the late 1980's and invested in a partnership with a friend who was an active stock broker. I loved the excitement of the chase and what the markets could provide in terms of rewards for accurate decision making. A little later I was introduced to the Futures markets where you could participate using leverage and of course the decision to go "Long" or "Short" was now equally available. With stocks I would always have positions taken Long and now Futures provided the opportunity to go either direction, this really caught my attention.

In 1998 I discovered Forex - the markets traded globally and 24 hours a day, add to it the huge liquidity of at least 10 times greater volume the NYSE just knocked me over. Here we had a CURRENCY Spot market which traded all day with staggering liquidity and no expiration date. I was sold - the internet and computers had now brought this all together and we no longer needed to call the broker but could make trades directly on a Trading platform on our personal computer – this fired me up and my PERSONAL Forex journey had now begun.

Educating myself and gaining a full understating as to what moves these markets and most importantly learning to come to grips with the reality that losses are an integral part of trading. Once learning to accept this fact – this was the turning point in my trading career – acceptance of losses and acceptance of knowing one can't win every trade and losses are just another part of the journey. The understanding that as long as the gains at the end of the day are even slightly greater than the losses - that in itself constituted success. That same year 1998 I started a Forex training school in California and within 2 years had several locations in Canada, Australia and South Africa.

Q: What are some ways that other people you know have gotten started in this field?

A: I know people from all walks of life that have entered the field and attended my Forex education program. A few to mention were a Dentists, Kidney Specialist, Security guard, retired stock broker, salesman and others from many walks of life.

Q: What are the pros and cons of working in this field?

A: The biggest Pro for being in the field for me is being able to do what I love for a living – and the benefit of having my business at the end of my fingertips as long as I have access to the Internet I can work from anywhere in the world or even sitting on the beach. How do you beat that? The disadvantage of this business is dealing with a losing run which happens from time to time - fortunately that happens less often than winning trades win streak.

Q: I know you do not post any proof of your trading results in terms of money or percentage. Can you comment on this?

A: As there are no 100% identical experiences between Forex users due to different broker spreads and speed of execution we have opted to show our results as Pips earned rather than dollars made. Because no two traders experience 100% identical Entry and Exit point results, this is deemed as Hypothetical by the USA regulators therefore CFTC RULE 4.41 – HYPOTHETICAL OR SIMULATED PERFORMANCE RESULTS HAVE CERTAIN LIMITATIONS is adhered to in our decision making.

This has not been a negative in any way as most Forex traders with experience understand that results will vary between traders and any claims of earning the exact same dollar amount is unrealistic. However, because past performance is no guarantee of future results - the Pips shown earned from past trades provides a very realistic picture of past performance. The savvy Forex trader / investor usually does their due diligence and analyses or refers to a set of charts and compares the dates and entry point shown on the results page and can clearly see what has transpired.

At this stage they are now only interested in what is going to happen going forward and is first and foremost on a new followers mind. New clients are encouraged to test us out on a demo platform or to trade with a low risk leverage to try us out and compare what we show as our results to their own experience following our signals. This decision has added to our credibility, as our targeted client base are traders/investors looking to the long term and we don't want to in any way portray any unrealistic expectations of gain. Due to the risky nature of Forex we have opted and prefer to guide our business model towards clients who understand what is involved in Forex trading and it is our high quality of service as well that we offer to subscribers. Our 16 years of being in business is a huge advantage and serves to confirm our serious approach to Forex trading and we are proud and honored that we have clients that have been with well over 10 years.

Q: What would be your advice for those who are just starting theirs signal service now?

A: It is very tough but also very potentially profitable business. New Signal providers, even if they don't have much of a trading track record, need to know that it is a long term undertaking and will start with one then two satisfied clients. They will tell their friends and the friends will tell others and the business will grow from there. I don't know any successful Signal provider whose business has been an overnight success. Over time and with honesty and integrity the clients base will grow. Forex is here to stay and once your business has been established and client trust has been gained you can look forward to many happy profitable years as a Forex service provider.

Q: If you were me, what would you do to try to break into this field now?

A: Keep doing exactly what you are doing – I get your newsletters. I see you on the search engines and you are active in Social media. That is exactly where you need to be in my opinion. I also believe that offering to build EA's for clients is big business – so many traders especially new ones feel they have the magic formula and 90% of traders are looking for that quick 10-20 pip's in and out. They have a trading formula and do not know how to automate their trades, they will be glad to pay someone they can trust to build them an EA and most are not looking for a cheap deal but will pay gladly for an expert like you to do the job for them. (This is just my opinion and I feel it could be very big business once established.)

There are100's more people looking to be successful self-traders than those wanting to become signal providers (in my opinion). Many traders have big money and are happy to pay higher amounts for a professional to turn their trading ideas into an EA. The word will spread quickly as many traders are part of a club that with over 100 members – one happy club member tells another and it grows from there. Traders are not interested in a cheap deal but a solid deal with an expert. Again – just my opinion Rimantas.

Q: What publications, professional associations, or events should I check out for additional information on this field?

A: A web search will provide access to Forex blogs and portals – this could open you up to many hundreds even thousands of Forex traders.

Q: Do you know anyone else I can speak to for advice about breaking into this field?

A: I really don't know who to refer you to – there have been many books written on Forex and Forex strategies, possibly some of the authors.

Q: What was the funniest moment in your career?

A: During late 1998 – a brand new trader had just completed my trading course and proceeded to fund his account with $10,000.00. His very first trade was the USD/JPY with a Stop Loss and no set profit Limit. That was also the day the Bank of Japan intervened in the markets. The NET results were he more than doubled his account in about 15 minutes and he didn't even know. I seem to remember he was so traumatized by what happened, he withdrew the funds and bought a new car.

Q: What do you think about other signal providers?

A: I have not really given this much thought – as with any business some are good and some are outright junk.

Q: Are trading signals sent by SMS message still popular?

A: Yes we still have a demand for this – but automated trading is definitely growing also.

Q: Which is the most popular trading signal delivery method used by your customers? Is it SMS messages, email messages, trade copier service (auto delivery), live trading room or other?

A: I'm going to say it is equally spread .... We have a demand for all of the above. I believe whatever the Signal Provider feels to be his best method of approach and trading objective the market place is large enough to accommodate and be good for any of the above styles.

Q: Is there anything I can do to help you?

A: Nothing at this moment, thank you. You always do help us and we are very satisfied and happy with everything you have done for us. I and my family not only see you as work colleague but also as a friend. It's our pleasure to help!

Chapter 10 Takeaways

Chapter 10: Interview with the Trading Signal Provider
Bernard Lewis
- founder of Aforex.com and forexsignal.com
- Uses Remote Trade Copier to deliver trading signals to their customers

CHAPTER 11

Marketing Your Signal Service - Forums, Affiliates, and PPC

Marketing is an essential step towards increasing customer awareness about your online business. Currently, the most effective marketing methods for Forex trading signals service include content marketing, Forex forums, promotional partners (affiliates) and Pay per Click (PPC). We'll go over each of these marketing strategies in this chapter.

What is content marketing?

Content marketing consists of planned content creation and free online sharing with those who are interested. This may be in the form of a blog on your website or a video blog on YouTube or other video network, eBook, case study, etc. It also could take the form of an infographic that takes off and becomes more and more popular. There are many ways to create content that is useful for your audience... for Forex traders.

If you are writing a blog or creating videos, you can teach people various tips and tricks on how to do stuff in the Forex market. If you already have a service or some products, you probably have received many questions from your customers. Why not answer them in a blog post or a video post?

Things to write about on a Forex Signals website blog
- Daily technical analysis.

- Give screen shots of recent trades that were closed. Add both losing and winning trades. Be honest if you are doing this.
- Write how-to articles explaining to people how to do different things.
- Answer questions from your customers through a blog post. If one person asks something, it is likely that there will be more people looking for the same answer.
- Check the comments from your other blog posts or even on some other relevant websites. Look for questions that you could answer with a blog post.
- Check Out Other Blogs in Your Community and find what their readers like to post. Then do a great work and write an even better blog post on that topic, whatever that is.
- Look In Your Archives. You can always rewrite, update or just repost an old article. Two years ago my blog posts were terrible and now I often take one of those and rewrite it so that it would be valuable and interesting to my readers.
- Go to Google News and see what is going on in the Forex market right now. Writing reviews about certain important events in Forex is a good idea.
- Create a special blog post that explains every key term in the world of Forex trading signals. Obviously there will be people who will not know what "signals" are or what "trading session" means, etc.

Or maybe you have a blog where you post technical analysis of currency pairs several times a week. Why not create a video explaining how you are doing this also. YouTube is very user-friendly for uploading videos and allows you to add links to your website in a description of the video that you upload.

I never done videos of technical analysis personally, but I have watched some online and they were truly boring. My advice would be to not exceed 2 minutes for a video and make it short and to the point. You do not want people to be bored by your long videos, unless it's a webinar that you're doing.

It is easy to create videos using a software named Camtasia which is available for PC and MAC. It allows you to record your computer screen and later you can even edit that video by adding special effects like zoom-in, zoom-out, captions, pictures, etc. There is also a free version available that is not quite as robust called CamStudio. It is a bit more cumbersome to use and there are not as many options for video effects and production settings, but again, it is a free software and might be useful to you if you are starting your business on a limited budget.

Once you create a piece of content that your prospects are interested in, you should make it available on social networks like Twitter. Now I do not see much use in marketing Forex related content on Facebook, but on Twitter there are a lot of currency traders that you can reach.

I have tried marketing on Facebook, and to this day I still experiment with it, but it seems very hard to find serious Forex traders there. What I have learned is that most of the profiles on Facebook that seem to be Forex related come to the site just to share their content. You will find hundreds of thousands profiles that even have the word 'Forex' in their names, but what is common between those profiles is that mostly all of them have 5000 friend connections already which is the limit on Facebook. The chance that they will spot your post is almost zero when all of these people come to only post something they have to offer, but not see what others share.

Now with Twitter it's somehow different. I believe there are a lot of people there who come for marketing only, but you will see that it's easier to find Forex traders on Twitter.

If you just search for "forex trader" and filter the results to show people, you will see that there are thousands of people who call themselves forex traders. These are the people you are interested in reaching with your content. Try to connect with them by retweeting their tweets and by following them. This is how you can get noticed and find future customers, partners or even friends.

Benefits of Forum Marketing

Do a search for Forex related forums and use these platforms to advertise your services. To get started, you simply have to sign up using your email, a username and a password. Most forum memberships are free although a few might be charged a nominal one time registration fee. Now hold on, do not do this before you read this entire chapter.

When you sign up to a forex forum, you instantly gain access to a huge database of trading enthusiasts. Many struggling traders visit these sites to find a solution to their problems. A lot of forum goers are beginners, eager to jump into the market but not sure how and where to begin. They are looking for someone like you to guide them through the process. You in turn, are looking for prospective customers. If you know what you're doing, a forex forum could easily become a customer fishing ground in no time.

However, it's important to remember not to spam the forum. Some forums have stringent rules on marketing and even on the posting of any links to outside websites. Any improper conduct could have you banned.

Never post any links to any website on any Forum unless you have been a member for at least a few weeks and have made 10-20 posts that were relevant and useful to other members. If you won't follow this rule you might get banned from the forum rather quickly. I am not joking.

I would recommend only one method of advertising on forums. You should find a forum section which clearly states that it is for commercial products and services. Then you create a new thread with your domain name as a title. The very first post you make should be a clear, honest and brief description of your service, your results, yourself and your goals with the service. Do not brag about the results, no matter how good they are and try not to look like a salesman pitching a product.

When forum members start to interact with you and your service, they will definitely post dozens of questions, even those that you have answered on your website already. Be patient and answer all the questions with respect and kindness.

One rude post can ruin your whole reputation—not only on a single forum, but on others as well, because many members participate in multiple forums at the same time.

Accept criticism gently and do not start a fight or argue with others on the forum. Be polite. There are many people on forums that will ask all sorts of questions and make various comments. Be open minded and once you start a dialogue, you should visit the forum and speak with those involved at least 2-3 times a week. If you won't participate, the thread on forum will be dead in no time. What's the point of starting it if you won't manage and participate in it.

It's human nature to criticize new things, especially in Forex, because there are countless numbers of scam and low quality products online. They all should out to be the best in the world, but usually die and vanish from the Internet in a few weeks or months after they fail to work. So don't be like those products and services. Prepare to be attacked by forum participants as they will try to crush your product to the ground.

Promotional partners (Affiliate Marketing)

At a time when online advertising costs are spiraling out of control, affiliate marketing offers a safe haven. An affiliate (personally I like the name promotional partner) is someone who advertises your products and services in exchange for a percentage of every sale they deliver to your website.

There are websites where one can improve his or her affiliate marketing strategies. These places are teeming with affiliates who will be more than willing to take on the work of advertising for your signal service.

A good place to begin an affiliate marketing campaign is ClickBank. This digital platform connects business owners with marketers. The affiliate partners are the ones who do the actual promotions.

At the time of the writing of this book, there were more than 1 million affiliates operating on that site. You can use the site to expand your marketing to other countries since many affiliates live overseas.

Now, I also want to warn you to not dive straight into this too. Here is an example story for you from my experience that will show you how dangerous it can be for your brand name. When I first started to offer one of my products to affiliates through ClickBank, I got few dozen of them interested. Usually you do not see who is promoting you, because once you put your product on the ClickBank marketplace, it is available to many affiliates. You only see their usernames in the traffic and conversion reports.

A few weeks later I realized that if I searched for my product on Google, there were dozens of 3rd party websites on the first few search results and my own website was buried on page 2 and beyond. Now almost all of them looked like spammy websites with hundreds of other products from the CB marketplace on them. All they did was just copy and paste my content, and the description of my product, onto their website and use some images that were, of course, taken from my website too.

Now to my surprise, at first this did not made me any extra sales, well, maybe few. However, later it hit me and I understood. Who will ever buy something from these kinds of websites that look like just another page online that you want to run away from? Most of them had banners all over the place and had "ad links" between paragraphs of the text, formatted to have the same color and style where you can't even view the link because the text and the link were the same color and blended together. From my point of view, adding these confusing kinds of things to a site is just stupid, if you allow me to use such word.

Such websites will add many of those ad links just to get paid a few cents when someone clicks on it. And to make people click on them, website owners try to sneak them into every possible place on the page just to expect that people will click them accidentally.

From my point of view, this just ruins the reputation of any website, even if it's a huge blog network that earns thousands of dollars from these ads.

The right way to find promotional partners

So what is the right way of doing this, you may ask. If you are on the CB marketplace, I recommend to set your product up to require approval before someone can promote you. Next, you should clearly explain on your website that you are seeking for promotional partners and that anyone interested should contact you personally.

Another great idea is that these people, interested to becoming your promotional partners, would be added on your mailing list. So you can add a form on your website affiliate page that will ask them to input their name and email. After they submit their contact details they will get the information and rules for promoting your product.

Be smart and do not just let everyone promote your product, otherwise you risk ending up with your product on dozens of low-quality websites that just look like spam. When you have affiliates on a mailing list, you will be able to reach all of them at the same time. This way you can provide them with news about upcoming launches, promotions, etc.

If you want to get real promotional partners—those who are big promoters and won't happen by your website on accident—you should search them out yourself. One of the best places for this is Twitter. Just do a search for "forex trader http" and then filter the results just to show people's profiles.

Let me explain what I mean by those search keywords "forex trader http". This obviously will find people who describe themselves as a forex trader and I add "http" to the search to make sure that they have a link to some website in their profile description. In most cases that link will lead you to their website. Usually it's a blog or a page where they offer their own product or services.

Spend at least one hour a day searching and reaching for such people and after a few weeks you will have a good list of people that may be your promotional partners or even friends. You may find it a good idea to promote their products to your customers as well and make extra income too. This is how promo partnerships work, even on stage during live seminars.

Now do not be too nervous about all this, when you are just starting your business of trading signals, you should focus on creating a good, high-quality product first. Do not look for promotional partners unless you have all the systems and website in place. Beta test everything you have for at least a few weeks, or even months, to see if everything is working fine. You can make a fool out of yourself if you contact some big affiliate and ask him if he can promote you if the kinks are not first ironed out of your systems. You first want to have everything up and running smoothly when you approach others to promote your service.

How much profit should you share with promotional partners?

An interesting question that people often ask me is how much they should pay to promotional partners. Well, for higher priced products of $1000 and above, the usual share is 50%. But your signal services usually won't cost that much. So if you charge your customers something like $50-$200, it might be wise to share 75% for the first subscription payment and then at least 50% for the rest of the payments for as long as the customer stays with your service.

Yes, these numbers are correct. It looked like a mistake when I first stumbled onto these numbers, but this is just how it works. Keep reading to learn more about how powerful it is to give generous commissions.

If there is someone who wants to promote you, first ask what size email list (s)he has. If it's less than 500 emails, then my advice is to not to work with such an affiliate. It might be a different story if it is a targeted list of people, or that email list has an open rate of at least 20%. At first, you might be glad to get any amount of customers and that is completely fine. But later you will realize that email marketing does not do wonders in most cases.

Calculate it like this. If your promotional email is sent to 500 recipients and 20% of people open that email, which is considered very good, especially in a Forex industry where the average open rate is about 10%. Then the click through rate (CTR), the number of people that will click the link inside your email to visit your website, will be even lower—normally around 10%-

15% when open rate is 20%. So this means that only about 50 people will visit your website, and with a conversion rate of 2%, you will get only one customer. And that customer may even cancel your service after the trial period.

So now that you see how these numbers work you may want to search for promotional partners that have large mailing lists. Never turn your back to someone who has a small list, but is doing a good job and works in the Forex industry being honest. There are so few people like this and you should have an Excel file where you keep all such contacts. Make friends with 20 of these kinds of people and you will find that your way to the top is definitely much easier.

There will be people who dream about making money by selling your product and you will work hard to setup an affiliate system on your server so they can drive traffic to a special affiliate link. You will need to create banners, write promotional emails, etc. And finally you will learn that they do not produce much traffic. But do not be too sad about this, because you learn this by doing. Yes, you learn how to connect with promotional partners by connecting with promotional partners. You learn how to setup promotional campaigns by setting up promotional campaigns.

A lot of people do not understand how this works. They think that if they find a huge affiliate they will become rich with thousands of customers in no time. Even if that is true for some, these things happen only after hard work and only when you and your service are ready to handle such a large number of customers.

Now by that I mean, your product should be so good that the world will need it. Imagine if you are just a farmer standing with a shovel. Do you think you are ready to work and use the land of 1000 acres? Are you ready to sow, grow and harvest all the yield? My guess that it will be too much for just one man with the shovel.

But once you have people to help you and the right agricultural equipment, you are ready for big yield. So the same with business, even a business of trading signals.

Do not expect that someone will find your product and deliver hundreds of thousands of visitors that will convert to thousands of paying customers. It's not how this works. I know someone who has 100,000's of emails on his list and when I asked if he can send a promotion for my signals website, he asked me questions that I had no clue about at that time.

- What is the conversion rate of your product?
- What ROI (return on investment) do you normally have in your other promotional campaigns or your own advertising?
- What CTR (click-through-rate) do you normally see when others email your offer?

I did not know what to answer, as I did not knew such numbers. So the promotion was not possible for me at that time.

He also said, that big affiliates will ask 75% or more on each sale, which sounded like complete nonsense for me. I would not make money with such a promotion after paying for servers and other expenses.

So he explained how it all works. When affiliates send you a customer, you pay at least 75% to affiliate. No big affiliate will promote you if you pay less for a low-tier priced product which costs $50-$200. You should look at this sale only as getting the lead/customer and still getting 25% of the money (well actually a bit less as you will pay commissions to PayPal or ClickBank, etc.). Once you have the new customer, even though you did not made much money initially, you offer the customer an upsell or cross-sell. This means you offer him another product or service to buy. Now you basically have him on your email list and can offer him products and services for life and that is much valuable than just getting the full revenue for that first sale.

If a big affiliate is not promoting you, you are not getting new leads/customers. So it is better to pay 75% and get a customer than end up with no customers and no sales anyways.

Now here is a trick to avoid paying monthly payments to your promotional partners. It will not work all the time, but it is something for you to consider. Instead of having an affiliate promote your monthly service, create another one-time fee product that will peak the interest of Forex traders that may be interested in subscribing to your signals service later.

Now by this I mean that you could create an indicator or some trading tool, or even write an eBook. Then have your promotional partners advertise it to their audience and give 75% of each sale or even more. When you get new customers on your list then you can offer them your trading signals service.

"Hey there, if you like that indicator that gives pretty good entries for Forex trading, why don't you check out my trading signals service that is based on the same, and even more advanced technology. And a link to your website goes here".

Eventually you will not care about the profit made from sales from your promotional partners, but you do care about the new customers that you will offer your other services to.

My advice is to simply look into promotional partnership only after you have everything setup and already have some clients. When you know all your systems work, and the trading signals are delivered with no issues, and there are no problems with the billing system, etc., then you can approach potential affiliate partners.

For example, imagine getting a big affiliate to promote you who can drive 50,000 visitors to your site and 10% of them will convert. This would result in 5,000 new customers. Will your existing server space be able to handle a load like that?

You cannot rent a server that big just before you find promotional partner as that will cost huge amounts of money. Instead, you grow in steps and you will see all of it happening when you live with the right positive attitude and manage your business with honesty and integrity.

I personally have this problem of being a "perfectionist" and always wanting to "think about every detail" before I do something. But this never happens in real life, especially for the things we do for the first time. So you just start, and do your best the way you know how to, nice and easy. Then once that is accomplished, you move to the next step like getting affiliates, buying another server, etc.

PPC or Pay per Click Marketing

Similarly to affiliate marketing, Pay per Click offers a way to launch an inexpensive advertising campaign. Pay per click is an advertising model in which advertisers pay a website owner whenever their ad is clicked on. When it comes to search engines, advertisers bid on keyword phrases relevant to their market.

For example, with Google's AdWords you can bid on forex, trading or signals related terms like "trading forex", "forex signals", "free forex signals" etc. Now whenever a user searches for "free forex signals" on Google, your ad will appear in the sponsored results section. If that user clicks on the ad, he will be directed to your website and Google will charge the amount you bid on for that click.

Now don't be too excited about adding hundreds of keywords, even though I know Google will offer you that for sure. First try with only a few keywords, set up a sales funnel correctly that will track sales, and only then start using paid ads. Only with a properly configured sales funnel will you be able to track which keywords convert better and which don't. Then you can eliminate bad keywords and try to add new ones as time goes on and you continue testing.

Conversion optimization is another topic altogether and honestly I am no expert in this matter. At the moment, the best expert I know in this field is Neil Patel. So, when the time is right for conversion optimization, you should read his blog to learn about this and other online marketing topics also.

Use the marketing practices I covered above to successfully promote your services online. They are cost-effective strategies that can give increased exposure to your business both locally and globally.

Chapter 11 Takeaways

Chapter 11: Marketing Your Signal Service - Forums, Affiliates, and PPC

Content marketing
- Consists of planned content creation and free online sharing
- Can be in the form of a blog on your website or a video blog on YouTube or other video network, eBook, case study, etc

Forum Marketing
- a forex forum could easily become a customer fishing ground in no time
- important to remember not to spam the forum
- Never post any links to any website on any forum unless you have been a member for at least a few weeks and have made 10-20 posts that were relevant and useful to other members
- Find a forum section which clearly states that it is for commercial products and services
- The very first post you make should be a clear, honest and brief description of your service, your results, yourself and your goals with the service
- Be patient and answer all the questions with respect and kindness
- Accept criticism gently and do not start a fight or argue with others on the forum

Promotional partners (Affiliate Marketing)
- Hire someone who advertises your products and services in exchange for a percentage of every sale they deliver to your website
- ClickBank is good place to begin an affiliate marketing

PPC or Pay per Click Marketing

- offers a way to launch an inexpensive advertising campaign
- you will pay advertisers whenever the ad is clicked on

Search Engine Optimization -Is it Worth Your Time and Money?

Search Engine Optimization (also known under the acronym SEO) is the best way to bring in more visitors to your website, because it gets your website to a better position on the search engine results page (SERP). In other words you get visitors for free and it is called an organic traffic. Using SEO correctly can lead to more traffic (visitors) and greater online visibility for your business. This can make your Forex signal service more popular.

There are a lot of websites that offer SEO services. You will get SEO proposals each week or even every day, once you have your website established. There are also many websites that provide free tools to check your "SEO health" just to give you suggestions for improvement. Just like you will get tons of emails giving you "super exclusive and secret MT4 trading indicators that will make you filthy rich" in the same way there are a lot of SEO experts that will promise you that their exclusive and secret strategies will land your website on Google page #1 in no time at all.

Don't bother yourself too much with this. A lot of SEO "experts", "gurus" and online services will tell you really bad things about your SEO and your website. They will tell you how they can improve it. But believe me, that is just a waste of time and they are just trying to be different from their competitors or scare you into hiring them. They just want to find people who do not know much about SEO and then collect monthly payments in exchange for SEO services. They usually give you a monthly plan with the exact list what they will do, and once you know the process yourself you will be able to identify phony SEO experts. Actually, no reputable and authoritative SEO expert will contact you and offer his service. The real pros are busy working for huge companies and it's usually difficult to hire them because of their busy schedule.

If you have doubts, just compare a few of the top websites from the first page of Google using SEO tool like Quick-Sprout.com and see for yourself how many errors and mistakes they have. See the table below how many things can be upgraded and how many suggestions for improvements those SEO tools give. But you know what, they are still on top of the Google search results. So why worry that much if your site gets similar warnings?

So don't bother yourself and don't invest any time in this from day one. Just follow a few of the best practices that I am giving to you and your SEO will be fine. I know that I am no SEO expert, so don't just blindly listen to me... but because I have spent thousands of dollars over the past few years on SEO experts, and in the end my site rankings were brought down by Google's new algorithm, I do have some experience in this area.

	Forex factory.com	Forex magnates.com
Traffic Rank	#1 1.76 sec	#2 3.96 sec
SEO Score	81	76
Total Number of Warnings	8	6
Use of Top Keywords in Heading Tags	No	Yes
Use of Top Keywords in Title Tag	No	No
Use of Top Keywords in Meta Description	No	No

You may say that Google was the problem, not those SEO experts, but actually those who were working with good SEO experts stayed on top or even improved their rankings. What I have realized is that those who did SEO for me used Black Hat SEO strategies, even though some were telling me that they weren't. It helped initially but then wound up costing me when Google made their changes.

When should I start doing SEO?

The simple steps that I will give you are best SEO practices and should be used from the first day your website is created. If you already have a website and did not follow these steps before, you should apply them to every page on your website.

Months or years later, when there will be nothing to improve on your trading signals service, the trading strategy will be working just fine, the servers will be optimized for best performance, the sales conversion rate will be perfect at 10% or more and there will simply be no other things to improve, then you can take tall those SEO improvement suggestions from SEO tools and nail them. But for now, do not even waste your time.

Adding an icon for mobile devices for your page and eliminating some CSS error by removing a comma that was not in the right place (these are the tips those SEO tools may give you for example) will not make your search engine rankings better. Well, unless there is another website with the exact same ranking score (or whatever Google uses to determine ranking positions) and those 2 errors solved.

Phony SEO experts will hurt your site rankings

I have hired several SEO gurus and some of them charged $600 a month. This was a lot of money, and now I understand that I was just wasting it. I paid more than $5000 over the 2 years to do SEO for my website and all I got was terrible ranking of my website that was punished by Google Penguin and Google Panda.

Now please do not get me wrong, I'm not mad at them, they were just using the strategies that they knew and I am sure they believed in what they were doing too. Also, this gave me a good lesson, and after Google Penguin knocked down my rankings, I started to learn SEO myself. I then found out that true SEO experts like Neil Patel and Brian Dean deliver a lot of free training and content that can help anyone to learn how this SEO stuff works.

So I am trying to save you hundreds or even thousands of dollars and also save you time, which is priceless.

Don't experiment that much with this, like I did. Now I am so interested to learn more and more about this, that I even continue to study SEO every day and apply new tactics to my websites just to learn even more. Then I will be able to fulfil my mission even better - help you avoid the mistakes I have made so you can concentrate on your trading signals business and not bother about SEO too much.

As an example, you can go to Google and search for "mt4 trade copier". You will notice that what used to be my main website at www.ea-coder.com is not even in the search results of the first 10 pages or so. But my new website, www.mt4copier.com, which I created following only a few simple best practices of SEO will likely be on the first page of search results. Well, at least it is there at the moment when I write this book and it has been there for the last several months already.

This only proves how my rankings of the 1st website are hurt and the new website is doing just fine. No SEO expert that I have hired in the past was able to fix the damage my website has even though I have paid a lot of money for that. In other words my 1st website has a bad reputation in Google eyes and I am learning how to fix this.

How to identify a phony SEO expert

So how do those phony SEO experts work and how can we identify them? Usually they will offer you a variety of services. One of them will be content writing, where they will outsource this job cheaply and often to non-English speaking writers. They will write a 500 word article about Forex which is usually done only by rewriting other articles from other websites that were likely written the same way. So in the end it's just a piece of junk content that nobody will ever read, and the goal of using this content is just to show Google that your website has content about Forex or whatever niche you are into.

Also, they will write additional articles and post them on 3rd party websites that allow you to gain backlinks. It means at the end of that article there will be a link to your website. Great, now you have backlinks from the websites that have articles about growing potatoes, feeding a canary, teaching your horse to dance a ballet and other kinds of stuff other website owners and SEO's add just to get the backlinks to their websites.

Even if that content is posted on a website full of low quality Forex articles, Google will still see that it has no value and won't give you any benefit for that. Actually it will often bring your rankings down if Google sees that you are doing this constantly. So basically, you would be paying someone to do this to make Google love your site, but it will be opposite.

Does this make sense to you? How does this give anyone any value? Well, these articles show up on Google, and someone will visit them and may even read one or two, and click an advertisement... then an article network owner gets paid a few cents for that and Google charges the advertisement owner a significant amount of money too. There is some value, but not for you or your customers for sure, and many people believe that the internet works this way. Well, it used to in the past but Google has changed the rules as of 2012.

What SEO experts will tell you to do?

SEO experts will say that one way to get your site to a better position in Google is to incorporate relevant keywords. For example, say you want to optimize your website or a webpage from the site for the term "forex signal".

The correct way to do this (also known as White Hat SEO) is to sprinkle the keyword all over your selected webpage. You put "forex signal" in the title of your webpage. Next, you find a way to insert the keyword at the start, middle and near the end of the page.

Sometimes even including "forex signal" at the beginning of different paragraphs can make a positive difference toward improved search engine rankings. If you successfully perform the SE Optimization process, search engines like Google and Yahoo will index your website for the term "forex signal". Now whenever a user makes a search for "forex signal" on Google, your website should come up in the top results.

A good SEO campaign will propel your website to a high rank in the search results for your chosen keywords. In order to get an idea about which keywords to pick for your website optimization, use keyword search tools, SEO software or consult marketing experts in this field.

Does it sound like good advice? If you want to rank for "forex signals", then just add that to your website a bunch of times and that should give you top results. I love the word "should" in this explanation as that kind of removes the promise. Well, let me tell you this. Whether you put that keyword on your website once or twice or 100 times, you will not get top ranking position. In fact I don't think you will appear in the first 100 pages either unless you have 100+ backlinks from other reputable forex websites.

Yes, it's that difficult. I don't want to scare you, but I want to save you time, energy and money. So does it mean that keywords do not matter? Of course they do, but it does not work that way. Let me give you an example. Let's take a look at two sites that rank for the keyword "forex signals" on Google. The first site ranks at #1 on Google.co.uk and the 2nd site ranks at 300+ position.

In the table below you see two sites compared. These results are from a SEO tool QuickSprout.com. You can see that the 2nd site has a better SEO score, its load time is faster, it has less SEO warnings, zero errors, and uses "forex signals" keyword in the heading and title tags and this keyword is even the top 2 words key phrase. However, this does not have better ranking position, and it even ranks 300+ while the other site ranks #1 on Google.co.uk.

	Fxmarket leaders.com	Dailyforex signals.com
Traffic Rank	#1 2.89 sec	#2 2.40 sec
SEO Score	64	86
Total Number of Warnings	7	5
Total Number of Errors	1	0
Total Number of Indexed Pages	97	7
Total Number of Back Links	66	2
Top Keyword	forex	forex
Top 2 Word Key Phrase	forex trading	forex signals
Top 3 Word Key Phrase	open trading account	daily forex signals
Use of Top Keywords in Heading Tags	No	Yes

Use of Top Keywords in Title Tags	No	Yes
Use of Top Keywords in Meta Description	No	No

This is just one example, and there are hundreds of thousands of these online. So the next time when some SEO guru will tell you that you can get on the 1st page of Google results page by repeating your main keywords more on the webpage or by optimizing meta tags, remember this example. Sure, all these things are important SEO factors, but they alone won't get you on top. Google needs to see the results of your work and they do this by analyzing visitor and customer behavior on your site. If they are visiting your site often, thousands of people are talking about it online on forums, emails, communities, and social networks, then they know that you are worth a closer look and a higher rank.

How and what keywords to use

Do not worry about what keywords to use and how to use them. You should use them normally like you were speaking with another person. For example, would you say something like this to another person in a conversation?

"Hi, let me introduce you to my forex signals service. My forex signals service offers good forex signals and these forex signals will make you money. So don't wait another day without forex signals and join my forex signals service today".

Does this sound like a proper conversation to you? Of course it doesn't. It's just plain stupid to think Google will see you are using that keyword (I don't want to repeat it again and make you sick) 10+ times and then give you top rankings? Yeah right, do this just once and you will get thousands of customers.

It is obvious that in the text on your website you will use words "Forex" and "currency" and "MetaTrader" instead of words like "potatoes", "cucumbers" and "mushrooms". It's a website about a Forex service, not a recipe website, so why bother so much about keywords when your natural content will already contain such words.

You've already saw an example of poorly ranking site. It is possible that they have too much of the keyword "forex signals" which is called "keyword over optimization".

Types of Search Engine Optimization

There are two main types of SEO optimization. I will explain both of them to you in the simplest way I can. I know that maybe you are not a website designer or programmer, not a SEO expert and probably just a good Forex trader or trying to become one. I also understand that learning SEO might not be the thing you are after, but believe me, if you want to have a website, you should at least know the most important things about SEO.

You definitely want to understand what your SEO experts will be talking about and, more importantly, understand if they are doing it right. Otherwise, you risk getting your site on the last page of search results page.

So two main methods of SEO are called on-page SEO and off-page SEO. Let's look deeper at both.

On-page SEO

On-page SEO refers to the process of optimizing anything that appears on the pages of your website. These are the things like page title, description, H1, H2 and H3 tags, image description tag, etc. So these are the things that you are in control of, and these are the things you should be focusing on from the start. Once you learn a few simple methods, and develop them as your habits, you can move on to off-page SEO optimization.

The most important on-page SEO ranking factors are:
- Page Title (Meta tag).
- Page Description (Meta tag).
- Header tags (H1, H2, and H3).
- URL.
- Page content.
- Alt attribute for images.

- Links to other pages on your website from within the body of each page/post.
- Links to highly relevant 3rd party websites from within the body of each page/post.

The "Perfectly" Optimized page

(for example keyword phrase "Forex signals")

Page Title: Forex signals | Vavatrade's Currency Trading Solutions

Meta description: Vavatrade Currency Trading Solutions is a monthly-subscription based Forex trading signal service that have been profitable for more than 2 years already.

H1 Headline:

Forex signals from Vavatrade's Currency Trading Solutions

Image file name:
forex-signals.jpg

Body Text:
_____forex signals_____

_____signals_____

_____forex signals_____

_____signals_____

forex signals_____

_____forex signals_____

_____forex_____

_____forex signals_____

Photo of signals
(with alt attribute)
Forex Signals

Now let's take a look at each of those on-page ranking factors.

Page Title.

This is the very first thing people will see when your site appears in the Search Engine Results Page (SERP). So, if you forget to update it and leave it as "Untitled", you won't appear on SERP, at least on the first 10 pages. So make sure your site title stands out from your competitors and explains well what the customer going to find if they visit your site.

Page Description.

This is the second thing people are going to see in the SERP. So take your time to write a couple of sentences that will tell people more details about what they are going to find if they choose to visit your site from the SERP.

The Page Title and Page Description are known as Meta tags. Usually WordPress does not give an option to edit these, but with the help of a special plug-in called All-in-One-SEO, you will be able to edit those with ease for each page or post. And, of course, it will give plenty of other options for on-page optimization too. This is a must-have plug-in for every WordPress website, and the best part about it is that it's free.

Headline (H1).

Every page text (body) you create should start with a headline and its style Headline (H1) should be "Header 1", which in HTML programing language stands as H1 tag. There should be a single H1 tag per page. Avoid having duplicates.

Sub-headlines (H2, H3).

These are the sub-headlines of the content you write. These are like blocks or chapters.

If we were talking about this as a book, for example, then the title would at the top would be the H1 tag. The name of each chapter would be H2 tags and the blocks of each paragraph inside each chapter would be H3 tags. Now there are H4, H5 and H6 tags as well, and you could use those to break paragraphs into smaller chunks of information if that is needed, but the first 3 are the most commonly used.

URL.

I hope everyone knows what this is. It's an address of the particular page on your site and it can look something like this:
http://www.ea-coder.com/?p=123
Or it can be converted to something more human readable which will also benefit your on-page SEO. So the same page can be opened using this URL:
http://www.ea-coder.com/contact-us/
I am sure you will agree that the second URL looks better for everyone. And this also allows you to use additional keywords to rank for. Here is an example. Say your Page Title says "How to install Forex software" and your URL might look like this:
http://your-domain/how-to-setup-forex-trading-robots/
Now you can see that both say the same thing, but because in the URL we use additional keywords, your page will get a higher chance to rank for those as well. Note that I said "get a higher chance", not guarantee.

Page content.

This is where 80%-90% of the text on your site is. Make sure it is well structured using H1, H2 and H3 tags described above and make sure it is relevant content which is useful to people. Putting some mediocre content online and expecting it to do any good is useless and simply a waste of time.

There is a saying "if you don't know anything wise to say then don't speak at all". The same with websites. Don't hire just any writer to write something Forex related. If you can't write the content yourself then give it to a good writer to proofread and add his own knowledge as well. Make sure there is no similar/duplicate content online and that it will be useful to people. Why waste your time on something that no one will be interested in?

Image alt attribute. This is a special attribute that every image needs to have that you place on the website. It will help search engines to understand what that image is about. So, if you post an image of today's EURUSD chart, you should use something like "eurusd chart January 13th 2014" as the Alt tag attribute. This way, search engines will know what that image is about, and it then may appear in the SERP of image search.

Also, when you are using an image instead of anchor text (banners for example) the alt attribute will act as an anchor text for that link.

Links to internal pages.

This is one of the most important things to do. Each of your posts should link to at least three internal pages (other pages or posts on your website) using long tail keywords. Don't know which long tail keywords to use? Did you see how Google will try to give you suggestions when you type search keywords in their search box? Well, those are the most popular long tail keywords that people are using. So go find them and use them, just make sure that the page you are linking to talks about the same things that the long tail keywords say.

Links to relevant external pages.

The anchor text you should be using for those links should be the ones you are trying to rank for. If search engines see that you are linking to other pages with anchor text like "forex breakout trading explained" they will know that there is something important on your page about that topic too, and that you are referring people for more information on that topic.

So this kind of tells the search engines that your page is the smaller version of that page that you are linking to. Imagine if you have 5 web-pages on your site that explain 5 different types of "breakout trading". Now if someone is reading this and they know what breakout trading is then its fine, but if they stumble upon that page with no knowledge what the breakout trading is then it is not of great value for them to read about a "False breakouts technique" for example. First, the reader needs to learn what breakout trading is. But it is not wise to add the same explanation of breakout trading on each page where you talk about different breakout trading styles. Ideally, you have a 6th page where you explain what breakout trading is in general. Now all those 5 pages would link to that 6th page for a breakout trading explanation. If you do not have that 6th page, you just can link to some external site. But most importantly, you do not want to have any duplicate content on multiple pages. This is why you would not want to explain the same topic, using the same words, over and over again on multiple pages.

Linking to external sites is not only a benefit for SEO. It can also create relationships with other websites in your niche. When a webmaster, or an owner of another website, sees that there are a lot of visitors who come from your website to theirs, they may want to make friends and partner with you. This is how you might become well-known in your space and get backlinks from other sites without even asking. Remember, first giving, then receiving.

Off-page SEO

Off-page SEO includes those things that are not on your website, and usually you have no control over them. However, there are many well-structured systems about how to influence those things and make them work in your favor.

These two approaches, On and Off-page SEO, should be combined in order to maximize the impact of your Search Engine Optimization. Although, I would not bother too much with the off-page optimization until the on-page optimization is done correctly and is implemented on each page and post you create on your site.

The first major off-page SEO factor is backlinks. There will never be enough of them pointing at your site, and they should all come from reputable sites. So obviously, if your website is Forex related, the backlinks should come from other Forex related sites like Forex forums, Forex blogs, Forex software review sites, etc.

It is definitely better to have 1 backlink from www.forex-crunch.com then 50 backlinks from random article network sites. Usually this is where phony SEO experts will post the backlinks to your site because it is easy to do.

In order to get a backlink on forexcrunch.com, you will need to write a stunning piece of content and offer that as a guest post. Or, you will need to give outstanding service which will make a difference in many people's lives and will become the next sensation in the Forex trading world. Then forex-crunch.com will definitely spot you and probably blog about you, but that is no guarantee of course.

Anchor text in backlinks

Almost everyone will tell you that anchor text in a backlink should be your main keyword. For example, instead of using a generic term like 'click here" to mask your link, you would use "forex signal" instead. This will suggest to search engines that your website is highly relevant for this keyword. After all, there are other websites quoting you as a source and pointing back to your site with the term "forex signal" in the link, and what could be more relevant than that?

Yeah, right. If you don't use "forex signal" as an anchor text in the backlink to your site, Google will be stupid and won't understand that your website is about Forex signals. Oh come on, seriously, does this sound logical to anyone? You really think Google will not know that your site is about Forex signals if you will use your domain name or even your real name in the anchor text? In the old days of the internet you could get away with this through black hat SEO, but it just does not work like that anymore. You will definitely get punished by Google Panda or Google Penguin (two Google algorithm updates made since 2011) if you use such high competition keywords in the anchor text, so you had better not do this. I learned this the hard way, so don't repeat my mistakes.

What anchor text to use

The best anchor text you can use can be broken in 3 categories.

- Domain name.
- Your real name.
- Long tail keyword.

Domain name as anchor text is the best choice if you can't make up your mind which anchor text to use. You never go wrong with this one, ever.

Your real name as anchor text will help Google associate your website with your name. So if you do it right, your Forex site will appear in the search results if someone types your name. I know it may sound completely irrelevant right now, but if you are serious about this business for a long term, you will definitely want this to happen.

A long-tail keyword example would be "Read my story of how I doubled my Forex trading about in 12 months following my own trading signals". And obviously this would point to an article on your page telling a story about how you doubled your Forex trading account in 12 months like the anchor text said.

An important thing here to mention is that this example above comes from a high integrity website, and if you write and share such story with the world, it had better be the truth. Personally, I will never support anyone who operates their business based on lies and phony marketing.

Chapter 12 Takeaways

Chapter 12: Search Engine Optimization (SEO)

The best way to bring in more visitors to your website because it gets your website to a better position on the search engine results page

There are a lot of SEO experts that will promise you that their exclusive and secret strategies will land your website on Google page #1

Phony SEO experts will hurt your site rankings

It is important to note that no reputable and authoritative SEO expert will contact you and offer his service because real pros are busy working for huge companies

The Best way to get your site to a better position in Google

- White Hat SEO
- Incorporate relevant keywords and sprinkle it all over your selected webpage

Types of Search Engine Optimization

- On-page SEO
  - o The process of optimizing anything that appears on the pages of your website
  - o Things that you are in control that you should be focusing on them from the start
    - Page Title (meta tag).
    - Page Description (meta tag).
    - Header tags (H1, H2, H3).
    - URL.
    - Page content.
    - Alt attribute for images.
    - Links to other pages on your website from within the body of each page/post.
    - Links to highly relevant 3rd party websites from within the body of each page/post
- Off-page SEO
  - o Things that are not on your website and you have no control over them

- Backlinks
    - Should all come from reputable sites (e.g. forexcrunch.com)
    - Anchor text in backlinks
        - Domain name
        - Your real name
        - Long tail keyword

Conclusion

You now know all that is required to start your own online Forex signal service. Now we are going to recap and review what we have learned so far. Nothing will replace your raw experience when it comes to running this kind of business. As I mentioned before, the best way to gain experience is through experience. The best way to learn how to ride a bike is to work on riding a bike. You have to do, and you have to try, in order to make progress. The best way to learn how to drive a car is by driving a car. And the best way to learn how to run a Forex signals business is to run a Forex signals business. "There are no shortcuts to any place worth going," it could be said.

But even so, I have tried here, with this book, to help accelerate your learning curve so that you will be armed with enough information to be dangerous. I want you to succeed in this kind of business because I know how wonderful of a business it can be. I will warn you again, though, that this is not a business for the 'weak in spirit' because it will test you and try you. You will likely receive customer complaints at one point or another, because remember, you cannot please everyone all the time. It is indeed a challenging business, but at the same time, it can be a very fun business to run. It can certainly also be a very lucrative business.

Remembering the vision

Do you remember the kind of money that can be made? Assume you have just 75 customers who are paying you about $200 per month... I'm sure you've realized already, or you probably wouldn't have made it to the end of this book, that the earning potential from this kind of business is very good. The gross revenue would be approximately $15,000 per month from our example. This is some serious money and it can really carry you and your family a long way. Yes, there will be some expenses, but that is true of any business that can pay you this kind of money.

Let's not forget that this is the kind of business that you can build even if you aren't a trading pro. There are many ways, as we discussed, that will provide you with Forex trading signals—everything from robots to hiring another professional to do the trading for you. It is also the kind of business that can be run on relative autopilot once everything is up and built. The maintenance is not as demanding as many other businesses. Once you have secured your trading strategy, built your technology infrastructure, and gained some clients, your trading signals business can continue to bring you revenue month after month.

Here is a recap of the specific steps you will need to take in order to build your own **Forex signal provider business.**

Step One

You select a Forex robot and put it to the test. You may need to undergo a trial and error process until you find the right trading robot. After you make your pick, make sure to go through the robot's trading patterns over the course of a few months ideally.

Learn how it behaves, when it takes trades and under what market conditions. This will help you notice any irregular behaviors in the future. In addition, with some luck, you may be able to reverse engineer the robot and create your own version of it to avoid future subscription charges.

Make sure you are tracking all of your results with a 3rd party website like MyFXBook.com, which will help you compile your trading stats into a verifiable report that you can share with your clients and future clients. A tool like this is a great credibility booster when you have a strong track record and trading history that is verified as legitimate. This performance record is what other traders and investors are going to use when evaluating your trading signals business. If you are using one of the social trading websites like ZuluTrade or Currensee then they will take care of tracking your performance record for you and displaying it for potential investors.

If you are not going to use a robot and would rather do the trading yourself, or otherwise hire a professional to do the trading for you, then you will still want to create a track record and measure the results at all times. Would you ever sign up for a trading service that did not offer you a performance history? No, and neither will anyone sign up with you if you do not have a record of success. Building this track record takes time. Do not be discouraged your first few months or even your first year—this is a long term process and requires much patience at all times.

Step Two

The second step involves the copying of trading actions from your master account to other accounts. This is where the trade copier software comes in. Any trading related changes in your own account will get instantly reflected in your customers' accounts with the help of this software.

(QTE)"Don't let what you can't do get in the way of what you can do."- John Wooden, hugely successful American college basketball coach

It can be a little difficult to set everything up if you are not very technically inclined, but just hang in there. There is always a possibility of hiring out all of the 'tech' work to someone who specializes in this area. "Do what you do best and delegate the rest," is a popular business expression for entrepreneurs and highly-skilled professionals who know their time is valuable, and also know that they don't need to handle every aspect of their business in order for it to be very successful. Just remember, if you don't know how to do something in your business, someone else does. You can work with them as a partnership or hire them to help you do what you don't know how to do.

Step Three.

Every online based enterprise should have a website. To complete this step, you need to purchase and register a domain name. Pick a name that is relevant to your business but also try to be unique and stand out from the competition.

Remember, if you don't know how to build a website, don't let this stop you—hire it out if need be! There are tons of tutorial videos on how to set up a WordPress website. You can learn from these and set it up yourself or otherwise just hire someone to do it for you. There are great sites like Elance.com, Odesk.com, and Freelancer.com where you can hire professions for relatively small amounts of money—sometimes as low as $2/hour for skilled help.

You will also need to write the content for your site. Again, if this is not a strength of yours, or you do not know how to do this at all, hire it out! Don't get caught up in the littlest details, but instead, push forward steadily. Always watch your budget at all times though. If you don't have the money to hire it out, see if there is someone you can trade services with. Maybe you can reward your employees with access to your trading services. This won't appeal to all people, but at the same time it might be a real win-win for everyone involved. This type of can-do attitude can really help you get your business started in the right direction and with some strong momentum.

Step Four

Work on creating a demand for your service. This is the time to reach out to prospective customers and offer them your trading services. Offering your trading signals/service to beta testers is always a good idea. They can help you iron out the kinks in your technology, will ask you many questions that can become content on your website, and will help you gain invaluable experience at the start of your business. Do not be afraid of offering some of your services for free in the beginning like this. These customers might even become referral partners in the years ahead.

Step Five

Get your website up and running. This virtual storefront is where customers will come looking to buy your Forex products and services. Make sure that their visit to the site is as hassle free as possible. Make your website easy to navigate. Post new content regularly to entice your visitors to keep coming back to the site.

In the process of building your site, make sure to ask for feedback regularly. You can ask of friends, acquaintances and also those beta testers who you have been working with. Alternatively, you can also hire some product and website reviewers on the sites like Elance and Odesk. For just a few dollars you can hire someone to take a good strong look at your site. Listen to the comments you receive and implement all of the good ideas that come from such a project. This is a great learning experience for you as well and provides a very valuable outside point of view.

Make sure also to ask for positive reviews on a regular basis. These reviews can be in the form of feedback and reviews on sites like ForexPeaceArmy.com, or posted on your site, or also posted in one of the many Forex forums online. Positive reviews and testimonials will always help you build your business and entice other customers to join.

Step Six

Tie your website to a safe payment gateway. This will make your service more reliable and easier to maintain. You can use a merchant account or a tool like Clickbank to help promote your service and gain access to new clients, but one of the easiest ways is to do it yourself with a service like PayPal. Since everyone knows about PayPal now, it's a great option and can help you build your business with a secure payment solution.

Step Seven

The seventh step calls for promoting your business on forex related trading forums. These places are frequently visited by traders, trading enthusiasts and experts. Forum promotion is a proven way to build on your other advertising methods. Some people like spending time on forums more than other people. Again, if this is something that you don't do well, or don't like to do, remember that you can hire out this step as well. Don't be afraid to build a small team of employees who can help you build a large business.

Think about Bill Gates of Microsoft... do you think that he could have built a very large business without hiring other people? Entrepreneurs have talents in hiring and providing leadership to their employees. If you want to build a truly strong business that brings in multiple five-figures each month, you're going to need some employees along the way to help you. If you've noticed, this principle of outsourcing work can be used in every single step so far, and is equally true with step eight coming up.

Step Eight

The eighth and final step involves maximizing the productivity of your website through search engine optimization. There is great power in ranking well for some search terms that professional investors and other Forex traders are using to look for business services. If you rank highly for good terms then people will find your website and you might gain many monthly clients. Search engine optimization is a very important part of your overall business and a great long-term focus. It should be worked on each and every day ideally.

There are a few more things you may need to consider overall with this business:

Money

You should have enough funds to complete all the steps I covered above. You don't have to do all the steps at once, you can work on them in stages. If you decide to do this, calculate the cost of each stage beforehand and set aside that amount. If you are short on funds, consider the trading-of-services scenario and be willing to barter for the work that you need. If you have the right mindset, you will be able to build your business no matter what the obstacles.

Licensing

Whether you're trading or sending signals, make sure you have the required permits in place. Every country has its own laws and regulations when it comes to forex trading and providing signals to others. If you need to, obtain a valid license BEFORE you begin your signal service. One of the worst things that could happen is to build a strong business with good monthly revenue, only to have your business seized by the authorities because you have failed to obey the financial laws of your country. The United States is the most heavily regulated country for all financial/currency matters, so if you are a citizen of the US then it is your job to work twice as hard at following the regulations. For the rest of us, the task is a bit easier, but you still must be diligent with this part of your business and hire a legal attorney to help you if you feel it necessary.

Staffing

Any successful business has many departments like customer support, marketing and sales. Once your business grows, you will need to have the necessary staff to perform all the different tasks that your business requires in order to function properly. Remember what I said about Bill Gates of Microsoft. There is no human way possible that he could have built a multimillion dollar per year business on his own. Can you think of any other businesses that are very successful and are only run by one person? Your ambitions may not be to build a million-dollar business, but even a business that makes $5-10k per month can be a challenge if you try and run it without any help. As always, protect your budget and try and be as wise as possible with your available funds. Once you have some recurring monthly income, it will be easier to afford hiring staff.

Taxes

You need to pay your taxes if you want to continue to operate legally. Hire a tax attorney or other profession when getting started, and when it comes time to pay your business taxes. This is not an area of your business that you want to leave to chance. The best practice with the money you receive is to take a portion of it and save it away for when taxes are due. Don't get yourself in trouble by falling behind on your tax payments/bills. It is often a good idea to hire a bookkeeper to help keep track of your finances so you can focus on building your business. Remember, do what you do best and hire out the rest if necessary.

A great, but still challenging business

It's one thing to manage your own money in the Forex arena. It's a completely different ballgame to manage other people's money. As a service provider you have to constantly be on top of your game.

The Forex signals market can be very lucrative, but it is also very demanding and competitive. There has been a rapid growth in the number of service providers in the past few years. It is best that you set a practical and realistic target for your forex signal service. The greatest confidence you can offer to your future subscribers is a long and solid track record of success. You can even be the best by being the steadiest.

But don't get discouraged, there is always money to be made by those who work harder, and most importantly, smarter than the competition. Working smarter is where my book here comes in—I wanted you to have every advantage possible. Make sure that you go over each chapter and implement the actions described in this book. Never stop learning and improving—running a business requires constant experimentation and innovation.

Remember to treat your clients and customers well because they are the lifeblood of your business. Keep in mind that your business is made possible by your customers—no customers, no business, no income. Treat your clients like gold and your excellent reputation will be spread and talked about in the industry and your business future will be bright. Good luck with your new Forex signals business! I wish you the very best!

Recap of the specific steps you will need to take in order to build your own Forex signal provider business

1. Select a Forex robot and put it to the test
2. Copy trades from master account to slave accounts using a trade copier software
3. Create a unique website that is relevant to your business
4. Reach out to prospective customers and offer them your trading services
5. Get your website up and running
6. Tie your website to a safe payment gateway
7. Promote your business on forex related trading forums
8. Maximize the productivity of your website through search engine optimization

Few things to consider with this business
- Money
  - Calculate the cost of each stage beforehand and set aside that amount
- Licensing
  - If you need to, obtain a valid license before you begin your signal service
- Staffing
  - Once your business grows, you will need to have the necessary staff to perform all the different tasks that your business requires in order to function properly
- Taxes
  - You need to pay your taxes if you want to continue to operate legally

And finally...
- Don't get discouraged, even when things get difficult. Remember, everything is difficult before it becomes easy.

- You learn how to ride a bike by riding a bike. You learn how to drive a car by driving a car. And you learn how to build a Forex signals business by building a Forex signals business.
- Experience is your best teacher.
- Run your business only with honesty and integrity. Build a firm foundation that can support your business for years to come. A long term focus is better than a short one.
- Treat your customers well and they will earn you income for years and years. Remember that your customers and clients are your business' lifeblood. Without customers you would have no business and no earnings, so treat your customers like gold.
- The financial rewards that can come from a successful signals business are amazing. The reward for helping people do well financially is a reward of its own and a wonderful feeling.

About the Author

My name is Rimantas Petrauskas and I am the author of the book "How to Start Your Own Forex Signal Service". I am also a Forex trader, a programmer with 16 years of experience, an entrepreneur, and the founder of www.ea-coder.com, www.vavatrade.com and the creator of two of the most popular trade copiers for the MetaTrader 4 platform—the Remote Trade Copier and Local Trade Copier.

I have been creating software for currency trading and signal delivery since 2009, and have created hundreds of trading robots for my customers. Although I did not test or use any of them myself (as that would violate customer agreements and copyrights), I developed a good understanding of what people were looking for the most in Forex.

I strongly believe that with a Positive Mental Attitude we can achieve any goal. We are one of the most important people in our own lives and we are responsible for everything that happens to us. I like my personal quote:

> *"People need to go through hard times on a regular basis so they will have a reason to improve, and also appreciate how well they lived before."*
>
> *- Rimantas Petrauskas*

Isn't this something that often happens in Forex trading when we experience a drawdown in our accounts? The same applies to life and once you educate yourself to deal with those "life drawdown periods" you will eventually become a better currency trader.

My goal is to show people that a Forex signals business can be legitimate and honest and that Forex is not as complicated as many people tell you. Also, that it is not as easy as many marketers try to convince you it is. Not all signal providers are a scam and not all marketers lie to people. My goal is to teach people to avoid, and also not be like, the crappy the Forex signal providers that are out there.

A Forex business can take as little time as possible so that you can spend it with your family and living your life like it matters to you. My priority is my family and I never work on weekends and after 5 PM. I get up at 5 AM every morning so I can have an extra 3 hours before my work day starts at 8 AM and I spend that time learning new things, deepening my knowledge, studying and reading books on Forex and how to improve the life of my family and myself. Those are golden hours and I am proud to say I have learned to do that from Robin Sharma. He is my hero who changed my life and I follow many other great people and their work to constantly develop myself and grow personally and professionally. People I follow the most are Robin Sharma, Brandon Burchard, Jeff Walker, Chalene Johnson, Mike Filsame, and Andy Jenkins. Those are the people that will teach you to be a better person and make your business a success.

I spend lots of time writing books, articles, case studies, blog posts and upgrading my currency trading tools. I have created several applications that help people trade currencies easier and I never claim that my tools make you money. They usually do not work without human intervention and you need to know what you are doing before you use them. Once you do, however, these applications will help make your job easier and help you to do things faster and with less effort. I have been creating Forex trading delivery software and upgrading it over and over again by adding more useful features. This is how I became a programmer who know a lot about running a trading signals business, and even started one on my own.

I also have created my trading signals business at www.vavatrade.com and been successfully making profit on my real money account and my customers' accounts since 2012. I started to make my first income with just a demo account until

I could afford to have my own real money account. I do not give any guarantee that you will make money by following my automated trading signals, but there is a good chance that you will, especially if I make money on my own live account.

I am a Positive Minded person and choose to work with people with the same attitude. I believe everything happens for a reason.

After work you probably won't reach me as I will be playing toy cars with my children or spending romantic moments with my beloved wife.

I have built my Forex business in a way that it does not steal the time from my family. Hours after work belong to them.

Honesty and Sincerity are the things that I care the most in any human being I work with or make friends with.

I also apply those attributes to my business, which is quite unusual in the Forex niche. Most of the vendors just try to sell "anything" to anyone, while I care who my customer is and how I can help him or her achieve their goals.

I am a charitable minded person who donates money each month to World Vision Australia and other charity organizations. I also sponsor a child in Sri Lanka and am very happy about that.

My key priorities:

1) Be present and actively engaged with my family. Have as much quality family time with them as possible. Always put their needs before anything else.

2) Achieve financial freedom so that I am able to provide the best for my family and deliver more value to my customers.

3) Have perfect health to live for 120 years. I always like how people laugh at that last one, but many of you will agree that big goals lead to a big life.

"Believe in yourself, take the plunge and get to first base. From there things will be easier."

- Rimantas Petrauskas

About This Book

"How to Start Your Own Forex Signals Service" is like a treasure map to buried gold not only for every currency trader, but for all those trading in other markets as well. It is the true story of how a struggling currency trader was able to make thousands of dollars a month with just a demo trading account. Included in this book is:

- A road map for building a fully-automated trading signals business. Why struggle to learn this business yourself when you can have an experienced signal provider show you all the ropes.

- The exact same steps used to build and run a successful Forex signal service business. These steps are very important to the success of your new business.

- Details of the many ways to find profitable sources for trading signals that you can sell to your customers. Using just one of these methods can help increase your monthly cash-flow.

- Time and money saving strategies that cover everything from A – Z of a signals business. These will help you get up and going in less time than going at it on your own.

- All you need to know about starting an online Forex signal service. This will save you potentially years of struggle in trying to figure out things yourself.

- How to start your own website and what software you will use to deliver trading signals. These are great gems that can help you turn a profit much faster and easier.

- What different methods you can use to run this business. It is important to use this information to get the right start from the beginning and avoid all of the most common newbie mistakes.

- How to create financial freedom and help others around the world with your business, just like I did. This is a reward of its own and one well worth the read.

Even if you are struggling right now and have no money to invest in your own live trading account, you can still build a successful trading business. You will be able to start earning income with just your demo account by using the information and roadmaps provided in this book.